Money Matters

Published in association with the
Social Policy Research Unit, University of York

MONEY MATTERS

Income, Wealth and Financial Welfare

edited by
Robert Walker
and Gillian Parker

SAGE Publications
London • Newbury Park • Beverly Hills • New Delhi

SAGE Publications Ltd
28 Banner Street
London EC1Y 8QE

SAGE Publications Inc
2111 West Hillcrest Street
Newbury Park, California 91320

SAGE Publications India Pvt Ltd
C–236 Defence Colony
New Delhi 110 024

SAGE Publications Inc
275 South Beverly Drive
Beverly Hills, California 90212

British Library Cataloguing in Publication Data

Money matters: the distribution of
  financial welfare.
  1. Public welfare—Great Britain
  I. Walker, Robert L. (Robert Lloyd)
  II. Parker, Gillian
  361.6'0941   HV245

ISBN 0–8039–8128–7
ISBN 0–8039–8129–5 Pbk

Library of Congress catalog card number 87–062228

HC
260
I5
M65
1988

Typeset by Photoprint, Torquay, Devon
and printed in Great Britain by J. W. Arrowsmith Ltd, Bristol

Contents

1 Introduction
Gillian Parker and Robert Walker   1

FINANCIAL NEEDS AND COSTS

2 The Costs of Household Formation
Robert Walker   9

3 The Costs of Childrearing
Deborah Mitchell and Kenneth Cooke   27

4 The Costs of Ageing and Retirement
Robert Walker and Sandra Hutton   46

5 The Costs of Disability
Caroline Glendinning and Sally Baldwin   63

6 The Costs of Unemployment
Kenneth Cooke   81

7 The Costs of Marital Breakdown
Jane Millar   99

FINANCIAL RESOURCES

8 Wages and Salaries
Chris Pond and Robin Smail   115

9 Non-wage Benefits from Employment
Robin Smail   132

10 New Patterns of Wealth:
The Growth of Owner Occupation
Stuart Lowe   149

11 Welfare Benefits
Jonathan Bradshaw   166

12 Credit
Gillian Parker   182

MAKING ENDS MEET

13 Earning, Sharing, Spending:
   Married Couples and Their Money
   Jan Pahl   195

14 Indebtedness
   Gillian Parker   212

THE DISTRIBUTION OF FINANCIAL WELFARE

15 Income Distribution over the Life Cycle
   *Michael O'Higgins, Jonathan Bradshaw
   and Robert Walker*   227

Index   255

Contributors

Sally Baldwin — Director, Social Policy Research Unit, University of York

Jonathan Bradshaw — Head of the Department of Social Policy and Social Work, University of York. Formerly Director, Social Policy Research Unit

Kenneth Cooke — Research Fellow, Social Policy Research Unit, University of York

Caroline Glendinning — Research Fellow, Social Policy Research Unit, University of York

Sandra Hutton — Research Fellow, Social Policy Research Unit, University of York

Stuart Lowe — Lecturer, Department of Social Policy and Social Work, University of York

Jane Millar — Lecturer, Department of Social Administration and Policy, University of Ulster. Formerly Research Fellow, Social Policy Research Unit, University of York

Deborah Mitchell — Economist, Australian Department of Finance. Formerly Visiting Research Fellow, Social Policy Research Unit, University of York

Michael O'Higgins — Managing Consultant, Price Waterhouse Management Consultants, London, seconded to the Social Affairs Division, OECD, 1987/88. Formerly Reader in Social Policy, University of Bath

Jan Pahl — Senior Research Fellow, Health Services Research Unit, University of Kent. Member of the Social Policy Research Unit Advisory Committee

Gillian Parker   Research Fellow, Social Policy Research Unit, University of York

Chris Pond   Director, Low Pay Unit

Robin Smail   Research Officer, Low Pay Unit

Robert Walker   Assistant Director, Institute for Research in the Social Sciences, University of York and Research Fellow, Social Policy Research Unit

1
Introduction

Gillian Parker and Robert Walker

The fourteen original essays included in this volume aim to further understanding of the nature and distribution of financial welfare in Britain today. The term 'financial welfare' is used instead of the more familiar 'economic welfare' in recognition of the fact that no attempt is made to measure the value of the public services which individuals receive. Financial welfare, therefore, has to do primarily with levels of monetary resources in relation to need. As such, account is taken of the main forms of cash resources over which people have direct control including, for example, bank loans and physical and financial assets, as well as the value of certain informal services provided within and between households.

The intention is to contribute to the literature on the distribution of income and wealth and with the advantage of more recent information to relocate the discussion in the 1980s. Conclusions based on earlier research will have been overtaken, in many cases, by social changes such as the substantial rise in unemployment and the associated contraction in the length of working life, the changing economic role of women, particularly older married women, and Britain's ageing demographic profile. Wherever possible these changes are taken into account in the essays that follow.

A difference from earlier studies, and one which also reflects the rapid pace of social and economic change, is the broader range of financial resources which is considered. One chapter examines the economic benefits which accrue from employment over and above the basic wage or salary. Another examines the changing nature of wealth holding brought about, not least, by the steady rise in home ownership. Yet another looks at the growth of consumer credit and underlines the extent to which this can serve to reinforce existing inequalities in financial welfare.

However, perhaps the most radical departure from more conventional recent studies concerned with the distribution of income and wealth is that *Money Matters* explicitly grounds consideration of financial resources in the context of household needs. 'Needs', in this instance, are taken to be those claims on a household's budget which, if not met, are likely to result in some form of stress for some, or all, members of the household: financial hardship, psychological suffering, social exclusion, etcetera. The yardstick used to measure these needs is the monetary cost that can be ascribed to them (see below). There is no presumption that the needs defined in this way are 'social' in the sense that a collective response is warranted in order to meet them (Charles and Webb, 1986). Rather, the point is that account should be taken of them in deciding whether households with identical resources enjoy equivalent standards of living. However, considering resources together with needs inevitably focuses attention on issues of *horizontal* equity (the equal treatment of people with identical circumstances and the differential treatment of people with the same resources but different needs) as much as on matters of *vertical* equity (the differential treatment of people with different resources and identical needs) (Knapp, 1984; Charles and Webb, 1986).

The examination of household needs also encourages readers and contributors alike to think beyond simple equivalence scales — which take account solely of the *average* needs of adults and children — and to consider other contingencies, some associated with particular stages in the life cycle, which might generate additional needs. Household formation, disability and ageing are three examples which are explored in this volume.

Explicitly taking account of household needs also directs attention to the ways in which people seek to match financial demands and resources: the process of making ends meet. Until very recently next to nothing was known about the budgeting behaviour of households and the topic was rarely considered in studies of income distribution. However, it is now apparent that there are significant inequalities in living standards within households as well as between them. Moreover, the budgeting skills of individuals, and particularly those of women within the household, serve to mediate the consequences of different levels of resources. It is through the difficulty and outcomes of budgetary decision-making that the seemingly arcane topic of income distribution acquires meaning in individuals' lives.

The book is organised so as to reflect the parallel interests in resources and needs. The three main sections cover the financial needs of different households, the distribution of resources at their disposal, and methods of money management. A final chapter provides a statistical recapitulation of many of the themes which emerge earlier in the volume.

It should be stressed that *Money Matters* is largely about the nature and distribution of financial welfare and not about policy imperatives. It is a book about the world as it is and, for the most part, it is left to the reader to decide how the world ought to be.

Financial Needs and Costs

Appropriately enough for a volume whose contributors mostly have close connections with York, the approach adopted in *Money Matters* owes much to Seebohm Rowntree's pioneering studies of the city (Rowntree, 1901, 1941; Rowntree and Lavers, 1951). At the turn of the century he recognised 'five alternating periods of want and comparative plenty' in the life of a labourer: childhood, early working adulthood, early middle life with two or three children to rear, late middle life when children are earning and, finally, old age. The continued relevance of this formulation, which is applicable across the social classes, has been demonstrated by a recent follow-up of the children of people interviewed by Rowntree in his 1950 survey (Atkinson et al., 1983; see also Chapter 15). The three periods of relative need are covered by Deborah Mitchell and Ken Cooke in their chapter on the costs of childrearing and by Robert Walker and Sandra Hutton in their chapter on old age. Chapter 2 on household formation overlaps with Rowntree's period of early working adulthood.

The first section also includes three chapters which cover contingencies that fit less easily into Rowntree's model: unemployment, disability, and separation and divorce. Rowntree's 1901 study was conducted at a time (1899) of economic boom and unemployment was little in evidence although mass unemployment was a feature of his second study in the 1930s. Disability, other than that associated with old age, is a much more recently visible phenomenon and the appreciation of its associated costs is more recent still. Likewise, the growth of marital breakdown and remarriage is a feature of the late twentieth century (although the severe financial consequences of widowhood attracted Rowntree's interest in each of his three studies). Any given individual is more likely than ever before to experience life in a series of households, any one of which may be characterised by relative affluence or poverty. As a result, analyses of financial resources at a single point in time provide an increasingly inaccurate portrayal of the true distribution of financial welfare and also have a reducing predictive value over time.

While the notion that there are costs attached to having children, losing one's job or getting divorced is intuitively reasonable, how these might be defined is far from being self-evident. The various contributors necessarily approach their task of establishing costs in different ways. However, a number of common concepts are evident. First, all six chapters in the first section are concerned with the *additional* costs which are incurred though having children, separating or whatever. In each case, therefore, a *comparison* must be made with individuals or households in otherwise identical circumstances. The appropriate comparison naturally varies. Mitchell and Cooke in their analysis of the cost of children take childless couples as the 'index group'; Jane Millar compares single parents with married couples who have the same number of children; Walker and Hutton compare retired households of differing compositions with similarly-sized households where the household head is not retired. The comparisons are not always straightforward, however, nor the results unequivocal. It is often difficult, if not theoretically impossible, to find other households whose circumstances are identical. For example, families with children are, by definition, at a different stage in the life cycle than families without children, thus their incomes and resource base will reflect *this* difference as well as the simple fact of having children. Care has also to be taken in making the conceptual leap from increased costs to financial needs. Mitchell and Cooke, for instance, in Chapter 3 show that the costs of additional children vary according to the income of the household and, perhaps, also according to its size. This problem is discussed extensively in the literature on equivalence scales (see, for example, Prais and Houthakker, 1971; McClements, 1977; Muellbauer, 1979) but has yet to be satisfactorily resolved. When costs appear to vary with context one has to use a somewhat elastic yardstick.

A second common feature is a concern with costs that have a monetary expression. Having children may bring with it sleepless nights and increased stress. Disability may, on occasion, cause depression. Arguably these 'non-monetary' costs could be translated into money units but for the most part this is not attempted. A related distinction is between the costs of, say, childrearing, as experienced subjectively by parents and those identified 'objectively' or, more accurately, 'externally', by means of behavioural studies or normative 'basket of goods' approaches (see, especially, Chapters 2 and 3). In all chapters the emphasis is placed on externally derived estimates of costs.

A number of chapters distinguish between direct and indirect costs. The former relate primarily to extra expenditures arising directly from the presence of, for example, children: toys, children's clothing, food. What Baldwin (1985) has termed 'spillover' costs might also be included. Spillover costs, in the case of disability, would cover expenditures arising from the need to pay for routine jobs that would previously have to be undertaken by family members, and more expensive shopping and compensatory spending on non-disabled siblings that can arise because of pressure on parental time. Indirect costs (a subset of what economists term 'opportunity costs') relate not to increased expenditure but to losses in income. This is most obvious with respect to retirement (Chapter 4) and unemployment (Chapter 6). But many mothers give up work to look after young children and disability may result in a loss of earnings both for people with disabilities and for those who care for them.

A further distinction made explicitly by Cooke (Chapter 6), and implicitly in other chapters, is between costs measured in terms of income and those which are manifested in the form of expenditure. This again draws attention to the importance of budgeting in mediating living standards but also highlights the many ways in which life styles may be maintained by, for example, eating into savings or building up debts.

Finally, a number of the chapters show that additional costs associated with contingencies and stages in the life cycle do not fall equally on all concerned. The costs of household formation will probably not be met solely by the new household (Chapter 2). Likewise, the financial costs of childhood disability are borne by parents and by other members of the family rather than by the child itself (Chapter 5). Frequently, too, additional costs are carried disproportionately by women. The assumption that all members of a family or household necessarily share equally all its resources is no longer tenable. Intra-household inequalities are no less real simply because they cannot easily be measured.

Financial Resources

Chapters 8 to 12 examine the distribution of financial resources. For many readers this part of the book will be more familiar, with fewer new concepts introduced. There remain, though, formidable problems of definition and measurement which are discussed in the individual chapters.

Chapters 8 and 10, on wage income and on wealth, cover topics of long-standing interest. Wages and salaries still constitute the main sources of income for the majority of households and substantially affect the living standards of many outside the labour force, for example pensioners drawing earnings-related pensions. Most important, from the perspective of financial welfare, is income after deductions for tax and national insurance contributions. Fiscal changes since 1979 have, as Chris Pond and Robin Smail demonstrate, done much to alter the distribution of after-tax income.

Stuart Lowe chooses, in his chapter on 'New Patterns of Wealth', to focus on owner occupation, which now accounts for around half of all personal disposable assets. Home ownership, along with the 'partial privatisation' of pensions, have broadened the base of wealth ownership and although they will eventually alter the balance of relative poverty and affluence in old age, they also paradoxically strengthen existing divisions in the pattern of welfare.

In Chapter 9, Robin Smail's careful sifting of the evidence shows how employment confers many financial benefits in addition to wage income. These fringe benefits, perks and opportunities for tax avoidance and evasion are largely hidden from official statistics and, hence, typically from studies of income distribution. So, too, are informal resources which are available in kind — having a room decorated in exchange for repairing a car, for example (Pahl, 1984) — which may be more intrinsically valuable than their cash equivalents. These non-wage benefits of employment have an effect on the distribution of financial welfare in at least two ways. First, they increase the 'value' of employment and thereby increase inequality between those who are in employment and those who are not. Yet, because much of this 'added value' is hidden, the increased inequality is obscured. Secondly, the added value, because hidden, is untaxable and thereby exempt from any redistributive intention that might underlie patterns of taxation.

Outside the labour market, household income is very largely determined by the state through the provision of benefits. Moreover, the benefit system is far more important than taxation in reducing vertical income inequalities generated by people's position in, or relationship with, the labour market (Central Statistical Office [CSO], 1985). Jonathan Bradshaw's chapter details the contribution made by benefit income to financial welfare but also identifies occasions when the benefit system widens horizontal inequalities.

In the last chapter in the section on financial resources Gillian Parker considers credit. As forms of credit proliferate, many people are increasingly able to spread the burden of financial demands and to mortgage future income to present consumption. When present income is less than present needs credit is available to bridge the gap and to refute Mr Micawber's famous maxim. But credit is not universally available and with the extension of home ownership and pension holdings, which increase opportunities for obtaining low-cost credit, access to credit facilities is likely to become less equitable.

Managing Resources

The two chapters in this section address important behavioural issues which are often neglected in studies of income distribution. The first, by Jan Pahl, examines the issue of money transfers within households, drawing on recent empirical research with married couples. The chapter outlines the distinctions between earning, controlling, managing and consuming resources and between household and individual consumption. These distinctions are then used to illustrate potential and actual inequalities in access to, and use of, resources which can arise between members of the same household.

The second chapter in this section, by Gillian Parker, concentrates on one of the eventual outcomes of a mismatch between needs and resources — indebtedness. Consumer debt has grown substantially in Britain since the 1950s, particularly since the late 1970s. The chapter examines the size of the problem, reviews what is known about the precursors of debt, including budgeting and financial decision-making, and gives a brief insight to the experience of being in debt.

The Distribution of Financial Welfare

The single chapter in the final section *begins* the task of bringing together the main themes of this volume in an empirical synthesis. Using Family Expenditure Survey (FES) data it first examines the impact of recent economic, social and demographic developments on the pattern of financial welfare, then explores the ways in which some people are able to manage their resources across the different stages in their lives and, finally, briefly considers the role of the state in response to the financial inequalities revealed in British society.

The synthesis, however, is incomplete. The focus in Chapter 15 is primarily on life-cycle factors, although some attention is paid to lone parenthood and the impact of unemployment is clear. However, the analysis cannot take full account of access to 'hidden' financial resources, intra-household inequalities or, even, the complete gamut of costs associated with the contingencies and life stages described in the first section of the book. Nevertheless, the door is now ajar. It is for others to decide whether the case is successfully made that the door should be pushed fully open.

References

Atkinson, A.B., A.K. Maynard and C.G. Trinder (1983) *Parents and Children*. London: Heinemann.

Baldwin, S. (1985) *The Costs of Caring: Families with Disabled Children*. London: Routledge and Kegan Paul.

Central Statistical Office (CSO) (1985) 'The Effect of Taxes and Benefits on Household Income', *Economic Trends*, 376.

Charles, S. and A. Webb (1986) *The Economic Approach to Social Policy*. Brighton: Wheatsheaf.

Knapp, M. (1984) *The Economics of Social Care*. Basingstoke: Macmillan.

McClements L.D. (1977) 'Equivalence Scales for Children', *Journal of Public Economics*, 8: 191–210.

Muellbauer, J. (1979) 'McClements on Equivalence Scales for Children', *Journal of Public Economics*, 12: 221–310.

Pahl, R.E. (1984) *Divisions of Labour*. Oxford: Basil Blackwell.

Prais, S.J. and H.S. Houthakker (1971) *The Analysis of Family Budgets*. Cambridge: Cambridge University Press.

Rowntree, B.S. (1901) *Poverty: a Study of Town Life*. London: Macmillan.

Rowntree, B.S. (1941) *Poverty and Progress: a Second Social Survey of York*. London: Longman.

Rowntree, B.S. and G.R. Lavers (1951) *Poverty and the Welfare State*. London: Longman Green.

2

The Costs of Household Formation

Robert Walker

Setting up home is a costly business. Traditionally it was a once in a lifetime event; leaving the parental home on, or shortly after, marriage to start a new life with the marriage partner. This is still the typical pattern but an increasing number of people now spend spells in a series of different households. Young people may leave home either to live by themselves or to share with friends; a few, for one reason or another, are obliged to live in hostels or even on the streets rather than continue living at home. Single mothers are more likely than in the past to resist pressures to get married and instead bring up their children alone. Higher separation and divorce rates (see Chapter 7) often mean a fracturing of households into two units with one, or both, of the partners spending spells as lone parents, or as single persons, before possibly entering into marriage for a second time.

This chapter examines some of the financial costs involved in setting up home. For the most part attention is focused on the situation of young married couples since, statistically, this is still the largest group involved in household formation, although passing reference will be made to other categories of 'home-maker'. This applies particularly to the following section which briefly records recent trends in the number and characteristics of households. Thereafter the chapter divides into three. The first part considers some of the financial hurdles which confront anyone looking for a place to live; the second details some of the ongoing expenses associated with running a home and, finally, the third part attempts to cost a 'basket of goods' needed to set up home.

Patterns of Household Formation

Table 2.1 shows that in England and Wales the rate of increase in the number of households has, in recent years, far exceeded the growth in the population. In 1961 there were 14.6 million households with an average size of 3.2 persons; by 1981 the number of households had increased to 18.3 million while the average size had fallen to 2.7 persons. Within the overall increase the number of 'simple' households, that is households consisting solely of a single individual, married couple or one- or two-parent family, grew by 55 per cent while the number of complex households containing more than one basic unit, for example a married couple living with the wife's parents, fell by 21 per cent.

TABLE 2.1   *Changes in the number and composition of households, 1961–81, in England and Wales*

Household type	Percentage of households			Percentage change	
	1961	1971	1981	1961–71	1971–81
Simple					
One person	12	18	22	73	32
One-parent family with dependent children	1	1	3	74	102
Married couple with no children	23	25	25	24	12
Married couple with dependent children	24	24	25	11	15
Complex					
Two or more unrelated adults	9	8	7	−3	−2
One family with dependent and independent children but no others in the household	11	9	6	−5	−22
Other complex households	20	15	12	−14	−11
Total households (thousands, $N = 100\%$)	14,624	16,619	18,264	14	10
Total population (thousands)	46,196	49,152	49,634	6	1

Source: adapted from Overton and Ermisch (1984)

Changes in the number and composition of households reflect the outcome of a multitude of socio-economic and demographic processes. Take, for example, the marked growth in the number of one-person households which alone accounted for 62 per cent of the total increase in the number of households that occurred between 1961 and 1981. The growth, which has continued since 1981 (see Table 2.2), was largely due to an increase in the number of elderly people. This, in turn, reflected both high birthrates during the first few years of the twentieth century and increased longevity. But there has also been an increase in the propensity for elderly persons to continue to maintain separate households rather than move in with their children or siblings — the number living with other people fell by a third between 1961 and 1981 (Office of Population

Censuses and Surveys [OPCS], 1984). However, the growth in single-person households has not been due entirely to changes in the behaviour of elderly people; the increase in young people living by themselves has also been a factor (Harris, 1983). The General Household Survey (GHS), for example, shows that the number of single people aged under twenty-five and living by themselves doubled as a proportion of all households between the early 1970s and the early 1980s. Nevertheless, in 1984, people under the age of twenty-five still represented only 5 per cent of all single-person households whereas pensioners accounted for 55 per cent.

TABLE 2.2   *Household composition, 1981 and 1984, Great Britain*

Household type	1981 (%)	1984 (%)
Simple		
One person	22	25
One-parent family with dependent children	4	4
Married couple with no dependent children	26	26
Married couple with dependent children	32	29
Complex		
Two or more unrelated adults	3	4
Lone parent with no dependent children	4	4
Married couple with independent children only	8	8
Two or more families	1	1

Columns add up to more than 100 per cent due to rounding.

Source: GHS (1986)

Figure 2.1 illustrates some of the processes of demographic fusion and fission which generate new households and is useful when thinking about the developments described in Tables 2.1 and 2.2. Dependent children become adults and while, as already noted, increasing numbers are leaving home prior to marriage, around 80 per cent of men and 70 per cent of women who are not married in their mid-twenties still live with their parents (Ermisch and Overton, 1985). Finance is one factor keeping these households together: an extra annual income of £1,000 increases the probability of a person aged between sixteen and twenty-four leaving home by 3.5 per cent and a person aged between twenty-five and thirty-four by 17 per cent (Ermisch and Overton, 1984).

The main reasons why young people leave home before marriage

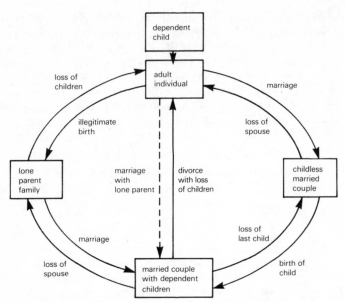

FIGURE 2.1   *Patterns of household formation (adapted from Overton and Ermisch, 1984)*

are in order to study (if they are from middle-class homes or are themselves upwardly mobile) or to find work. However, around 12 per cent say they leave for negative reasons, because of poor accommodation, friction at home or because they were no longer allowed to stay. Many young people live with friends in what are sometimes termed 'intermediate households' (Jones, 1987).

Marriage, however, is the main factor which causes young people to leave home and overwhelmingly the main generator of new 'permanent' as opposed to transitional households (Jones, 1987). First marriages in England and Wales (that is, marriages between people both of whom have not previously been married) are currently running at around a quarter of a million annually (OPCS, 1986). On the basis of studies undertaken in the late 1970s (Madge and Brown, 1981; Dunnell, 1979; Holmans, 1981; Ineichen, 1981), it seems that about 70 per cent of couples begin married life in a home of their own (albeit, on occasion, rented) and about 80 per cent of marriages involve one or both partners leaving their parental home.

The household type which has shown the largest percentage increase (see Table 2.1) comprises lone parents; by 1984 they accounted for 4 per cent of all households and 12 per cent of those with dependent children (General Household Survey [GHS], 1986).

Of the two formative mechanisms illustrated in Figure 2.1 — marital breakdown and illegitimate births — the former has been numerically the more important, at least when a simple cross-sectional view is taken. In the decade to the early 1980s, the number of lone-parent families resulting from divorce or separation increased by over 200,000 while the number caused by an illegitimate birth rose by 135,000. Also, lone-parent families caused by marital breakdown are more likely to live independently than are single mothers: in the two years 1983–4, 86 per cent of female divorcees with children lived by themselves whereas only 59 per cent of single mothers lived alone (GHS, 1986). However, this disparity is being eroded quite rapidly. As recently as 1977–8 44 per cent of single mothers lived with their parents, a proportion which had fallen to 30 per cent by 1983–4.

Published research (Overton and Ermisch, 1984; Ermisch and Overton, 1985) suggests that lone mothers are more likely to form separate households, rather than to live with their parents, if their child is teenaged or if they have more than one child. This may reflect differences in the ages of single mothers and divorced women (it is not clear that the cited research controlled for the cause of lone parenthood). However, the finding also reflects the impact of local authority housing policies and underlines the importance of access to independent housing which is the topic of the next section.

Access to Housing

Once the decision to set up home has been taken the next task is to find a suitable dwelling. The vast majority of people would prefer to buy: 82 per cent of married couples, 86 per cent of households with children, 96 per cent of middle-class households and 59 per cent of semi- and unskilled manual workers express a preference for home ownership (Kleinman and Whitehead, 1985a). The one exception to this rule is single people. Among this group only a small majority (52 per cent) prefer owner occupation. The reasons for this are complex and probably differ according to age. The young may be constrained by lack of money and, more especially, by the shortage of small flats and bedsits available for purchase. Some may not want to own because they feel that it would tie them down. At the other end of the age range, elderly people living alone may be content with the tenure that they have always occupied, or prefer to avoid the upheaval of moving, or simply not want the responsibility that ownership entails.

However, while the majority of people would prefer a home of their own, clearly not everyone manages to buy one. Moreover the preference gap is greatest among younger households and those with children, that is among those who are probably setting up home for the first time. Whereas, in 1982, 84 per cent of people aged twenty to twenty-four expressed a preference for owner occupation, only 30 per cent were in fact owners.

Owner Occupation

From a lifetime perspective, buying a home is an investment that is heavily subsidised by government (see Chapter 9). However, for many couples at the start of their married lives house purchase constitutes a major financial burden. Not only is there the mortgage to pay, but in many cases there is also a substantial deposit to find and legal and survey expenses to meet.

Table 2.3 records the average price paid for dwellings by first-time buyers with building society mortgages. Not every first-time buyer will be a young newly married couple: 27 per cent are aged over forty-four and a lot of these will be purchasing their council house under the 'Right to Buy' legislation. Nevertheless, most recently married couples will be included in the table which shows that, in 1985, 570,000 first-time buyers paid an average of £23,742 for a new house. The average advance was £20,260 indicating that buyers put an average of £3,482 of their own money towards the purchase price. However, Table 2.3 obscures the important, and growing, regional differences in house prices (see Table 2.4) which

TABLE 2.3   *Trends in house prices paid by first-time purchasers*

Year	Average dwelling price (£)	Average advance (£)	Average income of purchaser (£)	Ratio of average advance to average income of purchaser	Ratio of average advance to gross weekly income of male age 21–24	age 25–29
1976	10,181	8,073	4,285	1.9	2.7	2.3
1977	10,857	8,515	4,800	1.8	2.6	2.2
1978	12,023	9,602	5,283	1.8	2.6	2.2
1979	14,918	11,286	6,290	1.8	2.7	2.3
1980	17,533	12,946	7,749	1.7	2.5	2.2
1981	18,166	14,361	8,248	1.7	2.5	2.1
1982	17,762	15,109	8,602	1.5	2.5	2.1
1983	19,513	16,611	8,899	1.9	2.5	2.1
1984	22,174	18,786	9,754	1.9	2.7	2.2
1985	23,742	20,260	10,466	1.9	2.7	2.2
1986[1]	26,965	23,271	11,511	2.0	2.9	2.4

[1] Second quarter.

Source: BSA (1986a) and author's calculations

TABLE 2.4 *Regional variation in the cost of owner-occupied housing*

Region	Average house first-time buyer[1] (£)	Weekly outgoings[2]	
		3-bed terrace (£)	3-bed semi (£)
Greater London	36,829	84	109
South-east	29,855	61	77
South-west	25,313	43	57
East Anglia	14,449	41	58
Scotland	20,572	59	64
Wales	19,635	35	52
West Midlands	19,188	30	46
East Midlands	19,044	29	44
North-west	18,984	28	49
Northern Ireland	18,863	23	38
Yorks and Humber	17,604	29	46
Northern	17,295	29	47

[1] Figures for 1985.

[2] Repayments on a 68 per cent mortgage, rates, do-it-yourself expenses assuming current house prices, July 1986.

Sources: BSA (1986b); Reward Regional Surveys (1986)

means that the buyer in Greater London is faced with an average house price almost twice that in the northern region.

To reduce their outgoings younger people look for cheaper homes and, in 1985, first-time buyers paid about 40 per cent less for their homes than other purchasers (Building Societies Association [BSA], 1986a). Purpose-built, small, low-cost homes are still rare (though see Littlewood and Mason, 1984) so that first-time buyers tend to buy older and less desirable properties. Thirty-five per cent of the homes purchased by first-time buyers in 1985 were built before 1919 compared with only 21 per cent of those bought by other purchasers (BSA, 1986b). Twenty-six per cent of the first homes purchased by a sample of young married couples in 1975 needed outside decoration, 21 per cent inside redecoration, 13 per cent were reported to have insufficient light, 6 per cent were damp, 6 per cent required structural repairs and 4 per cent lacked modern amenities (Madge and Brown, 1981).

Table 2.3 compares house prices and the size of mortgage advance with the incomes of first-time buyers and the average gross weekly wage of younger male workers. It is evident that for much of the last decade men aged between twenty-one and twenty-four earning average wages could not have afforded a house unless they had accumulated a sizeable deposit, and were able to negotiate a mortgage of more than two and a half times their annual earnings (which only 23 per cent of first-time borrowers managed in 1985). Indeed, in the early months of 1986 this group would have been virtually excluded from house purchase. For couples aged under twenty-four the income of the wife is crucial in opening the door to owner occupation and this in part accounts for the relatively high incomes of first-time buyers recorded in Table 2.3. By his late twenties, however, the average male worker should find owner occupation within his financial grasp and, in fact, 54 per cent of households headed by a person aged between twenty-five and twenty-nine are owner occupiers compared with 30 per cent of households headed by somebody younger.

However, some workers never attain average earnings. In 1985 over 63 per cent of male workers aged between twenty-one and twenty-four simply could not have afforded the average house purchased by first-time buyers. Moreover, more than 41 per cent of those aged twenty-five to twenty-nine were in a similar situation. Home ownership becomes a realistic proposition for low-paid workers only if they happen to live in a low-cost housing area or their partner can contribute a substantial second income. For people who are unemployed or for others outside the labour market, for example lone parents with young children, house ownership is out of the question (Murphy and Sullivan, 1986).

Private Rented Sector
Young couples with insufficient income to buy a house and low down on the local authority housing list have two main options: living with in-laws and renting privately. (Madge and Brown [1981] found that in addition 5 per cent of couples continued to live separately until they acquired a home of their own.) The younger people are when they marry, the more likely they are to have to share accommodation with their in-laws. For example, a study of marriages occurring in the first half of the 1970s found that 45 per cent of women who married before the age of twenty started married life in shared accommodation whereas only 21 per cent of those marrying later did so. Sixteen per cent of the younger group and 7 per cent of the older group shared accommodation for at least two years (Holmans, 1981).

More couples probably begin married life in privately rented accommodation than begin by sharing although it is not possible to be sure on the basis of published evidence. In the early 1970s the proportion was about 30 per cent. Since then the private rented sector has declined by 46 per cent and the proportion of couples aged under fifty-nine and living in private rented accommodation has fallen by 38 per cent. However, the number of households in private rented property that are headed by young people has declined by much less: by 26 per cent for those aged less than twenty-five and by only 20 per cent for those aged between twenty-five and twenty-nine (GHS, 1978, 1986). Moreover, there has been a marked increase in the number of first-time buyers moving out of the private rented sector: from 129,000 in 1975 to 154,000 in 1985 (BSA, 1986a).

For married couples the private rented sector is typically a staging post en route to other tenures. For example, Madge and Brown (1981) found that 74 per cent of couples moved out of private rented accommodation within the first two and a half years of marriage. Moves from unfurnished accommodation were predominantly into owner occupation but couples in furnished property were equally likely to move into council accommodation.

However, moves from the private sector can sometimes represent a step down the housing ladder. Madge and Brown (1981), for instance, found that 12 per cent of couples starting in private rented accommodation ended up sharing after two and a half years. It is also possible to get trapped in the private rented sector. An analysis of the 1978 General Household Survey showed that while 89 per cent of private renters (aged under sixty) would have preferred to own a house of their own only 41 per cent could afford to do so. In fact 78 per cent of people renting privately were found to have no mortgage potential whatsoever, that is 'they and their spouses earned insufficient to buy houses in their own region, even those in the bottom quarter of the price range paid by first-time purchasers' (Littlewood, 1986: 89). Moreover, access to local authority housing is becoming ever more restricted.

One advantage of private renting is that it is relatively cheap, certainly much cheaper than owner occupation in terms of the weekly cash outlay, although this ignores both the benefits of capital acquisition which purchasing brings and differences in the quantity and quality of housing between the two tenures. Illustrative of this fact, purchasers able to take advantage of various special, low-cost home ownership schemes being promoted by the government nevertheless ended up with average additional monthly outgoings of about £42 (Littlewood and Mason, 1984). High interest rates have pushed mortgage payments ahead of wage inflation (Figure 2.2) and, while registered rents have been moving ahead of wages since 1982, taking a longer time perspective the relationship between rent and wage levels in 1986 was virtually the same as in the late 1970s.

However, two groups of private sector tenants have seen their rents rise substantially in recent years. The first group includes tenants whose rents are not registered with the Rent Officer. Recent work for the Department of Environment (Thomas and Hedges, 1987) has shown that rents for houses in multiple occupation are, in practice, deregulated and fixed in relation to what the market will bear. Likewise, circumstantial evidence presented by housing benefit officers (Walker et al., 1987) points to a marked increase in rents outside the fair-rented sector.

The other group of private tenants which has experienced large rent increases comprises people who have lost entitlement to rent allowances due to changes in the housing benefit provisions (Homes and Bennison, 1985). Table 2.5 shows that tenants who have remained within the scope of the scheme have experienced the same rent increase as other tenants. However, the net rents paid by those on slightly higher incomes, young couples and families on average incomes for example, will sometimes have doubled since 1982 if, as is the case with many, they are no longer eligible for rent allowances.

TABLE 2.5   *Net weekly rent paid by young 'model' households in private rented accommodation*

Household type and wage level[1]	1982 (£)	1986 (£)	Percentage increase 1982–6
Single person			
85% mean wage	14.90	25.04[2]	68
mean wage	17.06[2]	25.04[2]	47
Couple			
85% mean wage	11.79	17.40	48
mean wage	14.72	25.04[2]	70
Couple plus child			
85% mean wage	10.03	14.94	49
mean wage	12.95	25.04[2]	93
Average (gross) registered rent, furnished tenancies[3]	17.06	25.04	47

[1] Gross weekly wage, all full-time male workers aged 21–4.
[2] Not receiving a rent allowance.
[3] For England and Wales.

Finally, it is worth mentioning that the private rented sector has provided housing for a large proportion of the increase in young single householders noted above. Indeed, Holmans (1981) argued that the fall in the proportion of young married couples in rented accommodation which occurred in the early 1970s was a response to competition from single people. By 1981, 40 per cent of all tenants in private furnished accommodation were single people of working age; in the conurbations the corresponding figure was 49 per cent, although it was less (26 per cent) in rural areas (Kleinmann and Whitehead, 1985b). In practice the young have little choice since only the private sector provides relatively low-cost housing suited to their needs. For example, 52 per cent of all converted flats, maisonettes and bedsits are available only for rent. If proposals to lessen the effectiveness of fair rent legislation and the planned housing benefit reforms facilitate an upward movement in rent levels, this group will be particularly badly hit.

Local Authority Housing
For *families* unable to afford owner occupation, local authority housing has typically been the next choice. The emphasis on families in the preceding sentence is deliberate because access to mainstream public housing, which is allocated on the basis of need, is effectively denied to newly married couples and single young people. Even in the early 1970s, when local authorities were building six times as many houses as they are today, Holmans (1981) found that only about 5 per cent of couples began their married life in a council house. Of those who subsequently moved into local authority accommodation 66 per cent had children before they moved. In the Madge and Brown (1981) study, 50 per cent of the couples moving to council housing were previously sharing (mostly with parents) and another 13 per cent were lodgers, squatters, caravan dwellers and others in very inadequate accommodation.

Of the three household-types that have grown disproportionately in recent years — single young people, elderly people living alone and lone parents — only lone parents have benefited as a group from the 'need criteria' employed by local authorities. Indeed, Overton and Ermisch (1984) argue that local authorities have been largely responsible for providing separate housing for one-parent families. Certainly, the proportion in local authority accommodation has risen from 52 per cent in 1974 to 62 per cent in 1983–4 despite the large overall increase in numbers, although both of these figures include those living in their own parents' home (GHS, 1985). However, the local authority accommodation provided has not always been very suitable: 21 per cent of single parents live in purpose-built flats or maisonettes compared with only 6 per cent of other families with dependent children.

The collapse of local authority house building, the sale of over a million council houses, and the consequent reduction in new lettings (in London from 21,440 in 1975 to 2,300 in 1984; Conway, 1985) has meant that the local authority sector has increasingly been restricted to priority need groups (Forrest and Murie, 1987). Ironically, at the same time, the cost of local authority housing to tenants, other than those protected by supplementary benefit, has risen dramatically: between 1979 and 1986 average local authority rents increased by 256 per cent (see also Figure 2.2). Moreover, certain local authority tenants have lost entitlement to housing benefit in the same way as in the private sector and have consequently witnessed an even larger increase in their net rent. Indeed, it is now quite possible for the weekly housing costs of a moderately low-paid council tenant who is paying a partially rebated rent to exceed those of his higher paid neighbour who has purchased under the 'Right to Buy' legislation.

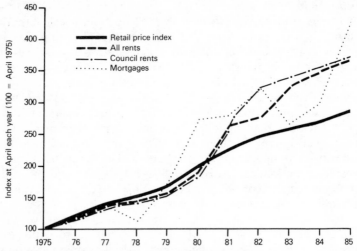

FIGURE 2.2   *Indices of housing costs (CIPFA, 1986)*

The *retail price index (all items)* is recalculated by CIPFA from the series based at January 1974 = 100 (Department of Employment). *All rents* is the housing rents component of the RPI. *Mortgages* is the mortgage repayments component of the RPI. *Council rents* is calculated by CIPFA from the net unrebated average rent figure for all dwellings shown in *Housing Rent Statistics* each year.

The Cost of Running a Home

The only housing expenses which have been considered so far are rent, the cost of house purchase and associated mortgage payments. Clearly there are many other on-going costs associated with being a householder which are to be briefly considered in this section. A point worth making at the beginning, and to be returned to later, is that these costs do not increase in proportion to household size. When an additional household is created, as when a teenager leaves home or two people leave their parental homes to marry, all the individuals involved lose certain economies of scale and the individual expenses rise accordingly.

Table 2.6 attempts to give a picture of average expenditure on housing-related items based on published information from the Family Expenditure Survey. The figures for owner occupation unfortunately include 'imputed rent', a statistical artefact which purports to be the rent that house buyers would be paying if they were renting. For this reason the amounts recorded in Table 2.4 (for example, £33.34 for a three-bedroomed semi-detached with a 68 per cent mortgage) perhaps give a better indication of the actual expenditure of owner-occupiers, although they relate to houses purchased in 1986 (and include rates and do-it-yourself repairs). The differences between gross and net expenditure in Table 2.6

TABLE 2.6   *Average housing costs, 1985*

Item of housing expenditure	(a) Average weekly expenditure, 1985 (£)	(b) Percentage increase over		(a) as % of average total expenditure, 1985
		1979	1982	
Rent, rates and water charges				
Local authority				
Gross	21.18	—	38	13
Net	11.65	N/A[3]	—	7
Private rented, unfurnished				
Gross	18.76	—	22	12
Net	13.95	89[4]	—	9
Private rent, furnished				
Gross	28.56	—	22[5]	18
Net	23.03	78	—	14
Owner-occupied (purchasing)[1]				
Gross	28.57	—	20[5]	18
Net	28.34	85	—	18
Averaged housing expenditure[2]	26.00	90	16	13
Repairs, maintenance and decorations[2]	4.46	109	42	3
Fuel, light and power[2]	9.95	90	19	6
Durable household goods[2]	11.61	64	20	7
Total expenditure	161.87	72	21(14[5])	100

[1] Includes imputed rent.

[2] Averaged over all households including rent free and owned outright.

[3] Changes in housing benefit make it impossible to calculate this figure. From 1983 the rents of council tenants on supplementary benefit have been paid direct to the local authority.

[4] In 1979 housing association properties were grouped with those of local authorities but not in 1985.

[5] 1983.

Source: Department of Employment (DE) (1986) and earlier years

reflect the impact of housing benefits. Adding in the cost of fuel, durable household goods, repairs and maintenance gives an average weekly expenditure of £47.56 which represents about 29 per cent of total household spending. Expenditure on housing rises with household income although in proportional terms it decreases. Thus, in 1985, the poorest fifth of households spent 40 per cent of their income on items related to housing whereas the richest fifth spent 35 per cent. (These figures include expenditure on a miscellaneous group of items which amounted to 7.7 per cent of total household expenditure in 1979.) The critical item was fuel which accounts for 13 per cent of the expenditure of the poor but just 4 per cent of that of the rich.

Table 2.6 also reveals that the costs of running a home have been increasing. Spending on all housing items, except household goods, moved ahead of general expenditure between 1979 and 1985 with the result that the proportion of expenditure tied to housing increased from 35 to 37 per cent. Virtually all of this increase was forced on households (by, for example, rising rents) and does not reflect a choice to spend more on housing. Moreover, for most tenants the increase has been much greater than that indicated by Table 2.6 which is necessarily distorted by changes in housing benefits.

As noted above, there are economies of scale in expenditure on housing items. Table 2.7 reveals that the housing expenditure of each household member is smaller in bigger households even though the incomes of larger families tend to be higher. A single person leaving their parents and an adult sibling to live alone could expect his housing costs to more than double, even on the unlikely assumption that he was previously paying his full share.

TABLE 2.7   *Economies of scale in household expenditure on housing, 1984*

Type of household (all with head of working age)	Weekly expenditure per household member (£)	Housing as a proportion of total expenditure (%)
Single person	33.73	38
Couple	26.80	32
Three adults	21.33	29
Three adults with children[1]	16.86	26
Four adults	15.67	21

[1] Using equivalences implied by supplementary benefit scale rates for a child aged 11 to 15 and the average of 1.5 children for households of this composition.

Source: DE (1986)

Another message from Table 2.7 is that the costs of household formation do not fall exclusively on the new household. For example, if two people without siblings leave their parental homes on marriage the total housing costs for the three new households would be expected to be 26 per cent more than for the original two. (This excludes the fact that the expenditure of new house purchasers is proportionately greater than for other households.) Not only would the new couple have to buy or rent a new home, the parents would pay only marginally reduced housing costs even though they no longer housed their offspring. Precisely where the increased expenditure falls depends in part on how much the young people were contributing to the costs of running the parental home: when the contribution is small, less of the *increased* cost will be borne by the parents. However, for housing benefit recipients this equation has been affected by recent changes in the provisions for 'non-dependants' (Cusack and Roll, 1985). Ten pounds forty pence — or the equivalent of about 60 per cent of the average council rent — is deducted from a claimant's benefit for each child in employment living at home. The amount that the parent stands to gain by way of increased benefit when the child leaves home is therefore £10.40, a sum which has increased in value by 330 per cent since 1982. Again the parents who gain most are those where the child contributes nothing to their keep but, in this case, the overall costs of household fission are reduced by what amounts to a government subsidy. Ironically, this subsidy is counterbalanced, in a probably unconscious system of bureaucratic checks and balances, by recent changes in the supplementary benefit board and lodging regulations which seek to prevent youngsters on benefit from living away from home.

The Cost of Setting up Home

The costs of furnishing and equipping a home are considerable. Traditionally wedding presents have served to share the burden between the family and friends of those setting up home for the first time. Table 2.8 provides two very different estimates of the costs likely to be faced by a young couple. The first estimate is very frugal. It is based on the items allowable as single payments under the supplementary benefit scheme except that new, rather than second-hand, purchases are costed. It covers the basic furnishing of a kitchen, two living-rooms and one bedroom; only two plates, mugs, etc., are allowed for, and no refrigerator or washing machine. The total cost of this basket of goods in York in January 1987 was £1,230.

TABLE 2.8   *The costs of setting up home for two*[1]

Household item	Extremely basic budget (£)	Recommended minimum budget (£)
Furniture and consumer durables	706	3,484
Soft furnishings and floor coverings	240	750
Bedding and linen	103	383
Kitchenware	74	473
Crockery, glassware and cutlery	26	227
General household items	50	216
Garden tools	31	159
Total	1,230	5,692

[1] Lists of the goods costed are available from the author.

The second estimate was derived from lists published in two popular books (Lawther, 1986; Grunfeld, 1982), one of which gives a very comprehensive list of 'basic' household items which might be asked for as wedding presents. In this case an allowance was made for the cost of furnishing a second bedroom, and for a refrigerator, automatic washing machine and vacuum cleaner, and for enough cutlery and crockery for six placings. The furniture costed for this estimate was at the very bottom of the Habitat range. The total cost was £5,692.

The two estimates mark out a substantial range in the cost of setting up home although most young couples would probably aim to acquire most of the items included in the more comprehensive list as soon as possible after setting up home. Indeed, in April 1986 the contents of an average two-bedroomed terraced house were valued at £10,120 and those of a medium-sized 'semi' at £13,629 (C.C. Lee and Co., Cambridge, personal communication). What is clear, however, is that both of the sums estimated in Table 2.8 are large when compared with the weekly earnings of younger workers (estimated to be £156 for men aged twenty to twenty-four in January1987). If the larger sum was to be borrowed from a bank, the weekly repayments would work out at about £49 over three years, or around 31 per cent of gross earnings.

Conclusions

In his 1899 study of York, Rowntree (1899) found early working adulthood to be a time of relative prosperity and current studies tend to confirm this generalisation (see Chapter 15). However, it is quite easy to overlook the substantial costs entailed in becoming a householder, not least because reliable expenditure data is hard to acquire. This chapter has sought to redress the balance by focusing explicitly on the costs of setting up and running a home. In so doing it has not only demonstrated that these costs are considerable but also that they are increasing at a faster rate than most people's resources. Many people, especially those who are not working, already have little real choice as to the nature and tenure of their housing. If present trends continue, the degree of choice will be constrained still further.

Note

I am most grateful to Lesley Warren who tramped the wind- and rain-swept streets of York to provide the figures for Table 2.8.

References

Building Societies Association (BSA) (1986a) *BSA Bulletin*, 48.

Building Societies Association (BSA) (1986b) *BSA Bulletin*, 46.

Chartered Institute of Public Finance and Accountancy (CIPFA) (1986) *Housing Rent Statistics 1985*. London: CIPFA.

Conway J. (1985) 'Capital Decay — an Analysis of London's Housing Problems', *Housing Review*, 34(4): 145–6.

Cusack, S. and J. Roll (1985) *Families Rent Apart*. London: Child Poverty Action Group.

Department of Employment (DE) (1986) *Employment Gazette*, 94(11): Table 7.3.

Dunnell, K. (1979) *Family Formation 1976*. London: HMSO.

Ermisch, J. and E. Overton (1984) *Minimal Household Units: a New Perspective on the Demographic and Economic Analysis of Household Formation*. London: Policy Studies Institute.

Ermisch, J. and E. Overton (1985) 'Minimal Household Units: a New Approach to the Analysis of Household Formation', *Population Studies*, 39: 33–54.

Forrest, R. and A. Murie (1987) 'The Pauperisation of Council Housing', *Roof*, 12(1): 20–23.

General Household Survey (GHS) (1978) *General Household Survey 1975*. London: HMSO.

General Household Survey (GHS) (1985) *General Household Survey 1983*. London: HMSO.

General Household Survey (GHS) (1986) *General Household Survey 1984*. London: HMSO.

Grunfeld, N. (1982) *The Complete Book of Lists*. Loughton: Piatkus.

Harris, C.C. (1983) *The Family and Industrial Society*. London: George Allen and Unwin.

Holmans, A. (1981) 'Housing Careers of Recently Married Couples', *Population Trends*, 24, 10–14.

Homes, P. and B. Bennison (1985) 'Downhill all the Way on Housing Benefits', *Community Care*, 30 May: 10.

Ineichen, B. (1981) 'The Housing Decisions of Young People', *British Journal of Sociology*, 32(2): 252–8.

Jones, G. (1987) 'Leaving the Parental Home: an Analysis of Early Housing Careers', *Journal of Social Policy*, 16(1): 49 –74.

Kleinman, M. and C. Whitehead (1985a) 'Who Becomes a Home-owner?', *Housing Review*, 34(5): 159–63.

Kleinman, M. and C. Whitehead (1985b) 'The Geography of Private Renting', *Housing Review*, 34(1): 13–16.

Lawther, G. (1986) *The Complete Wedding Planner*. Glasgow: Collins.

Littlewood, J. (1986) 'Is Home Ownership for Renters?' pp. 80–101 in P. Booth and T. Crook (eds) *Low Cost Home Ownership*. Aldershot: Gower.

Littlewood, J. and S. Mason (1984) *Taking the Initiative: a Survey of Low Cost Home Owners*. London: HMSO.

Madge, J. and C. Brown (1981) *First Homes: a Survey of the Housing Circumstances of Young Married Couples*. London: Policy Studies Institute.

Murphy, M. and O. Sullivan (1986) 'Unemployment, Housing and Household Structure Among Young Adults', *Journal of Social Policy*, 15(2): 205–22.

Office of Population Censuses and Surveys (OPCS) (1984) *Britain's Elderly Population — Census Guide 1*. London: HMSO.

Office of Population Censuses and Surveys (OPCS) (1986) *Population Trends, 46*. London: HMSO.

Overton, E. and J. Ermisch (1984) 'Minimal Household Units', *Population Trends*, 35: 18–22.

Reward Regional Surveys (RRS) (1986) *Cost of Living Report. Regional Comparisons*, September.

Thomas, A.D. with A. Hedges (1987) *The 1985 Physical and Social Survey of HMOs in England and Wales*. Birmingham: Centre for Urban and Regional Studies.

Walker, R., A. Hedges and S. Massey (1987) *Housing Benefit: Discussion about Reform*. London: Housing Centre Trust.

3

The Costs of Childrearing

Deborah Mitchell and Kenneth Cooke

How much does a child cost? Asking the question as bluntly as that sounds somehow improper or unseemly, even inhuman, as if one were thinking about children in the same way as a new car or a dishwasher. It is none the less a crucial question. Children bring a mixture of pleasure and pain to parents, but they also invariably represent an economic cost. It is of fundamental importance to know what this cost is because, for various reasons, it has become part of public policy in Britain and all other developed economies that the cost of childrearing should not be allowed to lie entirely where it falls.

Governments have had a mixture of reasons for supporting the costs of children. One purpose has been to arrest a declining birthrate; not a principal argument in Great Britain but one presented in the Beveridge Report in support of a system of family allowances for second and subsequent children. In addition, child support has been an anti-poverty device of enormous importance.

British governments only gradually recognised a need for intervention to prevent children being brought up in poverty. Even then intervention came about not without opposition, and not always for the immediate reason of promoting the health and welfare of children. Few social security schemes in the early part of this century made provision for children. Workmen's Compensation, introduced in 1897, included no dependants' additions because wages did not include any. The early social insurance schemes contained no child support at the outset on the grounds that it would undermine the insurance principle (equal benefits for equal contributions) and government conceded the introduction of child dependant's additions only as a cheaper alternative when demands for a general increase in the basic benefits could no longer be held off. Pre-war health insurance never included child support. By 1941, the child support that did exist lacked coherence, consistency and rationale (Brown, 1984: 23). The development had been 'typically British — hesitant, haphazard, opportunist' (Rathbone, 1940: 69).

The Beveridge Report (Cmd. 6404, 1942) brought with it not only sustained criticism of what had gone before but also a reasoned approach to the future. One of the proposals was for child support for non-employed families based (like other benefits to be introduced) on the basis of 'subsistence'. The case for universal family allowances for working parents had been developing before the war and these also were included in the Beveridge proposals, although only for second and subsequent children. The rationale for child support for working parents was partly practical and partly philosophical. The practical purpose was to prevent poverty among families without the requirement of an increase in wages. The philosophical purpose is seen in the fact that no means test was to be applied to family allowances (although they were to be taxable). Family allowances thus represented a form of collective responsibility for some of the economic burden of raising the next generation.

Much of the consensus out of which the post-war 'welfare state' developed has now disintegrated. In a period of economic retrenchment, what was once axiomatic is now the focus of attack. What was once widely recognised as a legitimate and desirable role for the state to perform has been put in doubt. Child support is no exception to this change. The economic burden of welfare has moved to the centre of political debate with the recent reviews of social security and the 1986 Social Security Act raising 'the political temperature' (Wicks, 1987: 22). In the course of taking evidence in the Review of Benefits for Children and Young People, for example, members of the review team were asking, 'Why should someone who consciously decided not to have children be expected to pay for others who decide to have children?' Another member stated:

> I have always thought that if one reaches a decision to bring a child into the world, one takes responsibility, including financial responsibility, for that situation. I do not think I would particularly want someone else to relieve me of it or share it with me. (See Lister, 1984)

The proposals for child support developed by the Institute for Fiscal Studies at the same time were similarly predicated on a principal that parents have chosen to have children and have done so for reasons of personal pleasure rather than social obligation (Dilnot et al., 1984: 5 and 142).

In such a highly charged political atmosphere, where one party to the debate seeks to defend and reassert a 'shared burden' principle which the other scarcely even recognises, or at best regards as unaffordable, it is more than ever important to know what this burden is. So the question must be asked: how much does a child cost?

It is important.to be clear about what is meant by 'costs' and how realistically these costs can be measured. There are, broadly speaking, two kinds of costs faced by families, which can be characterised as direct and indirect. Direct costs are represented by the extra expenditure incurred by families in respect of children. Food and clothing are two obvious examples but account also has to be taken of shared goods and services which are not consumed uniquely by children themselves but whose cost is normally increased by the presence of children. Housing and heating are examples of these. Indirect costs are the opportunity costs of having children, that is, the value of income which is forgone during the time when they are in the care of their parents. Thus the indirect costs are measured by differences in the long-term financial outcome between one course of action (having children) and another (remaining childless). The direct and indirect costs of children are discussed separately in this chapter.

In neither of these senses is it possible to ascertain the full financial costs of childrearing. The best that can be done is to attempt to estimate them by a number of different methods. Some methods purport to represent the minimum cost of a child while others attempt to show the average amount that parents at different levels of income actually spend on children. But all of these methods require the use of assumptions and simplifications to a greater or lesser extent.

Direct Costs of Childrearing

There are three main methods which have been used to estimate the direct costs of raising children: normative estimates, based on skilled judgements about the requirements of children, and often purporting to represent some minimally acceptable level of requirements for children of different ages; budget standards, which are much more elaborate estimates of requirements, and not necessarily related to any concept of a minimum; and behavioural estimates, derived from the analysis of surveys showing not what children need, but what their families spend (although, as will be seen, there are difficulties in attributing this expenditure exclusively to the costs of children rather than other family members).

Normative Estimates
These estimates are formulated by identifying a notional 'basket' containing certain goods that are deemed necessary for a child to enjoy a prescribed living standard usually, but not always, at some minimally acceptable level. The basket of goods (which also

includes services) is then costed to show the resources which a family needs in order to support a child at this prescribed level. The main weakness of this approach is its total reliance on value judgements in order to identify the type, quality and quantity of goods and services that constitute the chosen living standard. Its counterbalancing strength is its (relative) simplicity and clarity; although personal judgements have to be employed they are, at least, explicit and open to scrutiny.

A recent review (Roll, 1986) of estimates of the cost of a baby drawn up by newspapers, magazines and the insurance companies clearly showed the heavy concentration of expenditure required for a child during the first year of life. One estimate (from *Parents* magazine) put the cost of a first-born baby during the pregnancy and the twelve months after the birth at roughly £1,500. This estimate included £157 for maternity clothing and fares to hospital, £755 for clothing and basic equipment for the baby (cot and bedding, pushchair, etc.) and £575 for baby food and other recurrent, week-to-week expenditure. This estimate excludes a number of what are called 'optional extras', for example toys, safety equipment, tumble drier, and makes no allowance for the extra food requirements of a nursing mother.

Other estimates broadly confirmed that of *Parents* magazine for baby clothes and equipment (£755): £803 by *Mother and Baby* magazine and £700–800 by the *Daily Mail* (Roll, 1986: 31).

In an attempt to develop a 'modern minimum' standard for children up to eleven years, the costs of food, clothing, household goods, toys and presents were included together with minimal additional costs for heat and light, school-related expenses, entertainment and holidays (Piachaud, 1979). Estimates of the cost of a baby were deliberately excluded because it was felt that these would be much more variable than for older children, depending partly on whether the baby was a first or later-born child. Although the aim of the study was to establish a modern minimum, the author stresses that the estimate of costs is not 'merely that necessary to maintain life' but rather is 'intended to reflect prevailing social attitudes and standards' (Piachaud, 1979: 6). Nevertheless, one review of the work claimed that the minimum was 'frugal to the point of inhumanity' (Lynes, 1979: 374).

In 1981 the original estimates were updated to take inflation into account. The weekly costs of children aged two, five, eight and eleven were at that time estimated as £8.32, £9.45, £11.42 and £12.10 respectively (Piachaud, 1981a). At current (April 1987) prices, these costs are £11.36, £12.90, £15.59 and £16.52.

This principle of a minimum amount of resources required to lead a normal life, rather than for mere survival, has been employed on an extensive scale in recent years in research on poverty and deprivation. This has been principally in an effort to shift the terms of the debate about poverty away from subsistence and towards participation.

This approach, pioneered by Townsend (1979), still involves a large measure of normative prescription, but what is prescribed is not a basket of specific goods but a general life style, characterised by the possession of certain goods but also by participation in activities considered as normal for the majority of the community at a certain time. Numerous indicators of participation (including for example diet, social activities, possessions and household amenities) are combined into an index and, by observation of survey data, income levels for different family types are established which correspond to the point at which this participation begins seriously to decline (the inflection point).

Table 3.1 shows the minimum weekly income levels for 'young' and 'older' families with different composition which were found to be consistent with participation in the prescribed life style. These income levels are given both at their original (1967) values and also revalued, according to changes in the General Index of Retail Prices, to mid-1981. Simply uprating these values according to price increases over the relevant period involves an assumption that the components of the index developed for the 1960s continue to represent what can be considered a normal style of living in the early 1980s. While it is not possible to justify that assumption here, it is none the less worthwhile making it for the interesting comparison which can then be drawn between these estimates and those of Piachaud (1979).

TABLE 3.1 *Minimum weekly income required for participation in community life style*

Family size	'Young' families		Cost of child(ren)	'Older' families		Cost of child(ren)
	1967 (£)	1981 (£)	1981[1] (£)	1967 (£)	1981 (£)	1981[1] (£)
Man and woman						
(neither over 60)	12.00	56.81	—	12.00	56.81	—
with one child	14.00	66.28	9.47	15.00	71.01	14.20
with two children	16.00	75.74	18.93	18.00	85.21	28.40
with three children	18.00	85.21	28.40	19.80	93.73	36.92
with four children	20.00	94.68	37.87	24.00	113.62	56.81

[1] Requirements of each family type, less requirements of adult couple (£56.81).

Source: derived from Townsend, 1979: 269

The costs of children shown in the table have been deduced by substracting the income requirements of the two-adult family from those of each family type with children. At 1981 prices, the costs of one, two, three and four children respectively in 'young' families appeared to be £9.47, £18.93, £28.40, and £37.87. According to Piachaud's (1981a) estimates presented above, the cost of one child (aged five) is £9.45; the cost of two children (aged two and five) is £17.77; the cost of three children (aged two, five and eight) is £29.19; and the cost of four children (two, five, eight and eleven) is £41.29. Except in the latter case, the estimates from these two different sources, employing entirely different methods, are very close indeed. Piachaud's estimate of about £13.00 for a single teenager (see below) is also close to the estimate for the cost of one 'older' child derived from the Townsend index (£71.01−£56.81= £14.20).

There are two further comments which ought to be made about Table 3.1 itself. First, the deprivation index suggests that older children cost appreciably more than younger children. Secondly, each additional child appears to cost roughly the same. This is certainly the case in 'young' families, although less so in the 'older' families. This implies that there may be few 'economies of scale' in larger families. This possibility is discussed below.

The element of subjectivity in the choice of indicators of participation has given rise to claim (Townsend, 1983, 1985; Desai, 1986) and counter-claim (Piachaud, 1981b; Sen, 1983) about the validity of the results. An econometric analysis of the data (Desai, 1981) supported the contention that an inflection point was validly identifiable, indicating a level of income at which participation ceases to be normal.

Budget Standards
Like the normative procedures already discussed, budget standards are, in essence, costings of a hypothetical basket of goods and services deemed necessary to achieve the prescribed standard. However, determination of the contents of the basket (that is, the types, quantities and quality of goods and services) relies more heavily on evidence from consumer expenditure surveys than on opinions or judgements.

Budget standards, generally devised by committees charged with the task of determining the level of income necessary to achieve defined standards of living, are officially prescribed in a number of countries, but not yet in the UK. Those which have been prescribed in other countries have been extensively discussed elsewhere (Parker, 1978; Cooke and Baldwin, 1984) and the case for a British budget standard has been strongly pressed (Parker, 1979; Cooke and Baldwin, 1984; Bradshaw et al., 1987).

In order to illustrate the potential of the budget standard approach for providing estimates of the costs of children, two standards are presented here. The first of these was prepared in 1982 by New York Community Council (NYCC) and has been adapted by Mitchell (1985) to fit the British context. The second has been created from data on British expenditure patterns in the 1982 Family Expenditure Survey (FES) and illustrates how such data might be exploited to construct a UK budget standard (Mitchell, 1985; Bradshaw et al., 1987).

The detailed budget standard shown in Table 3.2 is based on the standard prepared by the NYCC (1982). Each item in the NYCC budget was translated from US dollars to UK pounds sterling using purchasing power parities calculated by the OECD (Hill, 1984). The figures were subsequently uprated to 1984 terms according to movements in the Retail Price Index.

Various methods were used by NYCC to derive the expenditure required for each component. The food budget was constructed in two stages: first, age- and sex-related dietary needs were specified using an existing dietary schedule; secondly, items from each major nutrition group were selected according to consumption patterns revealed by New York survey data. Clothing budgets were based on survey data for quantities and types of clothing and then priced, taking into account average replacement rates for each item. For example the budget allowance for a winter coat was derived by first determining the unit cost (in UK terms, £30), then determining a replacement rate (one coat every three years), and finally spreading the cost evenly over the period for which the coat was to last (£30÷3=£10 per year).

Fuel and household equipment were treated on a per capita basis and reflect the additional costs per person of heating, additional furnishings (for example, bedding) and equipment (for example crockery, cutlery). These were assumed not to vary significantly with age. The personal care and leisure/education budgets were based on survey data, while the transport and miscellaneous components were simply allotted a certain percentage of the total budget.

Excluded from the NYCC standard are budget allowances for medical and housing costs. In the UK it is assumed that medical costs will be met by the NHS. Housing costs, while an essential part of any budget standard, cannot be realistically converted from estimates based on New York data since these are unlikely to bear any relation to housing costs in the UK. For low-income families it

TABLE 3.2 *Budget standards for children, 1984 (£ per week)*

						Budget item				
Group	Age (years)	Food (£)	Clothing (£)	Fuel (£)	Personal care (£)	Household equipment (£)	Leisure/ education (£)	Transport (£)	Miscellaneous (£)	Total (£)
Infant	0–1	4.71	3.80	0.70	0.42	3.00	—	—	0.25	12.88
Child	1–2	5.58	5.06	0.70	0.63	3.00	—	—	0.30	15.27
	3–5	6.71	4.18	0.70	0.63	3.00	—	—	0.30	15.52
	6–8	8.74	5.04	0.70	0.63	3.00	0.29	—	0.36	18.85
	9–11	10.88	5.04	0.70	0.72	3.00	0.29	—	0.42	21.05
Male	12–14	11.64	4.93	0.70	1.37	3.00	1.99	1.20	0.47	25.30
	15–19	12.77	6.25	0.70	1.59	3.00	3.78	1.40	0.65	30.14
Female	12–14	10.29	6.58	0.70	2.34	3.00	1.99	1.20	0.50	26.60
	15–19	10.29	8.37	0.70	2.34	3.00	3.78	1.40	0.57	30.45

Source: drawn from the NYCC Standard, 1982

might be assumed that children's housing costs are met by the housing benefit system. Alternatively, a standard could be based on local authority rents which reflect regional variations. This problem is considered further in the standard based on the 1982 Family Expenditure Survey outlined below.

As Table 3.2 shows, there is a wide, age-related variation in children's costs. Distinctive changes can be observed in costs of children in the following age bands: birth to one year; one to five years; six to eight years; nine to eleven years; twelve to fourteen year olds; and teenagers over fourteen.

In the discussion of the NYCC standard it was noted that there are problems with applying budget standards developed in other countries to the UK context. These problems arise from cultural differences in consumption patterns, the relative prices of commodities and variations in national living standards. Ideally, the estimation of children's costs in the UK would require a total reconstruction of a budget standard as detailed as that of the NYCC. This is a complex task requiring the establishment of a UK dietary standard and more detailed consumption surveys to supplement data from the Family Expenditure Surveys which are conducted annually.

While the FES data provide a great deal of useful information about household consumption and expenditure patterns, they are restricted in their direct application to the construction of a budget standard. For example, there are limitations in the ability of the data to be disaggregated to identify the expenditure of individual household members. The data are also limited for particular household types. However, the US Bureau of Labor Statistics (BLS), in constructing its budget standard, has developed a method known as S-curve analysis which, with some qualification, is suitable for applying to the FES data.

S-curve analysis is based on the assumption that consumption patterns for various commodity groups typically follow a progression whereby, as income increases, expenditure is directed first towards increased quantities of the commodity, then increased variety and finally, improved quality. The Bureau of Labor Statistics argues that a 'modest but adequate' standard of living is to be found at that level of expenditure where quantity gives way to variety, and at this point 'reduction [in expenditure] meets greater and greater resistance; above which expansions become more and more limited' (BLS, 1948: 9).

On this basis, plotting quantities of goods or services bought against level of income would generate a curve that was roughly S-shaped. The BLS budget standard for a commodity is thus determined at the inflection point on this curve, that is, the point where the rate of increase in expenditure shows a tendency to decline relative to income. This point is illustrated in Figure 3.1.

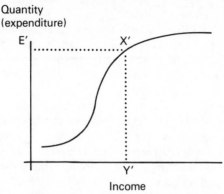

FIGURE 3.1 *S-curve showing the inflection point (X') which determines budget standard expenditure (E') on a commodity*

Essentially then, this method examines quantity–income elasticities. Since data on quantities are not collected in the FES, expenditure is used as a proxy measure in the following analysis.

In analysing the 1982 FES data it has been possible, using S-curve analysis, to derive inflection points for most household types for fuel, clothing and food expenditure. For other commodities this was more difficult and there were problems for some household types of small cell sizes. A further problem which is of particular concern here is that children's expenditure is not separately identified in the FES data. Thus the results shown in Table 3.3 are the *inferred additional costs* of a child when comparing a married couple's expenditure with the expenditures of a household with children in the age groups birth to ten years and eleven to fifteen years. The FES S-curve analysis produces a standard very close to that of the NYCC in terms of overall expenditure.

Table 3.4 summarises the information presented on budget standards in two ways: first, the NYCC and FES budget standard estimates of the costs of children are compared with similar estimates (at 1984 exchange rates) from a number of budget standards in use in other countries; second, the ages of children to which they apply are reduced to two broad age bands for ease of comparison. These age bands are those currently in use in the scale rates of supplementary benefit in the UK. The additions to supplementary benefit for children of these ages and the value of child benefit (which does not vary with age) are also shown. With

TABLE 3.3   *Budget standard based on 1982 FES data (updated to 1984 prices)*

	Age group	
	0–10	11–15
Item	(£ p.w.)	(£ p.w.)
Food	4.92	9.30
Clothing	2.24	5.47
Fuel	0.49	0.73
Household equipment	2.86	5.00
Transport	—[1]	3.22
Services	1.15	—[1]
Other	2.19	1.42
Miscellaneous	2.57	1.26
Total	16.42	26.40

[1] Expenditure in these categories did not differ significantly from households without children.

TABLE 3.4   *Comparative estimates of the weekly costs of children, 1984*

	Age group	
	0–10	11–15
	(£)	(£)
NYCC		
(purchasing power parities)	16.71	25.95
FES (S-curve) budget standard	16.42	26.40
Other budget standards		
(exchange rate estimates)		
North-Rhine–Westphalia	8.52	11.70
Germany	10.82	18.17
Montreal Diet Dispensary	15.48	22.32
US Bureau of Labor Statistics		
(Lower Standard)	18.22	24.59
Child benefit	6.85	6.85
Child additions in supplementary benefit	9.60	14.35

Source: figures for North-Rhine–Westphalia, Germany and Montreal Diet Dispensary from Parker, 1985

the exception of the two German standards, there is some consensus in the estimates shown, suggesting a weekly cost of about £16 for the 0–10 age group and about £25 for the 11–15 age group. Both of these estimates are considerably in excess of the child additions to supplementary benefit and child benefit.

Behavioural Methods
The third method of estimating the cost of children differs from the previous two in that the detailed prescription and costing of a basket of goods is replaced by observation of the goods and services

actually bought. The later of the two studies by Piachaud (1981a) used this method to estimate the cost of teenagers aged between thirteen and fifteen. The author's view was that, given the variability of views about what teenagers need, it would be pointless to attempt to list a set of requirements. The estimates were therefore based on a small survey of teenagers inquiring into what they (or their parents on their behalf) spent on a range of goods and services and what pocket money they received. On average, the teenagers (or their parents) spent £18.45, and on average received about £2 per week in pocket money. The teenagers were also asked what they felt was the minimum needed by someone of their age in order to lead a normal life without hardship. On average they felt they needed £13.15 per week.

More complex methods, based on large-scale expenditure surveys, have been used to attempt to derive estimates of the cost of children by comparing expenditure between families of different sizes. The object here is to determine how much additional income a larger family needs to have in order to share the same standard of living as a smaller family. In order to do this it is necessary to determine a scale of 'equivalence' — that is, a set of factors showing the relationship between the needs of adults and children of different ages. Of the various methods of estimating equivalence scales, empirical investigation of expenditure patterns is the one that has received most attention.

The major problem in this approach is that it is simply impossible to observe in any direct way when two families have a common standard of living. All that can be done is to identify certain circumstances which can be said to imply that their standard of living is the same. One proposition, deriving from the work of Engel (1885) in the nineteenth century, is that families who spend the same proportion of their budget on food have broadly the same standard of living. Engel observed that the proportion of the total budget allocated to food declined as income rose. Where two families of different composition and incomes devoted the same proportion of their budget to food, their incomes were assumed to be 'equivalent' in the sense of purchasing a similar standard of living. By comparing the equivalent incomes of families with and without children, it is possible to derive a set of factors which represent the amount by which the income of a family with children has to be increased in order to have the same living standard as a single adult or a childless couple: hence, the theoretical cost of a child.

Equivalence scales do not show the direct monetary costs of a child in the way that normative estimates and budget standards do.

Rather, they purport to show the relationship of the needs of a child to a reference individual — normally a single adult. Nevertheless it is important to remember that equivalence scales, like normative assessments and budget standards, need to be set at some chosen level, as indicated by the income of the reference unit. In the latter two methods, a particular target standard of living must be identified before the cost of goods and services required to attain that standard can be estimated. In equivalence scales, the costs of additional children vary according to the income of the reference unit. So in all cases, there is a distinction to be made between the *methods* used to determine the costs of children, and the *standard of living* on which these costs are based.

An underlying economic theory has been developed as a foundation for equivalence scales (Garganas, 1977; Deaton and Muellbauer, 1980) yet there is no generally agreed method of estimating equivalent incomes. This is a serious weakness because estimates of the cost of children are determined not only by the age of the child and income of the reference unit, but also seem to be particularly sensitive to the method used. One survey of the literature (Van der Gaag, 1981) revealed variations in the estimated cost of a single child ranging for 0 to 42 per cent of households' annual income.

Engel's method has been developed and extended to commodities other than just food, on the assumption that expenditure on these other commodities also indicates standards of living. Prais and Houthakker (1971) for example have produced an overall equivalence scale derived from a combination of expenditure on a variety of commodities. More recently, work by McClements (1977) has

TABLE 3.5 *Equivalence scale for children*

	(a) Equivalence ratio	(b) Cost of child at 1972 prices (£ p.w.)	(b) at 1984 prices (£ p.w.)
Married couple	1.00	26.50	113.41
Child aged:			
0–1	0.08	2.20	9.07 ⎫
2–4	0.17	4.67	19.26 ⎬ 19.27
5–7	0.21	5.77	23.79 ⎪
8–10	0.22	6.05	24.95 ⎭
11–12	0.26	7.15	29.49 ⎫ 30.04
13–15	0.27	7.42	30.60 ⎬
16–18	0.35	9.62	39.67

Source: derived from McClements, 1977

focused on equivalence ratios for children of particular ages. The equivalence scale shown in Table 3.5, derived from the 1972 Family Expenditure Survey data, is based on a reference unit of a married couple with a net weekly income of £27.50. This figure represents the average net weekly earnings of married couples without children in 1972 (gross earnings of male manual workers, less tax and national insurance contributions).

The factors shown in column (a) of Table 3.5 are those by which the incomes of families with children of different ages must be multiplied in order to retain the same living standard as a childless couple. In column (b), these factors are applied to the average net earnings figure of £27.50. The values shown are the 'costs' of a child in the sense that they represent the additional income needed by families with children on average earnings in order to have the same living standards as a childless couple also on average earnings.

The final column makes these values appropriate to 1984, for purposes of comparison with Table 3.4, by representing the values shown in column (b) at 1984 price levels. The costs are based on a reference couple with a net income of £113.41. An alternative method would be to apply the equivalence ratios of column (a) to the level of average net earnings of childless married couples in 1984. However, because this level (£115.50) is very close to the reference income shown in the table, the results are very similar, and the overall impression is the same. The costs of children up to ten and between eleven and fifteen calculated by this method (£19.27 and £30.04) are slightly higher than the composite figure derived from the different estimates shown in Table 3.4 (£16 and £25) but the ratio between the costs of the younger and older age group is exactly the same (1:1.56) in each case.

Economies of Scale

The equivalence scale analysis presented above indicates that older children are more costly to families than younger children. The next question is, 'Do second and subsequent children (independently of any effects due to age) cost any less than first children?' It is commonly assumed that people sharing a common household can live more cheaply than they could living separately because of economies of scale. For example, a second adult living in a household might add to the heating requirements of the household to some extent, but fuel bills would be unlikely to double. This assumption is currently embodied in British social security; a couple on supplementary benefit, for instance, receive about 40 per cent less than two individuals living in separate households. However, British social security makes no assumption of economies of scale in the case of children, for whom a specified amount is paid regardless of the number of children in the family.

If economies of scale exist for adults, there seems no a priori reason to believe that they do not also exist for children. In the case of second and subsequent babies, for example, there may be opportunies for reusing equipment already owned since the birth of the first baby, clothes may be handed down from older to younger children, and second and subsequent children might not have the same impact on fuel or housing costs as a first child.

A very detailed examination of economies of scale (Baldwin and Godfrey, 1983) took advantage of the larger than normal proportion of families with over three children in the 1978 *Family Finances Survey* sample. In general, their findings suggested little support for the suggestion that large families enjoy economies of scale. Housing was the only commodity which gave any indication that economies of scale might exist. However, the children in the large families tended to be older, and the complicated age structures of these families made it impossible to control for these differences. It was not therefore possible to separate the effect of age from that of family size.

Indirect Costs of Childrearing

Here the purpose is to place a monetary value on the time and labour expended in caring for children. This can be attempted in two ways, either by estimating the opportunity costs of childrearing (the value of the income the parent could expect to earn if he or she devoted that time and labour to work in the market economy) or by estimating the replacement cost of the services provided (the amount which parents would have to pay someone else to perform the equivalent services).

Opportunity Costs
When estimating the opportunity costs of children, the focus is, then, not on the extra costs that families incur but on the income that they forego. A child under five has no discernible impact on the employment of fathers in two-parent families, but a very great impact on that of mothers. Indeed, the presence of a young child is the most important determinant of whether or not married women are in paid work (Joshi, 1984). So in considering the income-effect of a young child it is principally the earnings of women that are lost, and the presence of a young child is more important than other

factors (such as educational qualifications) in bringing about this loss of income.

The period for which women are out of the workforce is obviously sensitive both to the number of children they have and the spacing of the births; it generally varies from seven years for one child to twelve years for four children (Joshi, 1987). However, it is not only the period out of the workforce that contributes to the loss of income, but also any ensuing period when women return to part-time, rather than full-time, employment. This reduction of hours is also, in a proportion of cases, accompanied by a downgrading of occupational status: the Women and Employment Survey showed that 37 per cent of women return to a lower level of occupation after having their first child (Martin and Roberts, 1984: 147). The impact of the period altogether out of the workforce on the number of 'reckonable years' on which pension entitlements are based is increased by about 40 per cent because of women returning to employment but earning less than the threshold at which national insurance contributions are payable (Joshi and Owen, 1983).

Joshi (1987) has made a bold attempt to quantify the impact of child-care on incomes (other than pension entitlements), on the assumption of an eight-year period out of employment followed by twelve years of part-time employment. The results are remarkable: having children costs £135,000 worth of forgone income — an average of £6,700 per year, or £130 per week, for twenty years. This total comprises £54,400 of lost full-time earnings, £48,800 of earnings lost as a result of working part-time rather than full-time, and £32,300 of earnings lost through lower rates of pay.

Replacement Costs

The great majority of child-care is undertaken by parents themselves, principally mothers (Oakley, 1974; Martin and Roberts, 1984), and is therefore unpaid. However, that does not prevent us from enquiring into the value of parents' child-care services.

Unfortunately, very little is known about this important aspect of family life. While surveys have provided data on the domestic division of labour in child-care tasks, there is little hard evidence on the time involved. Piachaud's study (1984) of fifty-five families suggested that child-oriented tasks — the most time-consuming of which was feeding, including preparation, supervision of meals and washing up — required about seven hours per day, or about fifty hours per week. For children under two, the time requirement was over eight hours a day. The cost of replacing these services commercially, at average earnings, would have been about £200 per week in 1984.

Conclusions

Clearly there is no single answer to the question: 'How much do children cost?' The answer varies according to the method used to estimate this cost and also according to the kind of living standard that is taken as the basis of the estimate. The answer also varies very considerably according to whether only the direct (i.e. money) costs of the needs of children are included or whether some estimate is also made of the lost opportunities for earning during the years of child-care or the value of the services that parents provide for children without payment.

Considering the indirect costs first, available estimates are tentative and few in number. These kinds of costs clearly require a great deal of further research. The best that can be said at the moment is that costs appear to be considerable: loss of earnings of the order of £130 per week or, alternatively, child-care services worth up to £200 per week.

In relation to direct costs of children, much more research has been done, but the results are not entirely consistent, always subject to methodological difficulties, and sometimes surrounded by controversy. By revaluing the results of normative estimates of the minimum requirements of children to current (September 1986) price levels, it is possible, with some trepidation, to suggest that the cost of a child aged under ten, at the minimum standard of living consistent with any concept of humanity, is in the range £10 to £11 per week, and that the equivalent for a child aged eleven to fifteen is in the range £13.50 to £15.50 per week. With similar trepidation, the direct costs of children at a standard of living somewhat beyond this minimum, and consistent with some concept of normality, are within the ranges £17.50 to £21 for up to ten year olds and £27.50 to £33 for children over ten. It must be emphasised that these estimates are crude averages for these age groups as a whole. In the case of babies, it is clear that there are very substantial direct costs of special clothing and equipment which may amount to £700–800.

Having drawn some conclusions about the costs of children, estimated by various methods, we end with a comment on the methods themselves. Clearly the indirect costs of children are under-researched and more confident estimates of these costs will emerge only as research and methodological development progresses. Research on the direct costs of children is relatively more plentiful but characterised by a diversity of approaches, some of which are more developed than others.

One approach which, we believe, has great potential and deserves much fuller exploration is that of budget standards.

44 *Deborah Mitchell and Kenneth Cooke*

Although these are used in the United States, Canada and several European countries, there is as yet no generally accepted British budget standard, either for children or for adults. Piachaud's (1979) normative study was explicitly an attempt to establish a modern minimum standard for children, and to compare this with current support given for children in the scale rates of supplementary benefit. Not surprisingly, in this kind of assessment, the tendency is to err on the side of stringency rather than generosity. The acid test of benefit adequacy is to ask the question: 'How well does social security compare, not with what most people spend on children, but with the very minimum that children require?'

Budget standards used elsewhere are not based on this kind of 'social minimum' but on a wider concept of participation. They allow for a much broader range of needs and attempt to reflect the requirements of individuals and families, living and participating in contemporary communities, who are neither affluent nor in poverty. One of the purposes of this chapter is to show the potential of budget standards as a method of estimating the costs of maintaining children at this more generally acceptable standard of living.

References

Baldwin, S. and C. Godfrey (1983) *Economies of Scale in Large, Low-income Families* (mimeo). York: University of York, Social Policy Research Unit.
Bradshaw, J., D.A. Mitchell and J. Morgan (1987) 'Evaluating Adequacy: the Potential of Budget Standards', *Journal of Social Policy*, 16(2): 165–81.
Brown, J. (1984) *Children in Social Security*. London: Policy Studies Institute.
Bureau of Labor Statistics (BLS) (1948) *A Worker's Budget in the United States*, Bulletin no. 927. Washington: BLS.
Cmd. 6404 (1942) *Report on Social Insurance and Allied Services*. (The Beveridge Report). London: HMSO.
Cooke, K. and S. Baldwin (1984) *How Much is Enough?* London: Family Policy Studies Centre.
Deaton, A. and J. Muellbauer (1980) *Economics and Consumer Behaviour*. Cambridge: Cambridge University Press.
Desai, M. (1981) *Is Poverty a Matter of Taste?* (mimeo). London: Department of Economics, London School of Economics and Political Science, p.8.
Desai, M. (1986) 'Drawing the Line: on Defining the Poverty Threshold', in P. Golding (ed.), *Excluding the Poor*. London: Child Poverty Action Group.
Dilnot, A.W., J.A. Kay and C.N. Morris (1984) *The Reform of Social Security*. Oxford: Clarendon Press.
Engel, E. (1885) 'Die Lebenscosten belgischer Arbeiter-Familien früer und jetzt', *International Statistical Bulletin*, 9: 1–74.
Garganas, N.C. (1977) 'Family Composition, Expenditure Patterns and Equivalence Scales for Children', in G.C. Fiegehen et al. (eds), *Poverty and Progress in Britain 1953–73*. Cambridge: Cambridge University Press.

Hill, P. (1984) *Real Gross Product in OECD Countries and Associated Purchasing Power Parities*. Paris: OECD.

Joshi, H. (1984) *Women's Participation in Paid Work: Further Analysis of the Women and Employment Survey*. London: Department of Employment.

Joshi, H. (1987) 'The Cost of Caring' in C. Glendinning and J. Millar (eds), *Women and Poverty in Britain*. Brighton: Wheatsheaf Books.

Joshi, H. and S. Owen (1983) *How Many Pensionable Years? The Lifetime Earning History of Men and Women*. London: DHSS, Economic Advisers' Office.

Lister, R. (1984) 'Foreword', in D. Piachaud, *Round About Fifty Hours a Week*. London: Child Poverty Action Group.

Lynes, T. (1979) 'Costs of Children', *New Society*, 50(893): 374–5.

McClements, L.D. (1977) 'Equivalence Scales for Children', *Journal of Public Economics*, 8: 191–210.

Martin, J. and C. Roberts (1984) *Women and Employment: a Lifetime Perspective*. London: HMSO.

Mitchell, D.A. (1985) *Constructing a Poverty Line for the UK: an Exploration of the Budget Standard Approach*. MA dissertation. York: University of York.

New York Community Council (NYCC) (1982) *A Family Budget Standard*. New York: NYCC, Budget Standard Service.

Oakley, A. (1974) *The Sociology of Housework*. Oxford: Martin Robertson.

Parker, H. (1978) *Who Pays for the Children?* London: Outer Circle Policy Group.

Parker, H. (1979) 'Why We Should Work out Family Budgets', *New Society*, 48(868): 450–51.

Piachaud, D. (1979) *The Cost of a Child*. London: Child Poverty Action Group.

Piachaud, D. (1981a) *Children and Poverty*. London: Child Poverty Action Group.

Piachaud, D. (1981b) 'Peter Townsend and the Holy Grail', *New Society*, 57(982): 419–21.

Piachaud, D. (1984) *Round About Fifty Hours a Week: the Time Costs of Children*. London: Child Poverty Action Group.

Prais, S.J. and H.S. Houthakker (1971) *The Analysis of Family Budgets*. Cambridge: Cambridge University Press.

Rathbone, E. (1940) *The Case for Family Allowances*. Harmondsworth: Penguin Books.

Roll, J. (1986) *Babies and Money*. London: Family Policy Studies Centre.

Sen, A. (1983) 'Poor, Relatively Speaking', *Oxford Economic Papers*, 35: 153–69.

Townsend, P. (1979) *Poverty in the United Kingdom*. Harmondsworth: Penguin Books.

Townsend, P. (1983) 'A Theory of Poverty and the Role of Social Policy', in M. Loney et al. (eds), *Social Policy and Social Welfare*. Milton Keynes: Open University Press.

Townsend, P. (1985) 'A Sociological Approach to the Measurement of Poverty: a Rejoinder to Professor Sen', *Oxford Economic Papers*, 37: 659–68.

Van der Gaag (1981) *On Measuring the Cost of Children* (mimeo). Wisconsin: University of Wisconsin, Madison, Institute for Research on Poverty.

Wicks, M. (1987) *A Future for All*. Harmondsworth: Penguin Books.

4

The Costs of Ageing and Retirement

Robert Walker and Sandra Hutton

Since time immemorial the spectre of poverty has haunted people in old age. The old Poor Law hospitals stand as red-brick testimonies to the destitution faced by the aged in Victorian Britain. Today's equivalents, less monumental but no less real, are the supplementary benefit pass book and the 810,000 elderly people who, for one reason or another, do not claim benefit, preferring penury to dependence on 'the Assistance' (Department of Health and Social Security [DHSS], 1986a). Poverty, then, is one unavoidable theme of this chapter.

However, not all the elderly are poor. Some enjoy a level of prosperity never before experienced and, indeed, 7 per cent have incomes which place them among the richest fifth of the population (Cmnd. 9519, 1985b). A second theme, therefore, is the existence of substantial inequalities in old age. These inequalities are in part an extension into retirement of inequalities present during working life. Of particular significance is the differential availability of generous occupational pensions which caused Titmuss (1963) to talk of 'two nations' in old age. But perhaps more important, certainly in the early years of retirement, is the ownership of assets, particularly a house, which is made possible by a lifetime of well-paid employment. Inequalities in old age also reflect processes during retirement — most notably inflation — which act to erode pensioners' resources at the same time as financial demands increase. Moreover, improving opportunities and better pension schemes have made each successive generation of pensioners more prosperous — or less poverty stricken — than earlier ones. The result is to set apart the 'old–elderly' as one of the most financially deprived groups in modern British society.

The final theme, again one linked to inequality, is gender. Most of the oldest pensioners and of those living alone are women. Most of those who reach pensionable age with few if any occupational pension rights are also women. The twin social phenomena of retirement and pension rights developed in response to the needs and life experiences of men. Women were left in the cold, sometimes quite literally.

The evidence concerning the financial circumstances of the elderly and the costs of retirement is first summarised before considering the class, temporal and gender divisions of welfare which affect the aged in Britain today.

Poverty and Affluence

Poverty

As elsewhere in this volume, poverty is defined in relation to the supplementary benefit scale rates. On the basis of official estimates for 1983 (Table 4.1), about 24 per cent of pensioner families (defined as the assessment unit for supplementary benefit) were in receipt of supplementary pensions or housing benefit supplement while another 13 per cent had income below supplementary benefit levels. These figures are over two and a half times those for other kinds of family. The incidence of poverty is even greater among single pensioners the majority of whom are women and tend, on average, to be older than other groups of pensioner.

TABLE 4.1 *Percentage of pensioners with incomes close to the supplementary benefit (SB) level, 1962–83*

	Married couples	Single person	Single male	Single female	Spinster	Widow
1962	23	—	29	—	—	—
1975						
On or below SB	18	44	35	—	41	48
Below 140% SB	60	79	77	—	70	83
1979						
Below SB	11	15	—	—	—	—
On SB	14	33	—	—	—	—
Below 140% SB	59	77	—	—	—	—
1982						
Below SB	15	26	20	28	—	—
On SB	14	37	23	41	—	—
Below 140% SB	59	78	66	81	—	—
1983						
Below SB	9	15	—	—	—	—
On SB	12	31	—	—	—	—
Below 140% SB	55	73	—	—	—	—

Sources: for 1962, Shanas et al. (1968); for 1975, RCDIW (1978); for 1979, DHSS (1981); for 1982, special analysis of the Family Expenditure Survey; for 1983, DHSS (1986b)

Table 4.1 also shows how the incidence of poverty has changed since 1962. The value of supplementary pension has not remained constant (Table 4.2). Largely as a result of the introduction of the long-term rate for pensioners in 1973, the scale rate for married supplementary pensioners has increased by 83 per cent in real terms since 1962 and by 161 per cent since 1948. Measured against rises in wages the increases are less striking; the supplementary pension for a couple has actually fallen since 1975 from 40 per cent of average male earnings to 36 per cent in 1983 (although the relative movement might be less if net disposable incomes were compared; see Fiegehen, 1986). Thus, while a supplementary pension would buy more goods in 1983 than in 1962, the supplementary pensioner's financial standing vis-à-vis the 'average earner' has changed very much less. As a consequence, supplementary pensions are now a more generous index of absolute poverty than in earlier years but provide an approximately stable yardstick against which to assess the incidence of relative poverty.

TABLE 4.2　*Real and relative value of supplementary benefit and retirement pension (married couple) 1962–83 (£ per week)*

	Supplementary benefit[1]		Retirement pension	
Year	Equivalent value (April 1985 prices)[2] (£)	Value as % of average earnings[3]	Equivalent value (April 1985 prices)[4] (£)	Value as % of average earnings[3]
1962	32.00	30.2	34.06	29.3
1975	53.33	40.2	54.97	34.3
1979	56.59	36.4	58.67	36.5
1982	58.84	37.8	60.25	37.9
1983	58.61	36.4	59.60	36.4

[1] Long-term rate.
[2] Using General Index of Retail Prices (RPI) excluding housing costs.
[3] Average earnings of male manual workers.
[4] Using RPI.

Source: DHSS, 1986a

According to this measure the incidence of relative poverty among pensioners may have fallen markedly over the last twenty years. If so, and unfortunately there is no consistent time series covering this period, the most likely reason is the spread of occupational pensions. Although the number of workers in occupational pension schemes remained virtually unchanged at about 11 million between 1962 and 1983, the decade to 1962 witnessed an increase of around four-fifths (Cmnd. 9517, 1985a). Only a minority of those retiring before 1962 could have had any substantial entitlement to an occupational pension but this was much less the case twenty years later.

State pensions, on the other hand, have contributed only marginally to the reduced incidence of poverty among the aged. In 1962, the married man's state pension stood at almost 97 per cent of the national assistance level while in 1983 the two rates were virtually the same. In both years, state pensioners with housing costs would almost certainly have qualified for national assistance or supplementary pension.

Increased take-up of welfare benefits may have further reduced the incidence of the very severest forms of poverty. Certainly there are reports of substantial numbers of pensioners drawing benefit after supplementary pensions replaced national assistance (Walker, 1983). Also, housing benefits, administered by local authorities since the early 1970s and thought by some to be less stigmatising than supplementary benefits, may have provided a source of income for pensioners unwilling to claim a supplementary pension. However, there is no evidence of a substantial improvement in take-up in recent years.

Affluence
While most pensioners live within the margins of poverty, 45 per cent of married couples and 27 per cent of single pensioners have incomes which exceed 140 per cent of the supplementary pension poverty line. Some have incomes that are high by any standard. Seven per cent, for example, have incomes which place them among the richest fifth of the population once account is taken of the size and composition of the tax units in which they live. Moreover, the proportion of affluent pensioners, defined in this way, increased by 30 per cent between 1971 and 1982 (Cmnd. 9519, 1985b). Forty-three per cent of pensioners own their homes outright, 76 per cent possess fridges and 34 per cent have either freezers or fridge-freezers while 65 per cent have washing machines. Fourteen per cent spend more than the average household on alcohol, 19 per cent on tobacco, 15 per cent on clothing and 13 per cent on food.

While it is impossible to say much in detail about the characteristics of affluent pensioners, it is clear that they have broken free from the constraints of living on state welfare benefits. The majority will, of course, still draw their state retirement pension but social security benefits constitute only a fifth of the income of pensioners with equivalent income in the top quintile compared with 88 per cent of the income of those in the bottom quintile.

Retirement

The reason why so many pensioners are dependent on state benefits is quite simply that they have retired from employment. For most pensioners the decision to retire will not have been made freely. For those aged below seventy state pensions are conditional upon retirement and so, for the most part, are private superannuation schemes. A study in the late 1970s showed that 46 per cent of the men who gave up work at sixty-five would have liked to continue working. Just over half of the men who retired did so compulsorily while three-fifths of men who changed jobs at sixty-five were responding to forced retirement (Parker, 1980). (The same study suggested that there was less pressure on women to retire at pensionable age.) Moreover, pressures to retire, and to do so before pensionable age, have increased markedly with higher levels of unemployment. The Job Release Scheme, introduced in 1977, is designed specifically to create vacancies for unemployed people by encouraging older workers to leave their jobs (Department of Employment [DE], 1980). Similarly, unemployed men aged over sixty no longer have to register for work and are not counted officially as being unemployed. The result has been a marked fall in the *de facto* age of retirement with the proportion of economically active males aged between sixty and sixty-four declining from around 85 per cent in 1971 to 73 per cent in 1981 and then, dramatically, to 53 per cent in 1985. In 1985, 18 per cent of men aged between fifty-five and fifty-nine were economically inactive compared with just 5 per cent fourteen years earlier (Office of Population Censuses and Surveys [OPCS], 1986). Similar, though less marked, changes were evident among unmarried women in the years before retirement age, but the economic activity rates of married women, though fluctuating from year to year, suggest no sustained trend towards early retirement.

Far from having the resources to retire early, many men and women retire into a life of financial hardship. They often retire from low status jobs after having previously experienced long spells of sickness and unemployment which will have eroded their pension rights and may, in some cases, have been the cause of their low status employment (Walker, 1985; Altmann, 1982).

The Cost of Retirement

Retirement can be a welcomed relief from arduous labour or monotonous routine (Phillipson, 1982) and pensioners with suf-ficient resources may be among the first to experience a future age of leisure (Neugarten, 1974). Be that as it may, for many the statutory retirement age establishes the beginning of 'old age': the final period of exclusion from the 'productive' sector of the economy and from the mainstream of social and political life (Walker, 1980; Phillipson, 1982). Only about a fifth of men and women stay in paid employment after retirement age and for both sexes post-retirement jobs are typically of a lower status than their lifetime occupation (Parker, 1980; Hunt, 1978).

Central to the creation of dependency in old age is the fall in income that generally accompanies retirement. Estimates vary from an average drop in income of 50 per cent (Central Policy Review Staff [CPRS], 1980) to more modest falls of 24 per cent and 32 per cent in the disposable income of one– and two-earner couples respectively (Fiegehen, 1986). The latter two estimates reflect the fall in taxation and the end of national insurance contributions which occur at retirement but nevertheless underestimate the drop in income experienced by the majority of people who do not continue working.

Table 4.3 contrasts incomes of elderly households with the incomes of a married couple in the ten years before retirement (see Chapter 15 for comparisons with other household types). The table does not measure the drop in income experienced by people at retirement and masks the inequalities in old age (see below). However, it graphically illustrates the low living standards of the elderly when compared with other groups. The average equivalent disposable income of elderly women who live alone (that is, their income after receiving benefits and paying income tax) is only 57 per cent of that of married couples before retirement while the relative position of elderly couples and lone men is only marginally better. Moreover, it is also apparent from the coefficients of variation included in Table 4.3 that the spread of disposable incomes among the aged is much less than among households of working age; this results from the fact that so many pensioners are dependent on some form of means-tested benefit. Indeed, were it not for means-tested benefits, 47 per cent of retired households would have had incomes which, in 1982, averaged £11.73 per week below the supplementary pension 'poverty line'.

Despite the fact that pensioners tend to have similar levels of disposable income, Table 4.3 reveals that there are considerable differences in the amount which pensioners spend. This is particularly true of lone women. Part of the reason simply reflects the way in which expenditure data are collected in the Family Expenditure Survey: they relate to a two-week period and no adjustment is made for the impact of a small number of people making unusually large purchases during the period. But other factors have to do with the favourable position of owner-occupiers (see below and Chapter 10) and the likelihood that some people may be more able, or more willing, to draw on their savings.

TABLE 4.3   *Weekly equivalent income and expenditure before and after retirement age, 1982 (£ per week)*[1]

	Pre-means-tested income[3] (£)	Disposable income (£)	Total expenditure (£)
Post retirement age			
Single men	55.83 (60)	53.96 (44)	48.82 (56)
Single women	44.84 (63)	47.91 (37)	46.87 (89)[4]
Married couple[2]	57.06 (61)	53.89 (46)	53.15 (70)
Before retirement age			
Married couple[2]	107.62 (61)	83.70 (57)	80.52 (66)

[1] Bracketed figures indicate the degree of variation by expressing the standard deviation as a percentage of the mean. The larger the figure, the larger is the variation in income between households in the group.
[2] Equivalent income based on supplementary benefit relativities.
[3] All income excluding disability benefits.
[4] One person with exceptional expenditure is excluded. Adding her increases average expenditure to £48.83 and the coefficient of variation to 140 per cent.

Source: Analysis of Family Expenditure Survey

Class Divisions of Welfare

The two nations in old age which were recognised by Titmuss (1963) in the 1950s survive to this day. To generalise, they comprise the retired with occupational pensions on the one hand, and state pensioners on the other. The former will typically have enjoyed a stable career in high status employment prior to retirement, while the latter will have worked in a succession of relatively low-paid manual jobs and experienced spells of sickness and unemployment. Many in the second group will be women.

Another division, perhaps less important or less visible in Titmuss's day, is between owner-occupiers and tenants. The former face much lower housing costs on retirement (although occasionally the cost of repairs may become excessive) and, in addition, they possess a valuable asset which may be used to generate income (Wheeler, 1985, 1986; Chapter 10 below).

Finally, the surest route to relative prosperity in old age is to continue in paid employment for as long as possible. However, this option is available only to a select few.

Occupational Pensions

In 1982 about half of elderly-headed households drew an occupational or private pension, but the proportion ranged from 66 per cent for married couples to only 36 per cent for elderly women living alone (see below). The average pension was over £25 per week and contributed about a quarter of the gross income of those households with private pensions. Without their occupational pension, 73 per cent would have qualified for a supplementary pension on income grounds, or 57 per cent after savings had been taken into account. However, not only did the pension lift them above the poverty line (only 9 per cent with occupational pensions also received supplementary benefit), it helped put a third into the highest quintile of equivalent income.

It is of the very nature of occupational pension schemes that they reflect inequalities in the labour market. Schemes are typically provided by larger employers, originally in an attempt to retain skilled personnel, and provide benefits linked to incomes. Not surprisingly, therefore, in 1983 only 58 per cent of manual employees belonged to occupational pension schemes compared with 79 per cent of professional, managerial and clerical staff (General Household Survey [GHS], 1985). In 1975, the latest year for which figures are available, 61 per cent of retired professionals and managers and 74 per cent of other former non-manual workers received occupational pensions compared with just 46 per cent of former semi- and unskilled manual workers. A 10 per cent increase in a man's former wage increased the likelihood of receiving an occupational pension by 10 per cent and, for those with an occupational pension, a 10 per cent increase in their former wage increased the size of pension by over 10 per cent (Royal Commission on the Distribution of Income and Wealth [RCDIW], 1978).

In the past, occupational pension schemes have seldom catered satisfactorily for the needs of the lower paid and more vulnerable sections of the labour force (James, 1985). Small businesses seldom provide pension schemes and even large employers often do not make provision for hourly-paid workers or part-time staff. Employees changing jobs before the 1975 Social Security Pensions Act typically lost their pension rights and, even today, few schemes make provision for redundancy. Moreover, those who in the past were lucky enough to retain all their pension rights when moving jobs saw a great deal of their value eroded by inflation. Consequently, in addition to those who have never belonged to a private pension scheme, there is a group of workers who, on arriving at retirement, receive little in return for their contributions. In 1982, 56 per cent of pensioner households with an occupational pension remained within 140 per cent of the supplementary pension level.

Owner Occupation

Despite the considerable tax concessions and the more recent 'Right to Buy' legislation described in Chapter 10, it is only the better off who can generally afford to purchase their home. This was even more true of the generation now retired. In 1982 about 50 per cent of pensioner couples and 38 per cent of single pensioners owned their homes outright. But, whereas only 35 per cent of pensioners who left school at fourteen own their own home, 69 per cent of those with more education are now owner-occupiers. The latter distinction is partly generational for, although the school-leaving age was not raised to fifteen until 1947, increasing numbers extended their education. However, it also illustrates the association between home ownership and class. Elderly home owners have higher incomes than other aged householders and are more likely to have investment income and occupational pensions. At the same time their expenditure on housing averages much less than the rents paid by elderly local authority tenants (even accounting for the impact of rent rebate and allowance schemes). In 1982 the differential was £4.75 per week although owner-occupiers may have been spending less than was needed on house repairs (Department of the Environment [DoE], 1983).

A further advantage for pensioners who own their own home is that it provides a means of generating additional income. On retirement owner-occupiers often trade down to release extra resources, while mortgage annuity schemes enable people aged over about seventy-five to use their home to purchase an annuity from an insurance company in order to provide further income (and receive a further state subsidy in the process; Wheeler, 1986). Both these factors may help to explain the higher level of investment income which is typically received by pensioner owner-occupiers.

Employment

Not surprisingly, pensioner households where somebody remains in employment have the highest incomes. Indeed, in 1982 they had incomes which were 57 per cent higher than those of other pensioners.

Opportunities for remaining at work beyond the state retirement age depend, among other things, on occupation. In 1975, 30 per cent of white-collar employees continued (or changed) employment beyond retirement age compared with only 16 per cent of skilled and semi-skilled manual workers (RCDIW, 1978). But it was former unskilled workers who, in 1975, were the most likely to continue working after retirement age; this perhaps reflects financial 'necessity' rather more than opportunity.

Often there is a downward shift in socio-economic status on retirement (affecting both men and women) and this is most marked among skilled manual workers (Walker, 1981). Nevertheless, the additional income from work adds considerably to living standards. In 1982, 76 per cent of employed pensioner households would have had incomes below the level of supplementary pension had not somebody been working. This was true of 87 per cent of employed women pensioners living by themselves.

Temporal Divisions of Welfare

Table 4.4 shows that the incomes of the old elderly are on average much less than those of younger people of pensionable age. This is partly because women predominate in the older age cohort (see below) and because only a minority of couples survive intact beyond the age of seventy-five. It reflects, too, the relative advantages which have been enjoyed by later demographic cohorts and the erosion of resources and increased costs that typically accompany increasing age.

TABLE 4.4 *Average disposable income by age and household type, 1982 (£ per week)*

Age group	Married couple (£)	Single male (£)	Single female (£)	Total[1] (£)
60–64	—	—	55.79	55.79
65–9	107.85	66.16	48.15	76.29
70–74	90.79	52.86	48.04	65.62
75–9	80.77	49.05	45.99	57.81
80–84	83.44	48.89	45.23	54.65
85+	81.04	38.79	43.46	44.30

[1] Elderly-headed single tax units.

Source: Analysis of Family Expenditure Survey

Generational Effects
Recent improvements in occupational pension provisions will be enjoyed only by younger pensioners. The very oldest will have been at work for some time before occupational pensions became commonplace while progressively younger pensioners will have been able to make pension contributions for a larger proportion of their working lives. Pensioners retiring in the last fifteen years will have gained from changes in occupational pensions stimulated by new legislation and, particularly, by inflation. Final income schemes, with non-taxable lump sum payments, have very largely

replaced money purchase schemes which failed to protect contributions against the ravages of inflation (Hannah, 1986). Widows'
pensions, too, have become commonly available. Legislation from
1973 onwards has attempted to increase the transferability of
pension rights and the conditions for contracting out imposed by the
1975 Pension Act have done much to improve the poorer
occupational schemes.

Successive generations of pensioners will have pensions based on
a final income that reflects the growth in real incomes during the
intervening period. This higher standard of living — which
continues into retirement — may also be reflected in the number
and quality of possessions that people bring into retirement.

During the early 1960s, in particular, there was a substantial rise
in the number of married women who continued working (or
returned to work after a spell at home). This pattern has continued
with the result that women are increasingly retiring with pension
rights of their own. However, many of the married women who
have already retired will have chosen not to pay full national
insurance contributions and so will not have a state pension in their
own right. Similarly, although the number of women in occupational pension schemes, especially in the public sector, has been rising
since 1967 at a time when the membership among men has fallen,
the bi-modal nature of married women's careers has prevented
many from obtaining maximum pensions (Groves, 1987; see also
below).

A still more potent generational effect arises from the growth of
owner occupation. Largely as a consequence of this growth, 80 per
cent of pensioner households with a head aged between sixty-five
and seventy owned, or were buying, their home in 1982 compared
with 50 per cent of those aged between seventy and seventy-four, 26
per cent of those aged between seventy-five and seventy-nine and
only 19 per cent of those aged over eighty. Later generations may
also have been able to cash in on the house price inflation of the
1970s by moving up-market and acquiring a much more valuable
house than would otherwise have been the case (see Chapter 10).

Process Effects
The same inflation which benefited owner-occupiers during the
1970s led to a substantial fall in the assets of many pensioners.
Income from occupational pensions fell very dramatically in real
terms. No private sector scheme provides full inflation proofing
(though some state sector schemes do) and, in 1979, the last year for
which figures are available, less than 5 per cent of private sector
pensioners had pension rises to match even 75 per cent of inflation

(James, 1985). Similarly, the real value of savings held in a building society account fell by 20 per cent between 1976 and 1986. The elderly, incidentally, tend to have more savings than other groups but the widespread belief that they tend also to save a higher proportion of their income is not correct (see Chapter 15).

At the same time as incomes are eroded by inflation, certain costs tend to increase as pensioners age. Consumer durables purchased before retirement wear out and have to be repaired, replaced or done without. Increased frailty may mean that the car has to be replaced by a reliance on public transport or else it may be used less often with the result that the unit cost of travel increases. Health may fail leading to increased expenditure on medical requisites (notably patent medicines), higher heating bills and the cost of home helps or private domestic care (see Chapter 5). Death will eventually destroy the economies of scale that come from couples living together and, if it is the woman who survives, she may lose a considerable part, if not all, of her husband's occupational pension.

Analysis of the 1982 Family Expenditure Survey reveals that although incomes fall with age, expenditure on food varies little while expenditure on fuel, seemingly greater for elderly women than for men, is highest among the very old. The older aged consequently have less to spend on non-necessities and expenditure on consumer durables, transport and services decreases substantially with increasing age and with decreasing income (Hutton, 1986).

Gender Divisions of Welfare

Table 4.5 shows that a much higher proportion of elderly women than men are dependent on supplementary benefit. Moreover, as Walker (1987) points out, because resources are not necessarily equally divided within married couples, a greater proportion of the women in elderly couples will be living at poverty levels than is suggested by the figures presented earlier in Table 4.4.

The greater incidence of poverty among elderly women is partly a reflection of their longevity. The life expectancy of women at sixty is twenty-one years while that for men is only sixteen years. Women constitute 67 per cent of people over retirement age and 76 per cent of those aged more than seventy-five. Inevitably the low resources of women in advanced old age reflect the impact of generational and process effects described in the preceding section. However, as Tables 4.4 and 4.5 show, within each age cohort women are more impoverished than men. The reasons for this have to do with the wide range of systematic disadvantages encountered by women,

TABLE 4.5   *Proportion of pensioners supported by supplementary benefit in 1982 by age, sex and marital status[1]*

Age group	Married couples (%)	Single men (%)	Widows (%)	Other single women (%)	All pensioners (%)
60–64	—	—	23	27	25
65–9	9	20	33	28	15
70–74	14	21	42	31	23
75–9	17	28	43	27	28
80+	18	20	38	21	26
All ages	13	22	35	27	23

[1] Single people (i.e. widowed, unmarried, separated and divorced) are included in this table if they are over pension age and married couples if the husband is over 65. Couples are classified by age of husband.

Source: DHSS, 1984

especially in relation to the labour market. A few of these are considered below.

Retirement Policies

A 'marriage bar' applied in much of the public sector and in many types of private sector employment until the end of the Second World War. This effectively forced women to choose between a career or marriage. The latter, in practice, usually meant 'retirement' from the labour market (Groves, 1987). Women who chose a career in one of the relatively few occupations open to them, such as teaching, the civil service, nursing, clerical and retailing work, might well have acquired rights to an occupational pension although access to the scheme was often prohibited for women before the age of thirty and retirement was imposed at fifty-five.

A lower retirement age is retained for women in the state scheme and, in practice, is enforced throughout much of the economy (although the 1986 ruling of the European Court of Justice that the enforced earlier retirement of women is contrary to the equal treatment directive may change this situation). Women, therefore, have a shorter working life in which to build up pension entitlement and experience a fall in income due to retirement five years earlier than men. For retired men and women of the same age, women will generally have experienced five years more attrition of their financial resources.

State Pension Provision

Women are much less likely than men to have a state pension in their own right and are even less likely to receive an earnings related addition (Walker, 1987). Indeed, according to the 1982 Family Expenditure Survey, women were three times more likely than men to report that they had no state pension whatsoever.

The reasons are moderately straightforward. A full state pension requires contributions to have been paid in nine out of every ten years of a working life. Many women fail to meet this condition because of time spent out of the labour market (or working part-time) in order to care for children or other dependent relatives. Until 1977 married women had the option of paying a reduced rate of national insurance contributions which still gave them the right to a dependent wife's retirement pension when their husbands reached sixty-five. (The dependent wife's pension is just 60 per cent of a single person's.) Indeed, married women had to work 50 per cent of their married life in order to be able to count on their contributions before and after marriage. One consequence is that many women not paying full contributions tend to retire in their mid-fifties, frequently to care for a sick spouse or relative (Martin and Roberts, 1984). Another is that married women frequently receive a small state pension of their own until the husband retires, at which point they lose an independent source of income.

Finally, although in some ways the State Earnings Related Pension Scheme (SERPS) introduced in 1978 represented a substantial improvement for women (for example, benefits are currently based on income in the best twenty years and widows inherit the whole of their husband's SERPS entitlement although both provisions are planned to disappear), the advantages are counterbalanced by the fact that the low average earnings of women inevitably place them at a disadvantage in an earnings related scheme. Also, the income from SERPS has yet to flow through to pensioners' pockets on any substantial scale.

Occupational Pensions
In 1982 only 36 per cent of single female pensioners received an occupational pension or annuity compared with 57 per cent of single men and 66 per cent of married couples. Moreover, the average pension received by single women was less than £20 per week compared with almost £28 for both of the other groups.

Occupational pensions typically pay benefits on the basis of final salary and according to length of service. Both factors place women at a disadvantage. Also, many women work part-time and in low-wage manufacturing and service jobs where occupational schemes are not provided. Of course some women do acquire pension rights and it is this differential access to occupational pensions which largely explains the very wide variation in income among retired women who have never married. Those who had careers in the professions or in administration, particularly in the public sector, frequently retire with generous and sometimes inflation-proofed pensions. Those who worked in non-pensionable occupations often have no supplementary income at all and are among the poorest in our society.

Nowadays occupational pension schemes typically provide for a widow's pension. However, this is a recent development and previously it was the rule for the pension to cease on the death of the husband (particularly when this occurred after retirement). Any payments to the widow would be entirely discretionary and generally very low. As a consequence, widows are most at risk of poverty in old age. But two other groups of women, as yet too small to show up in the aggregate statistics, are probably emerging with financial circumstances that are equally dire. They comprise divorcees whose entitlement to an occupational widow's pension disappears on divorce and, secondly, unmarried women living in 'marriage-like' relationships who, because of their non-married status, fail to acquire rights to a dependant's benefits (Groves, 1987).

Conclusions

There are, then, many divisions among the elderly in our society. The divisions reflect the outcomes of social processes, both past and present, and serve to frustrate policies which seek to treat the elderly as a single homogeneous group. Elderly people have a range of different needs and a host of gifts to contribute to society.

All of which is not to say that the elderly are getting a fair deal. Nor should the fact that 'since 1971 the number of pensioners in the low income population has declined sharply' (Cmnd. 9691, 1985c: 5) blind governments to the realisation that 'few pensioners are very well off' (Cmnd. 9519, 1985b: 11). Better occupational pensions and increasing unemployment may have caused some pensioners to be displaced from the bottom fifth of the income distribution by families with children, but those floated upwards have not risen very far. With 70 per cent of elderly households living in, or on, the margins of poverty, few can be convinced that the link between poverty and old age has finally been broken.

Note

Original analysis of the 1982 Family Expenditure Survey was made possible by the generous financial assistance of the Joseph Rowntree Memorial Trust.

References

Altmann, R.M. (1982) 'Incomes of the Early Retired', *Journal of Social Policy*, 11(3): 355–63.

Central Policy Review Staff (CPRS) (1980) *People and their Families*. London: HMSO.

Cmnd. 9517 (1985a) *Reform of Social Security*. London: HMSO.

Cmnd. 9519 (1985b) *Reform of Social Security: Background Papers*. London: HMSO.

Cmnd. 9691 (1985c) *Reform of Social Security: Programme for Action*. London: HMSO.

Department of Employment (DE) (1980) *Job Release Schemes*. London: DE.

Department of Health and Social Security (DHSS) (1981) *Low Income Families 1979*. London: DHSS.

Department of Health and Social Security (DHSS) (1984) *Population, Pension Costs and Pensioners' Incomes*. London: HMSO.

Department of Health and Social Security (DHSS) (1986a) *Social Security Statistics*. London: HMSO.

Department of Health and Social Security (DHSS) (1986b) *Low Income Families 1983*. London: DHSS.

Department of the Environment (DoE) (1983) *English House Condition Survey 1981*. London: HMSO.

Fiegehen, G.C. (1986) 'Income After Retirement', *Social Trends*, 16: 13–18.

General Household Survey (GHS) (1985) *General Household Survey 1983*. London: HMSO.

Groves, D. (1987) 'Occupational Pension Provision and Women's Poverty in Old Age', in C. Glendinning and J. Millar (eds), *Women and Poverty in Britain*. Brighton: Wheatsheaf Books.

Hannah, L. (1986) *Inventing Retirement: The Development of Occupational Pensions in Britain*. Cambridge: Cambridge University Press.

Hunt, A. (1978) *The Elderly at Home*. London: HMSO/OPCS.

Hutton, S. (1986) *Poverty and Affluence in Old Age: A Preliminary Analysis of the 1982 FES*. Working Paper 308. York: Social Policy Research Unit, York University.

James, C. (1985) 'Occupational and Private Pension Schemes', pp.34–9, in R. Silburn (ed.), *The Future of Social Security*. London: Fabian Society.

Martin, J. and C. Roberts (1984) *Women and Employment: a Lifetime Perspective*. London: HMSO.

Neugarten, B.L. (1974) 'Age Groups in American Society and the Rise of the Young-Old', *Annals of the American Academy of Political Science*, 415: 187–98.

Office of Population Censuses and Surveys (OPCS) (1986) *OPCS Monitor: Reference GHS 86/1*. London: OPCS.

Parker, S. (1980) *Older Workers and Retirement*. London: OPCS.

Phillipson, C. (1982) *Capitalism and the Construction of Old Age*. London: Macmillan.

Royal Commission on the Distribution of Income and Wealth (RCDIW) (1978) *The Causes of Poverty. RCDIW Background Paper 5*. London: HMSO.

Shanas, E., P. Townsend, D. Wedderburn, F. Henning, P. Milhøf and J. Stehouwer (1968) *Old People in Three Industrial Societies*. London: Routledge and Kegan Paul.

Titmuss, R. (1963) *Essays on the Welfare State*, 2nd ed. London: George Allen and Unwin.

Walker, A. (1980) 'The Social Creation of Poverty and Dependency in Old Age', *Journal of Social Policy*, 9(1): 49–75.

Walker, A. (1981) 'Towards a Political Economy of Old Age', *Ageing and Society*, 1(1): 73–94.

Walker, A. (1985) 'Early Retirement: Release or Refuge from the Labour Market?' *Quarterly Journal of Social Affairs*, 1(3): 211–29.

Walker, A. (1987) 'The Poor Relation: Poverty among Old Women', in C. Glendinning and J. Millar (eds), *Women and Poverty in Britain*. Brighton: Wheatsheaf Books.

Walker, C. (1983) *Changing Social Policy*. Occasional Papers on Social Administration, 70. London: London School of Economics.

Wheeler, R. (1985) *Don't Move: We've Got you Covered*. London: Institute of Housing.

Wheeler, R. (1986) 'Housing Policy and Elderly People', in C. Phillipson and A. Walker (eds), *Ageing and Social Policy*. Aldershot: Gower.

5
The Costs of Disability

Caroline Glendinning and Sally Baldwin

It has long been recognised that all forms of ill-health and disability can have serious financial consequences. Since the nineteenth century the range and variety of these consequences have been recognised in the legal system which provides full and generous compensation, though only to the tiny minority able to establish that their disability was caused by someone else's negligence. Social security has been slow to follow the example set by the law. Historically the war pensions and industrial injuries schemes reflected an official response to disablement which was both partial and very restricted, providing low rates of benefit for soldiers and workers alike and nothing at all for civilians disabled outside the work setting. The Beveridge reforms after the Second World War did little to change this situation. However, in the past two decades this limited provision and the rudimentary awareness on which it was based have been challenged by increasing evidence on the financial consequences of disablement, on their causes and effects, and on the effectiveness of the welfare provision designed to mitigate those effects.

The impetus for highlighting the financial consequences of disablement came initially from groups of and for disabled people, who were concerned to draw attention to their inadequate and inequitable financial circumstances, using evidence from their own and government-sponsored research to do so. More recently, critiques of 'community care' policies by feminists and by the carers of people with disabilities have further extended understanding of the financial effects of disability by drawing attention to the costs of disablement which are borne by (mainly female) carers and other family members.

It is now possible, therefore, to begin to map the complex relationships between disablement, money and living standards. The areas in which disablement is likely to have adverse financial consequences can be described and the person or people most likely to experience these effects can be identified. However, it is still difficult to assign accurate monetary values to some of the financial costs and disadvantages arising from disability. Despite the attempts of some pioneering studies to do this, difficult methodological problems remain.

There are three main reasons why disability may have financial consequences. First, disabled adults typically have lower incomes than average and are at greater risk of living in or on the margins of poverty. Secondly, extra expenses often arise, creating extra demands which may be impossible to meet from the resources available, or may be met only by sacrificing some other necessity. Thirdly, disability commonly gives rise to additional needs for personal care and practical help.

Cutting across these financial consequences, however, is a second important issue — that of who actually experiences or carries them. For example, people with disabilities directly experience disadvantage in the labour market but the reduced incomes they can command may affect other members of the households in which they live. Similarly, while people with disabilities may themselves have to accommodate extra expenses which arise in relation to their disablement, other household members may have to cut down on or give up certain items of expenditure in order to pay for the disabled person's additional needs.

State and, to a much smaller extent, private and occupational welfare systems also carry some of these financial consequences of disability: through sick-pay, invalidity pensions and other income replacement benefits; and through the attendance and mobility allowances which are specifically intended to offset some of the extra costs of disability.

The financial consequences of the need for personal care may be equally widely dispersed. Again, some may fall directly and solely on the disabled person who might, for example, buy in private domestic help at the going market rate. Some of the costs of providing care are met by the welfare state and voluntary organisations: through domiciliary services such as meals on wheels, home helps and care attendants; through day centres, holiday and respite care in hospitals or hostels, and through the invalid care allowance (ICA). However, much of the cost of providing care falls on the informal sector: on close friends and relatives, and in many instances on one principal carer. For these carers, financial costs through the loss of employment and earnings are becoming increasingly apparent as are other, less easily quantifiable, non-financial costs. The financial impact of providing care can also be experienced by other family members whose standards of living are reduced by the loss of the carer's earnings.

There is no clear or consistent relationship between any particular financial consequence of disability and where its main impact falls. Furthermore, the main burden of the cost of disability may shift between sectors over time, both for the population as a whole and for individual disabled people. Parker (1985), for example, has argued that over the past two decades responsibility for carrying the costs of caring for disabled people has shifted dramatically from the statutory to the informal and private sectors. Conversely, the financial impact of disability may shift in the opposite direction from the family to the state if, for example, a disabled person is admitted to long-term hospital care.

Those costs of disability which are borne by statutory services or income maintenance systems are not the focus of this chapter except in so far as they help to mitigate or offset the financial impact of disability on disabled individuals and their families. We shall be concerned with effects on individuals, and are particularly concerned to emphasise that these effects are frequently experienced by people other than the disabled person her or himself. These effects may not be readily apparent, so we shall draw particular attention to some of the hidden costs of disability.

The Impact of Disability

Lower Incomes
As indicated earlier, many adults with disabilities have lower incomes than their able-bodied counterparts, especially during their working years but also, to a lesser extent, in old age. The reasons for this are two-fold: first, their access to continuous well-paid employment tends to be restricted or prevented; secondly, the levels and structure of the social security benefits on which very many people with disabilities consequently depend are inadequate.

Loss of earnings. For disabled people of working age, disability is almost invariably associated with a reduction in, or complete loss of, income from paid work. Legislation does exist which is intended to promote the employment opportunities of people with substantial disabilities or handicaps, for example the 1944 Disabled Persons (Employment) Act. However, it is widely agreed that enforcement of the 1944 Act has been inadequate and that subsequent policy measures have worsened the employment opportunities of people with disabilities (Jordan, 1979; Darnborough and Kinrade, 1981; Lonsdale and Walker, 1984). Further, those who do enter the labour market are at greater risk of becoming unemployed, and for longer periods, than their able-bodied peers. In 1981, for example, 16 per cent of registered disabled people were unemployed, twice as many as in the workforce as a whole. Moreover, nearly three-fifths of the former, as against only a quarter of the latter, had been unemployed for more than a year (Townsend, 1981a). These official figures depend upon a disabled person having registered both as unemployed and as disabled; the actual rate of unemployment among disabled people may be much higher. Townsend (1979) estimated rates of 28 per cent for men and 56 per cent for women, and growing unemployment generally will have further increased the numbers of unemployed disabled people in recent years. The chances of being in employment also decrease further as the severity of disability increases (Harris et al., 1971; Townsend, 1979).

The difficulties of obtaining employment affect disabled people of all ages. School-leavers with disabilities are much more likely than their non-handicapped peers to experience unemployment or underemployment (Walker, 1982a; Hirst, 1983). At the other end of working life, disabled people are more likely to find themselves withdrawing early from the labour market through voluntary redundancy and early retirement (Walker, 1985; Dex and Phillipson, 1986; Piachaud, 1986).

The disadvantages associated with disability do not end once paid work has been found. The earnings of disabled workers are lower than those of non-disabled people, particularly in some sheltered workshops and training centres, and fall as the severity of disability increases (Harris et al., 1972; Layard et al., 1978; Jordan, 1979; Townsend, 1979; Lonsdale and Walker, 1984). On the whole, low take-home pay reflects lower hourly rates of pay rather than shorter working hours; indeed, disabled people tend to work longer hours than the non-disabled. They are also more likely than non-disabled people to have poor promotion prospects and a poor physical working environment (Townsend, 1979).

Unemployment, interrupted employment or employment in low-paid jobs with poor prospects also affect income after retirement. People with disabilities are less likely to work in jobs with the kind of occupational pension provision which will protect them from poverty in old age (Walker, 1986) and lower pay in employment affects the level of the pension received, whether occupational or provided by the state. Significantly, the intention to calculate the State Earnings Related Pension Scheme (SERPS) from 1988 on the basis of lifetime rather than the best twenty years' earnings will further disadvantage disabled workers (see Chapter 4).

Income from social security benefits. Disabled people who are unable to earn altogether, unable to earn an adequate income from paid employment, or to generate adequate occupational welfare provision for themselves when no longer working must necessarily look to state social security benefits as their main or only means of financial support. The last official national survey of people with disabilities, carried out in 1969, found that 74 per cent of the disabled people in the sample and over 80 per cent of the very severely disabled received one or more social security benefits (Harris et al., 1971). However, there is substantial evidence that these benefits fail to provide adequate incomes for the majority of people dependent on them.

First, successive governments have failed to maintain the real value of social security benefits for people with disabilities. Cuts in the levels of national insurance benefits — the abolition of the earnings related supplement to sickness benefit and the 5 per cent 'abatement' of invalidity benefit between 1980 and 1985 for example — have increased the numbers of people with disabilities who have to turn to means-tested supplementary benefit to top up their incomes (Disability Alliance, 1980). Further, the adequacy of supplementary benefit levels is widely questioned. There is clear evidence that the living standards of households dependent on supplementary benefit are much lower than those of the general population and lower than those of even the poorest households in work (Cooke and Baldwin, 1984). The position of supplementary benefit recipients has worsened in recent years as the relative value of their benefits has declined and access to discretionary extra payments for special needs has been restricted (Franey, 1983).

Secondly, the system of social security benefits for people with disabilities lacks coherence. The type and level of the benefits received by any individual often bear little relationship to the nature, extent and severity of their disability, or the practical difficulties which arise from it. Important new benefits have been created during the last fifteen years, but these developments have been ad hoc and piecemeal. Social security benefit provision for people with disabilities is characterised by inconsistencies and inequities which pre-date Beveridge's welfare scheme (Baldwin et al., 1981; Walker, 1981; Brown, 1984), and complexities to which recent developments and innovations have only added. In addition, a complex system of benefits with an increasingly heavy reliance on eligibility through means-testing inevitably leads to problems of take-up (Harris et al., 1971 and 1972; Simkins and Tickner, 1978; Casserley and Clark, 1978; Phillips and Glendinning, 1981).

Disability and poverty. Low earnings from paid work and heavy reliance on state social security income maintenance — particularly means-tested benefits — together render people with disabilities particularly vulnerable to poverty. The evidence for this is clear and depressingly enduring. In 1969 over a quarter (26 per cent) of impaired adults living outside institutional settings had incomes at or below supplementary benefit level (Harris et al., 1972: Table 10). Townsend (1979) similarly found that the proportion of people with even minor disabilities who had incomes below the supplementary benefit poverty line was more than double that of the non-disabled. The disabled adults in Townsend's study were also more likely to experience other forms of deprivation: they were more likely to be in debt; less likely to have savings or other assets; more likely to live in poor housing; and less likely to possess standard consumer durables. The risk of poverty also increases with the severity of disability. The proportion of adults with appreciable or severe disabilities whom Townsend found to be living in poverty (68 per cent was nearly three times that of the non-disabled (see also Layard et al., 1978: 13).

It is important to recognise that conventional measures of poverty — in particular the relationship of a person's income to her or his notional supplementary benefit entitlement — do not take into account any extra demands on income arising from disability. Even the more generous poverty line of 140 per cent of supplementary benefit, constructed to reflect the extra needs for which additional supplementary benefit payments are frequently made, may not match the extra costs actually incurred. These additional needs mean that conventional measures of poverty are likely seriously to underestimate both the extent and the level of the hardship and financial restriction experienced by people with disabilities. The nature and size of these extra demands are considered in the next section.

The Extra Costs of Disablement
Identifying the various types of extra need which may be occasioned by disability is relatively straightforward; calculating the actual amounts of money expended in meeting those needs is far less simple and, where it is possible, may oversimplify the financial impact of disability. Needs may remain unmet because there is simply not enough money to meet them. Conversely, they may be met by cheap, unsatisfactory alternatives or at the expense of other members of the family. Further, needs can sometimes be met because less money has to be spent on other items which are *not* needed because of disability; for example, the extra cost of a special wheelchair may be offset by greatly reduced spending on footwear. The timing of expenditure may be affected: items have to be bought sooner than planned, involving the reallocation of savings from

their intended purpose or the use of expensive credit. Some additional costs are not easy to calculate, for example the costs of buying 'convenience' foods rather than cheaper raw ingredients, or being unable to 'shop around' for bargains, or to make and repair clothes and household furnishings. In other words, simply calculating what people actually spend may tell us little about the true financial impact of disability, unless we also know something about the strategies which they employ to meet the various demands on their resources.

A number of studies have attempted to quantify the extra costs of disability and, to some extent, to place these in the context of families' financial strategies. Baldwin's (1985) study of disabled children and their families, for example, identified three main types of extra expenditure.

First, there were regular weekly or monthly expenses: on fuel and heating (78 per cent of Baldwin's sample said that their child's disability increased the amount of fuel they used); on food; on clothing and shoes (63 per cent of families spent extra on these); on transport, especially on cars which families would otherwise have managed without; and on household commodities such as telephones. All the families in Baldwin's study spent more, in total, each week than a similar 'control' group of families without a disabled child. However, the actual amount varied according to families' incomes, with the poorest and richest families spending a higher extra amount than those in the middle income range. The average extra weekly spending on housekeeping and household durables for families in this middle income range was £12 (1984 price levels). In addition, Baldwin found evidence that families' *patterns* of regular spending had altered; they were economising on some items in order to spend more on the extra items needed by their disabled children.

Secondly, there was extra expenditure which occurred less frequently, on items such as house alterations or moving house, and on special equipment, furniture or consumer durables such as washing machines, dryers or freezers. The average amount spent on these intermittent items of expenditure during the two years (1976–8) preceding Baldwin's survey was £184.

Thirdly, hospital costs loomed large for many families, both for outpatient appointments and when their children were admitted for treatment. Parents spent extra on transport, presents for the disabled child and child-care expenses for other children in the family.

With the less regular types of expenditure, some families bought items they would not normally have bought at all but more often it was the timing of the expenditure which was different. Washing machines were worn out more quickly by constant heavy use, unreliable cars had to be repaired or replaced immediately, while a child's serious illness or sudden hospital admission could disrupt budgeting for routine household expenditure and create financial difficulties which took months to sort out.

Families adopted a number of strategies for coping with the impact of the child's disablement on their finances. Some husbands, for example, reported attempting to increase their earnings, typically by working more overtime. Wives said that they had been forced to become much more efficient at handling money, bargain-hunting and buying in bulk wherever possible. Couples reported that they handled their money and took decisions together much more than before, with less of the man's earnings allocated to his personal spending than previously. For some families the child's disablement created involuntary savings — they found it too difficult to go out or on holiday. For others such economies were necessary if the disabled child's needs were to be met: parents and other members of the family had been forced to give up activities and small luxuries which friends without a disabled child took for granted. Even so, most reported chronic and depressing money worries, inability ever to pay bills on time and great difficulty in saving to replace furniture or cars or for possible emergencies.

Studies of adult wheelchair users (Hyman, 1977) and of children and adults with mental handicaps (Buckle, 1984) have demonstrated the extra costs which other groups of people with disabilities and their families incur. The wheelchair users in Hyman's study had extra costs at an annual average of £735 (1975 price levels), representing around 24 per cent of household income. Among people with mental handicaps families spent an average of £19.50 a week on additional needs — 8.9 per cent of average weekly household income (1981 price levels). In addition, an average of £3,645 (1981 price levels) had been spent on one or more extra items of capital expenditure during the mentally handicapped person's lifetime (Buckle, 1984).

There is much less evidence on the extra costs of disabilities which arise in old age, although elderly people constitute by far the largest group of moderately or severely disabled people. In part this lack of evidence results from a widespread failure to recognise the specific problems of disability and their consequences among the elderly (Townsend, 1981b). In addition, the substantially lower incomes received by men on retirement from the labour market (Walker, 1980 and 1986) and elderly women's unequal access to adequate state or occupational pension provision (Walker, 1987; Groves,

1987; see also Chapter 4) mean that elderly disabled people have fewer identifiable extra expenses simply because they have insufficient resources available to meet their extra needs.

Some of the extra expenses arising from disability in old age *are* relatively well known, such as the extra heating needed by people whose mobility is restricted by advancing age (Wicks, 1978). What are less easy to identify are the amounts, if any, which elderly disabled people can spend on meeting those needs without jeopardising other aspects of their material well-being (see Chapter 4); or which other family members spend on the elderly person's behalf.

In sum, disability causes extra needs which frequently give rise to additional spending. The areas in which these needs most commonly occur are heating and fuel, clothing, transport, housing adaptations and aids, food, household items, and needs arising from medical or nursing problems. The actual level of extra expenditure will vary with the financial resources available and the nature of the disability.

To some extent extra costs are recognised and may be offset by social security benefits, in particular by exceptional circumstances additions (till 1980) and additional requirements (from 1980 till 1988) for supplementary benefit claimants and by the non-means-tested attendance and mobility allowances. However, there is evidence that neither type of benefit adequately meets the actual level of expense incurred by many disabled people. The levels of additional requirements have been criticised as they do not cover the full range of additional expenditure and their take up is inadequate (Avery, 1983). Following the changes to the supplementary benefit scheme due to be implemented in 1988, the specific additional expenses incurred by people with disabilities will no longer be recognised. Despite the compensatory 'premiums' to be paid instead to people with disabilities, their overall financial situation is likely to be worsened (Disability Alliance, 1985). Further, the attendance and mobility allowances, also designed to meet the extra costs of disablement, do not cover all the extra expenditure associated with disability (Buckle, 1984; Baldwin, 1985).

The Financial Consequences of Caring

It is now accepted that disability may have financial consequences for people other than the person with the disability, both inside and outside the household. The costs identified in Baldwin's study of disabled children, for example, were borne principally by their parents. For disabled adults the picture is much less clear and the exact apportionment of costs between the disabled person and other household members can be established only from detailed research. Early research in this field tended, however, to overlook the costs carried by others. First, the costs incurred were identified on a household or family basis (Hyman, 1977) thus making it impossible to see on which individual(s) they actually fell. Secondly, no attempt was made to cost the care given to disabled people by relatives and friends. This was assumed to be entirely congruent with normal family obligations and commitments. The clearest articulation of this assumption appeared in the 1974 White Paper on Social Security Provision for Chronically Sick and Disabled People, which argued that social security provision for working-age carers should exclude married women 'as they might be at home in any event' (HMSO, 1974: 20; see also Groves and Finch, 1983). However, analyses of gender divisions in formal and informal systems of social welfare (see, for example, Land, 1978; Walker, 1982b) and critiques of the current implementation of 'community care' policies (Finch and Groves, 1980; Rimmer, 1983) have all questioned this assumption. Increasingly, therefore, attempts are being made to identify and quantify the costs of caring — those financial consequences of disability borne by carers rather than by the disabled person her or himself.

Loss of Earnings
One of the areas in which costs occur is in relation to carers' paid work. It is here that the most thorough research has been carried out — largely because it is relatively easy to compare carers' activities in the public domain of the labour market with those of their peers. This approach was taken by Baldwin (1985), who compared the labour market participation and hourly rates of pay of parents with and without disabled children. She found that the mothers of disabled children were much less likely to be in paid work. When they were, they worked fewer hours, at lower hourly rates of pay, than their control group counterparts. The differences between the two groups were the most marked between mothers whose youngest child had reached secondary school age. There was a difference of £5.70 in the average weekly earnings of women in the two groups who had a pre-school child; but among those whose youngest child was over ten this difference had virtually trebled, to £16.30 (1978 figures): 'These women [with disabled children] had a much smaller chance, than the general population of women with older children especially, of breaking out of part-time casual and unskilled work, of resuming former careers or of training for new ones' (Baldwin, 1985: 83).

Deviation from the typical pattern of women's labour market

participation increases as children with disabilities grow into young adulthood. Far fewer mothers of severely disabled young people (aged eighteen to twenty-two) are in paid employment than their same age counterparts and those in work are far more likely to be restricted to part-time work. Both part-time and full-time employees earn less on average than their counterparts in the general population (Hirst, 1985).

The impact of a disabled child on men's employment and earnings is far less clear. In Baldwin's study, fathers of disabled children in unskilled manual occupations were slightly more likely to be unemployed than their counterparts in the general population. Overall, however, the earnings of manual workers with a disabled child were very similar to those of other manual workers — possibly because low earnings and inflexible work conditions made it difficult for them to be involved in helping with the disabled child. By contrast, men in non-manual jobs earned considerably less than their control counterparts — an average of £18 a week less, rising to over £41 a week among managerial and administrative employees. As with women's employment, having a disabled child means that fathers in non-manual occupations are restricted in seeking improved employment opportunities with career prospects and better pay (Baldwin, 1985).

Among the people of working age whose employment and earnings might be affected by caring for a disabled person, the parents of disabled children are, however, a very small minority. The 1980 national Women and Employment Survey found that of the working age women who said they provided some regular help or service to a sick or disabled person, only 6 per cent were providing this for a child, as against more than two-thirds for a parent or parent-in-law. The highest incidence of extra caring responsibilities was among women in the forty to fifty-nine age group (Martin and Roberts,1984: 112). This suggests that caring is most likely to have an impact on women's paid employment at a later stage of the life cycle.

Nineteen per cent of the women providing care thought their employment or opportunity to work had been affected (though non-employed women carers were more than twice as likely as those still in employment to report some effect). However, only 24 per cent of the women lived in the same household as the person they cared for and a further 24 per cent said they saw the person they looked after every day. This means that just over half of those providing care lived separately from their dependants and saw them less than once a day — caring commitments which could more easily be integrated with employment commitments.

When the care of severely disabled adults living in the same household is considered, the impact on carers' employment is much more noticeable and consistent. Nissel and Bonnerjea (1982) found only two out of twenty-two married women who were looking after a frail elderly person to be in full-time work. Even these women earned an average of £5 a week less than the comparable (April 1980) average for their occupational group. Five women worked in part-time jobs paying well below the type of job they had previously had, with an average weekly loss of income of £37. Of the fifteen women not in paid work, nine had given up jobs to look after their relatives; ten said they would like to go back to work. The earnings lost by this latter group averaged £87 a week. Updated to 1986 earnings levels, the average annual loss amounted to £3,275 for the part-time workers and £7,750 for the non-employed women who would have liked to return to work.

Similar losses have been calculated using the Women and Employment Survey data (Joshi, 1987). This analysis calculated the immediate and lifetime effects of caring for children and other dependants on women's labour force participation and earnings. It was estimated that a childless woman would forgo £8,500 a year and a mother £7,000 a year if either gave up full-time employment at a later stage of the life cycle to care for a disabled relative.

Calculations such as these are essentially 'snapshots' of the earnings lost in any one year which could be attributed to caring for a disabled person. However, it is important to take a much longer-term view. Breaks in labour market participation are typically followed by lower wages on re-entry, reflecting factors such as loss of seniority and accumulated work experience. Periods in part-time rather than full-time employment have similar longer-term effects on rates of pay. Both breaks in participation and periods in very low-paid part-time work can affect eventual pension entitlements (see Chapter 4). Although the home responsibilities credits of the current (1986) state pension scheme protect basic pension rights during breaks in employment while caring for a child or severely disabled person, loss of earnings or lowered earnings will affect the earnings-related component of pension provision. As with disabled people themselves, carers with interrupted or low earnings will also be adversely affected by the 1988 changes to the State Earnings Related Pension Scheme.

Losses of such magnitude arising from interrupted or restricted employment while caring for a disabled person contrast starkly with current social security provision. Until June 1986 Invalid Care Allowance (ICA) was available only to men and single women to replace the earnings forgone by providing full-time care to a severely disabled person. The extension of ICA to married women following the implementation of EEC Directive 7/79 on equal treatment for men and women was clearly long overdue; it is anticipated that some 85,000 married women will be eligible. However, the level of the benefit — £1,209 a year in 1987 — is only a fraction of the earnings typically lost by those caring for a disabled person.

Non-income Costs of Caring
The evidence on the consequences of disablement for carers' employment and earnings is clear. However, helping or supporting a disabled person often creates costs of other kinds, whose financial value is far harder to impute. At a relatively straightforward level, carers (and their families) may bear some of the direct costs of the disablement itself. These are perhaps most easily identified when the disabled person and the carer live in separate households: heating bills may be paid; special equipment bought; or extra clothing given in the guise of Christmas and birthday presents. Subsidies from the carer to the disabled person can also be identified in situations where joint households are formed in order to provide care — for example when an elderly person moves to live with an adult child. Fuel and food bills may suddenly rise or extra equipment need to be purchased. Nissel and Bonnerjea's families complained of 'heavy additional spending especially for heating, laundry, linen and special foods' (Nissel and Bonnerjea, 1982: 49). However, costs such as these may be at least partially offset by the disabled person's contribution to the housekeeping and housing costs, by services such as housework or child-care which she contributes, or even by future capital transfers or legacies. It is probably hardest to disentangle the non-income costs borne by carers when it is a spouse who is being cared for in a marital relationship which has always been characterised by a pooling of resources or, alternatively, by considerable inequality in control over material resources (Pahl, 1980).

Far greater difficulties arise if we attempt to identify and quantify those costs of caring which do not arise directly from earnings loss or from extra expenses. Calculating and placing a value on the time spent in caring activities — whether that caring is done instead of or in addition to a paid job — raises enormous methodological (and political) problems. The problems stem primarily from the nature of the work, which is typically carried out within the private domain of the home, especially when that work involves the physical or emotional care of close relatives or kin and especially when — as is so often the case — it is performed by women (Graham, 1983).

Attempts have, nevertheless, been made to quantify the time costs of caring, notably in Nissel and Bonnerjea's (1982) time budget study of the care of frail elderly people. Twenty-two of the carers in their sample spent on average 149 minutes each day in 'primary' care activities and a further eighty-two minutes in 'secondary' activities — looking after the elderly person at the same time as doing something else. This time was costed on the basis of the current (1980 New Earnings Survey) market rate for home and domestic helpers of £1.80 an hour; the average annual cost to each carer was thus £2,500. Calculations such as these highlight some of the hidden costs borne by individual families and relatives rather than by statutory services. For example Henwood and Wicks (1984), using the 1982–3 hourly pay for local authority home helps of £2.90, calculated the cost of the time spent by an informal (unpaid) carer in looking after an elderly person to be between £71.05 and £101.50 a week (£3,695–5,278 per annum). On the assumption that there are around one million such carers, the total value of the unpaid care provided to dependent elderly people was estimated to be between £3.7 and £5.3 billion per annum.

Global estimates such as these are likely to underestimate the cost of caring. It is, for example, relatively easy to measure the amount of time spent directly helping or doing something for a disabled person. It is less easy to measure and place a value on the time which a carer spends at home not actually doing anything for the disabled person but *in case* she is needed, or because she is too tired and busy to arrange suitable substitute care. Further underestimation arises because some of the time spent in direct caring activities involves highly skilled nursing tasks. To pay someone to perform these tasks would cost considerably more than home help wage rates, so it is arguable that carers' time should be valued at a higher rate too. Above all, the jobs and rates of pay which form the basis of such calculations should be questioned. As already noted, caring is one of a number of private domestic activities which are usually performed by women without pay. When such tasks are performed in the labour market by, for example, home helps and nursing auxiliaries, the low rates of pay which they command reflect their essentially female and domestic characteristics. The paid jobs with which caring is often compared are not themselves independent, therefore, of the low status and remuneration accorded to 'women's work'.

Conclusions

The financial impact of disablement should by now be clear. It affects the incomes and living standards of disabled people, their families and those who help and care for them on a day-to-day basis. Despite developments since 1970 in social security provision and services, both for people with disabilities and for their carers, a very substantial proportion of the financial consequences of disability are still borne privately, by the individuals and families directly affected, rather than by the community as a whole.

The policy measures necessary to alleviate some of the material disadvantage experienced by people with disabilities are three-fold. First, measures are necessary to improve the employment opportunities and earnings of disabled people. These include a stronger and more rigorously enforced quota system, with all employers obliged — and enabled financially where necessary — to employ a stated percentage of disabled people (Jordan, 1979; Townsend, 1981a); anti-discrimination legislation; and stronger legislation to protect the rights and earnings of disabled people already in work. Secondly, a comprehensive disability income scheme to provide a total or partial replacement for income from paid work is long overdue. Such a scheme would provide an adequate income, as of right, based on the severity of disability and the needs which arise from it rather than, as at present, on how or when the disability occurred. This would be simpler to understand and claim and would end the reliance of so many disabled people on means-tested benefits. Such a scheme might include an element of compensation for disability, the replacement of earnings lost because of incapacity for paid work, and allowances to cover some of the extra costs associated with disability (Townsend, 1975; Disability Alliance, 1987). By compensating more adequately for the lower incomes and extra costs occasioned by disability, it would increase the capacity of people with disabilities to participate in the life of society and would help to shift some of the costs of disablement from the individual to society at large. There is by now universal commitment to the introduction of a comprehensive disability income. The results of the disablement survey carried out by OPCS in 1985, whose findings are due to be published in late 1987, will provide the basis on which this can be structured and costed.

Thirdly, much more consideration needs to be given to meeting the costs borne by carers. Invalid care allowance is only a very partial replacement of the earnings forgone by full-time carers, and overlapping benefit regulations prevent very many full-time carers from obtaining any financial advantage at all from this benefit. There is also no recognition or compensation for the caring which is done on top of a paid job, by people over retirement age, or by those in households receiving other social security benefits. It is also necessary to begin thinking about ways of shifting some of the non-financial costs of caring so that these are borne less unremittingly by carers and their families — without, of course, devaluing the bonds of commitment and concern which underlie most caring relationships.

For some ten years now governments have, in theory at least, pursued the dual goals of 'community care' and 'equal opportunities'. If the tensions between these goals are to be resolved, and theory to become practice in each case, collective recognition of the full costs of both disablement and caring is an urgent necessity.

References

Avery, L. (1983) *Disability: Counting the Costs*. London: Disability Alliance Educational and Research Association and RADAR.

Baldwin, S. (1985) *The Costs of Caring: Families with Disabled Children*. London: Routledge and Kegan Paul.

Baldwin, S., J. Bradshaw, K. Cooke and C. Glendinning (1981) 'The Disabled Person and Cash Benefits', in D. Guthrie (ed.), *Disability: Legislation and Practice*. London: Macmillan.

Brown, J.C. (1984) *The Disability Income System*. London: Policy Studies Institute.

Buckle, J. (1984) *Mental Handicap Costs More*. London: Disablement Income Group Charitable Trust.

Casserley, J. and B. Clarke (1978) *A Welfare Rights Approach to the Chronically Sick and Disabled*. Glasgow: Strathclyde Regional Council.

Cooke, K. and S. Baldwin (1984) *How Much is Enough?* London: Family Policy Studies Centre.

Darnborough, A. and D. Kinrade (1981) 'The Disabled Person and Employment', in D. Guthrie (ed.), *Disability: Legislation and Practice*. London: Macmillan.

Dex, S. and C. Phillipson (1986) 'Social Policy and the Older Worker' in C. Phillipson and A. Walker (eds), *Ageing and Social Policy*. Aldershot, Hants: Gower.

Disability Alliance (1980) *A Very High Priority?* London: Disability Alliance.

Disability Alliance (1985) *Social Security White Paper: Summary and Comments*. London: Disability Alliance.

Disability Alliance (1987) *Poverty and Disability — Breaking the Link. The Case for a Comprehensive Disability Income Scheme*. London: Disability Alliance.

Finch, J. and D. Groves (1980) 'Community Care and the Family: a Case for Equal Opportunities?' *Journal of Social Policy*, 9(4): 487–514.

Franey, R. (1983) *Hard Times*. London: Disability Alliance.

Graham, H. (1983) 'Caring: a Labour of Love' in J. Finch and D. Groves (eds), *A Labour of Love: Women, Work and Caring*. London: Routledge and Kegan Paul.

Groves, D. (1987) 'Occupational Pension Provision and Women's Poverty in Old Age', in C. Glendinning and J. Millar (eds), *Women and Poverty in Britain*. Brighton: Wheatsheaf Books.

Groves, D. and J. Finch (1983) 'Natural Selection: Perspectives on Entitlement to the Invalid Care Allowance', in J. Finch and D. Groves (eds), *A Labour of Love: Women, Work and Caring*. London: Routledge and Kegan Paul.

Harris, A.I., E. Cox and C.R.W. Smith (1971) *Handicapped and Impaired in Great Britain*, Part 1. London: HMSO.

Harris, A.I., C.R.W. Smith and E. Head (1972) *Income and Entitlement to Supplementary Benefit of Impaired People in Great Britain*. London: HMSO.

Henwood, M. and M. Wicks (1984) *The Forgotten Army: Family Care and Elderly People*. London: Family Policy Studies Centre.

Hirst, M. (1983) 'Young People with Disabilities: What Happens After 16?', *Child: Care, Health and Development*, 9(5): 273–84.

Hirst, M. (1985) 'Young Adults with Disabilities: Health, Employment and Financial Costs for Family Carers', *Child: Care, Health and Development*, 11(5): 291–307.

HMSO (1974) *Social Security Provision for Chronically Sick and Disabled People* Cmnd.276. London: HMSO.

Hyman, M. (1977) *The Extra Costs of Disabled Living*. Horsham, Surrey: National Fund for Research into Crippling Diseases.

Jordan, D. (1979) *A New Employment Programme Wanted for Disabled People*. London: Disability Alliance and Low Pay Unit.

Joshi, H. (1987) 'The Cost of Caring', in C. Glendinning and J. Millar (eds), *Women and Poverty in Britain*. Brighton: Wheatsheaf Books.

Land, H. (1978) 'Who Cares for the Family?' *Journal of Social Policy*, 7(3): 357–84.

Layard, R., D. Piachaud and M. Stewart (1978) *The Causes of Poverty*. RCDIW, Background Paper No. 5. London: HMSO.

Lonsdale, S. and A. Walker (1984) *A Right to Work: Disability and Employment*. London: Disability Alliance and Low Pay Unit.

Martin, J. and C. Roberts (1984) *Women and Employment: a Lifetime Perspective*. London: HMSO.

Nissel, M. and L. Bonnerjea (1982) *Family Care of the Handicapped Elderly: Who Pays?* London: Policy Studies Institute.

Pahl, J. (1980) 'Patterns of Money Management within Marriage', *Journal of Social Policy*, 9(3): 313–35.

Parker, G. (1985) *With Due Care and Attention*. London: Family Policy Studies Centre.

Phillips, H. and C. Glendinning (1981) *Who Benefits?* London: Disability Alliance.

Piachaud, D. (1986) 'Disability and Unemployment', *Journal of Social Policy*, 15(2): 145–62.

Rimmer, L. (1983) 'The Economics of Work and Caring', in J. Finch and D. Groves (eds), *A Labour of Love: Women, Work and Caring*. London: Routledge and Kegan Paul.

Simkins, J. and V. Tickner (1978) *Whose Benefit?* London: Economist Intelligence Unit Ltd.

Townsend, P. (1975) *Poverty and Disability*. London: Disability Alliance.

Townsend, P. (1979) *Poverty in the United Kingdom*. London: Penguin Books.

Townsend, P. (1981a) 'Employment and Disability', in A. Walker and P. Townsend (eds), *Disability in Britain: a Manifesto of Rights*. Oxford: Martin Robertson.

Townsend, P. (1981b) 'Elderly People with Disabilities', in A. Walker and P. Townsend (eds), *Disability in Britain: a Manifesto of Rights*. Oxford: Martin Robertson.

Walker, A. (1980) 'The Social Creation of Poverty and Dependency in Old Age', *Journal of Social Policy*, 9(1): 49–75.

Walker, A. (1981) 'Disability and Income', in A. Walker and P. Townsend (eds), *Disability in Britain: a Manifesto of Rights*. Oxford: Martin Robertson.

Walker, A. (1982a) *Unqualified and Underemployed: Handicapped Young People and the Labour Market*. London: Macmillan.

Walker, A. (1982b) 'The Meaning and Social Division of Community Care', in A. Walker (ed.), *Community Care: the Family, the State and Social Policy*. Oxford: Blackwell/Martin Robertson.

Walker, A. (1985) 'Early Retirement: Release or Refuge from the Labour Market?', *Quarterly Journal of Social Affairs*, 1(3): 211–29.

Walker, A. (1986) 'Pensions and the Production of Poverty in Old Age', in C. Phillipson and A. Walker (eds), *Ageing and Social Policy*. Aldershot, Hants: Gower.

Walker, A. (1987) 'The Poor Relation: Poverty among Old Women', in C. Glendinning and J. Millar (eds), *Women and Poverty in Britain*. Brighton: Wheatsheaf Books.

Wicks, M. (1978) *Old and Cold: Hypothermia and Social Policy*. London: Heinemann.

6

The Costs of Unemployment

Kenneth Cooke

For the majority of people, a spell of unemployment involves financial costs in one form or another. Understandably, many studies of the unemployed have drawn attention to hardship where it occurs, particularly in long-term unemployment, but the majority of the unemployed incur some costs as a result of a spell out of work, even if hardship is not the way in which these costs are manifested.

Costs can be measured either quantitatively, as the loss of income arising from a period without earnings, or qualitatively as the impact of such a period on the individual or family's living standards and life style. It is important to consider costs in both respects because, as will be seen, those with the greatest loss of income are not necessarily those whose living standards are sacrificed to the greatest extent. Focusing exclusively on income loss would suggest that for some families the cost of unemployment is slight, when in fact their material living standards are seriously disrupted. By contrast, focusing only on living standards would ignore the fact that those who are able to maintain them do so by incurring costs in other ways.

Income Forgone

A very great deal of research has been devoted to attempting to explain employment behaviour by reference, among other things, to the relationship between incomes in and out of work. For the purposes of this chapter, this relationship is important because, very broadly, it expresses the personal monetary cost to the individual of being out of work.

The conventional term for the relationship between income in and out of work is the 'replacement ratio'. In fact, there are several different replacement ratios, each answering a different question about the relationship between unemployment and work incomes. When interest lies in the personal cost of unemployment the appropriate comparison is between what the level of income would have been had there been no interruption of employment, and what it actually was during the period out of work.

There is a number of ways in which these replacement ratios can be calculated. One of the most widely quoted calculations is that based on the Department of Health and Social Security (DHSS) tax-benefit model (DHSS, 1986a: 66). These ratios are derived from simulation of the incomes in and out of work of various hypothetical individuals or family types with assumed levels of earnings, rent and rates. Table 6.1 provides a number of examples of these simulated replacement ratios.

TABLE 6.1   *Replacement ratios (in per cent) in DHSS tax-benefit model (as at July 1986)*

	Gross earnings		
Family type	Two-thirds average (%)	Average (%)	One and two-thirds average (%)
Single person	57	33	18
Married couple	77	50	28
with two children (4 and 6)	87	70	41
with three children (3, 8 and 11)	91	81	49
with four children			
(3, 8, 11 and 16)	96	92	58

Source: DHSS, 1986a

According to the model, with two-thirds of average earnings all family types except single people and childless couples would have at least 80 per cent of their in-work income replaced by benefits. At average earnings, however, only couples with three or more children would be in this position. With earnings at one and two-thirds of the average, even couples with four children would expect to lose at least 40 per cent of their previous net income from work.

The disadvantage of these hypothetical calculations is that the results can be interpreted only within the confines of the particular model family types. Atkinson (1982) has demonstrated that these model family types correspond to only a very small proportion of families in the general population. One of the factors which limit the correspondence between these model types and families in the population is that the former assume only a single earner where the head is in work and no earnings at all when the head is unemployed. In reality, two-thirds of working husbands and a third of unemployed husbands have working wives (Office of Population Censuses and Surveys [OPCS], 1985: table 7.17). The model also assumes that means-tested benefits to which families are entitled are in fact taken up, while empirical research indicates that, in reality, replacement ratios are affected by non take-up or delays in receiving benefits (Moylan et al., 1984: 70). Hypothetical replacement ratios also depend crucially on the assumptions of the model, particularly the imputed values of housing and travel-to-work costs. As Dilnot and Morris (1983: 322) observe, 'it is possible to "prove" virtually anything by such a method, depending on the specific case chosen'.

An alternative method of estimating replacement ratios is to calculate them from empirical data drawn from large and nationally representative surveys. There are several ways in which this can be done. One method is to use cross-sectional data to compare the net incomes from employment of individuals or families in the sample with estimates of what their income would be if they became unemployed. For example, Layard et al. (1978), using data from the 1972 General Household Survey, calculated replacement ratios by expressing notional entitlements to social security benefits as a proportion of the head of household's net earnings from work, with any wife's earnings, child benefit and net unearned income added as constants to both in-work and unemployment incomes. By these calculations, those who were in work would have lost an average of 31 per cent of their net weekly income on becoming unemployed; that is, the average replacement ratio was 69 per cent. Eleven per cent had replacement ratios of 90 per cent or more and 25 per cent had replacement ratios of 80 per cent or more. The majority of the sample (two-thirds) had replacement ratios of between 50 and 80 per cent.

However, as the authors themselves point out, benefit receipts can only be estimated rather than observed empirically. It is also the case that wives' earnings, assumed as constant, may not in fact be so. There is a tendency for the wives of men who become unemployed also to drop out of the labour force, for reasons that are not altogether clear (see below). Assuming wives' earnings to be constant, regardless of husbands' employment status, may overstate the level of unemployment incomes and thereby make replacement ratios unrealistically high.

A second empirical approach to estimating replacement ratios is to carry out a survey of the unemployed and compare their current incomes with their previous incomes from work. This was the method adopted in the DHSS cohort study of unemployed men (Moylan et al., 1984), for which the fieldwork was carried out in 1978. In this study, 25 per cent of the sample had replacement ratios of 80 per cent or more, and a further 40 per cent had replacement ratios of between 50 per cent and 80 per cent.

This type of comparison, like the hypothetical examples shown above, presents what is, in effect, a snapshot picture of the impact of a week's unemployment on that week's income. But the impact of unemployment on income can be considered not only as a function of the relationship between income in and out of work, but also as a function of the duration of the spell of unemployment. Dilnot and Morris (1983) have thus calculated average replacement ratios for different durations of unemployment for families of different composition in the 1980 Family Expenditure Survey. Excluding any estimate for work expenses, but including the value of tax rebates, their estimates of average replacement ratios are shown in Table 6.2.

TABLE 6.2　*Replacement ratios in 1980, by duration of unemployment (per cent with replacement ratio)*

Replacement ratio	Duration of unemployment (weeks)		
	4	13	52
Up to 50 per cent	10.8	8.0	16.6
51 to 60 per cent	15.6	13.7	19.3
61 to 70 per cent	21.6	20.5	24.9
71 to 80 per cent	23.9	25.4	22.0
81 to 90 per cent	16.9	20.4	12.3
Over 90 per cent	11.2	12.0	4.9
Average replacement ratio	70.8	72.7	65.7

Source: Dilnot and Morris (1983)

These calculations show that, in 1980, family heads in the working population could expect 71 per cent, on average, of their net income from work to be replaced during a spell of four weeks' unemployment, 73 per cent during a spell of thirteen weeks and 66 per cent during a spell of fifty-two weeks' unemployment. After these durations of unemployment, respectively 28 per cent, 32 per cent and 17 per cent of family heads had replacement ratios of over 80 per cent. This slightly higher replacement ratio at thirteen weeks than at four weeks is probably due to payments of tax rebates and delays in either claims for, or payment of, social security benefits.

In 1980, earnings related supplements were still payable to the unemployed who received unemployment benefit, and tax refunds — varying in size according to the point in the tax year where the unemployment occurred — were a normal occurrence. The abolition of earnings-related supplements in 1982 and the taxation of benefits, introduced in the 1982–3 tax year, have altered the costs of a spell of short-term unemployment considerably. The effect of abolishing earnings relation was to bring within the scope of supplementary benefit families who had previously been kept above that level by the earnings-related addition. Effectively, supplementary benefit now determines the out of work income of the majority of families. Taxing unemployment benefit meant that tax refunds virtually disappeared, and tax liability on subsequent earnings increased.

The effect of these two measures was thus to increase sharply the cost of a spell of short-term unemployment. When Dilnot and Morris (1983) projected their estimates forward from 1980 to 1983 to take account of these changes, the thirteen-week average replacement ratio fell from 72.7 per cent in 1980 to 60 per cent in 1983. Over the same period the proportion of families with a replacement ratio of more than 90 per cent fell dramatically from 12 per cent to 2.9 per cent. These changes had no impact on the costs of a spell of unemployment of longer than twelve months, when unemployment benefit ceases to be paid. In 1980 the average replacement ratio for a period in excess of twelve months was 50.3 per cent, with 1.9 per cent of families having a replacement ratio of 90 per cent or more and 47.8 per cent having a replacement ratio of less than 50 per cent. In 1983 these ratios were broadly similar, with the exception that the proportion of families with a ratio of less than 50 per cent had increased slightly to about 53 per cent.

The conclusions that can be drawn from these analyses are that, in terms of lost income, the costs of a short or moderate spell of unemployment have increased in recent years, and such a spell is now likely to cost on average roughly a third of the employee's in-work income. Only a tiny proportion are now likely to have 90 per cent of their in-work income replaced. The position of the long-term unemployed has remained relatively stable in recent years. Over a period of longer than twelve months, more than half of the unemployed can expect to have less than half of their in-work income replaced.

Replacement ratios tell us something about the loss of income that is consequent on a spell of unemployment but they do not tell us anything about the quality of life of the unemployed. Neither do they tell us whether this loss of earnings has any knock-on effects which create other kinds of costs — for example, the enforced reduction or abandonment of particular forms of consumption or social activities, and the accumulation of debts — which may not be recovered immediately on returning to work. For this information it is necessary to turn to a number of specialised studies of the unemployed.

Impact on Living Standards

Hardship
Surveys of the unemployed have consistently indicated an associa-

tion between unemployment, particularly when long-term, and financial hardship. A study of the unemployed in Coventry, Newcastle and Hammersmith by Hill et al. (1973) concluded that the majority were 'living . . . on what can be described as no more than subsistence incomes' (Hill et al., 1973: 139). A similar conclusion emerged from a study by Daniel (1974), in which the most common concern about being out of work, expressed by 72 per cent of the sample, was simply 'lack of money' — having to cut down and not being able to afford things. The chief financial problems centred not on what might be called luxuries, but on meeting day-to-day living expenses such as buying food and paying the rent and bills. A later survey (Smith, 1980) found that more than half of the sample found it 'very difficult to manage'.

A study which focused on the unemployed on supplementary benefit (Clark, 1978: 385) found that incomes were 'barely adequate to meet their needs at a level which would allow them to participate fully in the society in which they live'. Clothing stocks were depleted and 80 per cent of those surveyed said they had outstanding needs for clothing and footwear that they could not afford. Only 5 per cent (mainly single men) said they were 'managing quite well'; 85 per cent had cut their expenditure since becoming claimants, mainly on basic essentials: more than half mentioned food and clothing and 18 per cent mentioning heating. Nearly half had cut down on drinking and smoking and a quarter went out less often.

More recently, the Manpower Services Commission (MSC) study of the long-term unemployed (MSC, 1980: para. 7.6) concluded that 'most respondents found money extremely tight — enough for existence rather than for living. Sacrifices were not unusual . . . Observation confirmed that many respondents — especially those households completely dependent on social security — led greatly impoverished lives'. An analysis of unemployed families in the Family Finances Survey (Bradshaw et al., 1983) also indicated that cutting down is a common response to lengthening unemployment, and that the budgets of the unemployed are dominated to a greater extent by necessities (food, fuel and housing costs) than those of comparable working families.

Debt

The accumulation of debt is one of the common features of the lives of the unemployed. In Daniel's (1974) sample, 37 per cent of those with bank loans had not been able to meet the cost of repayments and 33 per cent of those with HP commitments had fallen behind. One-fifth found it impossible to meet rent or mortgage payments, and problems were also reported with fuel and telephone bills. In a later study from the Policy Studies Institute (Smith, 1980), half of the sample had failed to meet either rent, mortgage, rates or fuel payments. Only 8 per cent were facing eviction, fuel disconnection or a court action for debt, but a third said that debts caused them hardship.

Falling into arrears is not an experience exclusive to the unemployed, but a number of studies have suggested that households with rent arrears are more likely to have an unemployed breadwinner than other households (National Consumer Council [NCC], 1976a; Alpren, 1977). The same is true of fuel debts and difficulties (National Consumer Council, 1976b; Parker, 1983). A comparative study of the unemployed and employed in the Family Finances Survey (Parker, 1986) indicated that about half of the unemployed were experiencing difficulties with rent or mortgage payments compared with about a quarter of the employed. Further, between a fifth and a quarter of the unemployed experienced difficulties in paying for fuel compared with only 6 per cent of the employed. Recently published research (Building Societies Association [BSA], 1985; Doling et al., 1985; Culley and Downey, 1986) suggests that repossession following default in mortgage repayments is becoming increasingly common as a result of unemployment.

The Differential Costs of Unemployment

While it is generally true that unemployment involves costs of one kind or another it is also true that these costs do not fall equally on all of the unemployed. If we measure the costs of unemployment simply as forgone income, then the variations are clearly those that arise from differences in previous incomes from work and in current incomes during unemployment. Since the phasing out of earnings-related supplement (ERS) in 1982, unemployment benefits have been paid at a flat rate which does not vary according to previous earnings. Even when ERS existed, the extent of earnings relation was limited in time (to the first six months of unemployment) and in value (a proportion of previous earnings, up to a fixed ceiling), and

TABLE 6.3 *Replacement ratios in 1980, by earnings*

Income group	Replacement ratio	Percentage of income group with replacement ratio over 90%
Up to 75 per cent of average earnings	81.3	28.0
76 to 150 per cent of average earnings	72.1	7.4
Over 151 per cent of average earnings	59.6	0.7

Source: Dilnot and Morris (1983)

replacement ratios varied considerably according to previous earnings. For example, Dilnot and Morris (1983) estimated the proportion of income replaced for three groups of earners in 1980 to be as shown in Table 6.3.

While unemployment benefit is no longer related to previous earnings, it is related to family composition in that additions are paid in respect of spouses. There are also additions for each dependent child in the case of those receiving supplementary benefit. For this reason, the replacement ratios calculated for the hypothetical 'model families' (Table 6.1) are higher both for lower earners and for larger families. This effect of family size on replacement ratios is also clearly seen in empirical investigation (Dilnot and Morris, 1983; Clark, 1978; Moylan et al., 1984). The DHSS cohort study of the unemployed (Moylan et al., 1984) is interesting in this respect in that the analysis indicated that larger families had, on average, higher replacement ratios than smaller families despite the fact that smaller families had had lower earnings.

The cohort study also suggested a number of other characteristics that are associated with high or low replacement ratios. Housing costs (including rent in full but only the interest portion of mortgage repayments) are provided for in social security and therefore might be expected to influence replacement ratios. However, the only important difference in replacement ratios in the cohort was between non-householders (who receive much lower amounts for housing costs) and householders. Within the latter group, differences were much less marked.

Moving on now to consider the costs of unemployment in their qualitative aspect, something of a paradox emerges. As indicated above, larger families are likely to have higher replacement ratios, but surveys have generally concluded that it is families with children, particularly larger families, who experience the greatest hardship during unemployment. This was true in Daniel's study (1974), in the study by Smith (1980) and in Clark's (1978) study of the unemployed on supplementary benefit. In the latter, only one in twenty of the unemployed said they were 'managing quite well' and most of these were single men. The majority of families with two or more children said they were 'getting into difficulties'. Most of the sample had to cut back on expenditure, but the major economising took place in families, and it was families who had the poorest stocks of clothes.

This paradox might be explained by parents being prepared to sacrifice their own well-being but resistant to the thought of sacrificing that of their children (Burghes, 1980: 32–3). Consequently the extent to which they are able to accommodate a drop in income — even a small drop — without incurring financial problems is more limited. However, the hardship experienced by families, despite higher replacement ratios, is almost certainly also related to the level of child support in supplementary benefit. National insurance unemployment benefit no longer carries additions for child dependants, but even when it did families with children nearly always fell below supplementary benefit level when entitlement to earnings-related supplement was exhausted. More will be said about benefit adequacy below, but one of the clearest conclusions of a review of the adequacy of the scale rates of supplementary benefit (Cooke and Baldwin, 1984) was that the costs of children are underestimated. Piachaud's study (1979) for example suggests that the children's rates would have to be at least doubled to provide even a frugal standard of living.

While financial difficulties are a common experience of the unemployed, particularly families, it is not all the unemployed that experience them, nor does the same fall in income necessarily precipitate the same financial problems in different families. Some of this variation in the impact of unemployment is due to purely interpersonal differences in the ability to manage money and avoid debts — differences that we know little about and which, perhaps understandably, research workers have felt reluctant to probe. But the general consistency of research findings implies that the differential impact has less to do with individual competence than with the resources to which the unemployed have access, in order to mitigate the costs of unemployment.

For example, in Berthoud's (1979) study of unemployed professionals and executives, while there were other kinds of problems, no one in the sample mentioned acute financial hardship even though replacement ratios were low. Similarly, in Hartley's (1978) study of redundant managers only one family experienced a reduced standard of living and there was generally very little evidence of any cutting down of expenditure. In contrast, while the low paid, from whom the unemployed are disproportionately drawn, may have much higher replacement ratios, at such low levels of income people are likely to have difficulty coping with the impact of *any* drop in income, however small (Sinfield, 1976).

One of the main reasons why Berthoud's unemployed professionals and executives appear to have avoided any sacrifice in living standards was because they had resources other than unemployment benefits — particularly savings — on which they could draw. The next step, therefore, is to consider the sources of support that are available to mitigate the costs of unemployment.

Mitigating the Costs of Unemployment

The most widely used source of support for living standards during unemployment is social security. Before considering the role of social security benefits, some additional sources of support which the unemployed might have available to them are considered: the use of personal savings; borrowing or buying on credit; selling assets; redundancy payments; and earnings. Of these, the first three differ from the last two (and from social security) in that, while mitigating the immediate impact of unemployment on living standards, they are costs in themselves; savings (and the interest they bear) are depleted, credit is repayable with interest, and assets have to be re-acquired.

Savings

As has been said, savings were an important resource for the unemployed professionals and executives in Berthoud's (1979) survey; 53 per cent of the sample had drawn on savings, although the level of savings they originally had and the amount they drew on them are not known. Moreover, a further 11 per cent had some private income from interest on savings or investments. More general studies of the unemployed suggest that savings are of very minor importance in maintaining living standards, because the unemployed are likely to have little or none on becoming claimants, and those that they have are quickly exhausted. In Clark's study (1978) of long-term unemployed supplementary benefit claimants, 86 per cent had no savings before they became unemployed. Among the unskilled men (who constituted the majority of the sample) nearly half said they had *never* managed to save. Similarly, in the DHSS Cohort Study (Moylan et al., 1984) 57 per cent of the sample had no savings at all at the time of the first interview (one month after the onset of unemployment). Men with dependent children were the least likely to have any savings; about 80 per cent of those with three or more children had none. About a third of the sample (i.e. nearly all of those who had any savings) had reduced the level of their savings since becoming unemployed. For most of these, savings had fallen by at least £50 and the results suggested that about 9 per cent had exhausted all their savings during this month. 'General living expenses' was the most common reason given for drawing on savings.

Borrowing and Credit

There is no doubt that resort to borrowing money is a relatively frequent response to the loss of income from work (Clark, 1978;

Daniel, 1974; Moylan et al., 1984; Berthoud, 1979; Parker, 1986), although the proportion who have borrowed varies in different samples. Clark (1978), for example, records that half of the sample of long-term unemployed families had borrowed money while on supplementary benefit. Parker's (1986) comparative analysis showed that the long-term unemployed were more likely to have borrowed money (21 per cent) than either the short-term unemployed (16 per cent) or working families with low incomes (7 per cent). However, the amount of the loan outstanding at the time of interview (a rough proxy indicator of the size of the original loan) was in inverse proportion to the likelihood of borrowing: the long-term unemployed had the smallest loans. In view of all the other evidence it is inconceivable that this indicates less need for extra resources among the long-term unemployed. As Parker suggests, it is more likely to reflect the more difficult access of the unemployed to formal (and larger scale) lending institutions. Without exception, all of the studies mentioned above, including that of professionals and executives, indicate that the majority of borrowing is from friends or relatives.

Clark's (1978) study also shows that the majority of long-term unemployed families were making regular payments to clubs, HP companies, mail order firms or check traders, although these credit arrangements were not necessarily taken on after the onset of unemployment. Parker's (1986) analysis suggests that unemployed families are about as likely as those with low incomes from employment to take on new credit commitments.

Sale of Assets

The resale value of most small consumer durables is low, and while there is fairly clear evidence that the unemployed are less well equipped with consumer durables than working families (Clark, 1978; Bradshaw et al., 1983) it is less clear to what extent this is due to disposal of assets in response to unemployment. This was mentioned in the MSC (1980) survey and Bradshaw et al. (1983) found some evidence of disposal of assets in cross-sectional analysis of the Family Finances Survey, using multivariate techniques. However, a longitudinal analysis comparing the assets which families had in this survey with those they had in a follow-up survey twelve months later (Cooke, 1987) showed no clear or consistent pattern either of disposal or acquisition as families' employment position changed.

Redundancy Payments

Only a small proportion of the unemployed receive redundancy payments. The statutory redundancy payments scheme was established in the mid-1960s to ease labour market restructuring and encourage redeployment, but the eligibility criteria restrict entitlement to certain age and income groups, and payments are weighted in favour of older workers receiving higher pay who have worked for the same employer for longer periods (Parker et al., 1971). In 1980 only 491,000 of 3.85 million workers who experienced a spell of unemployment (13 per cent) received a statutory payment, and for those who did, the average payment was under £1,000. In 1981 this had increased to 20 per cent of the flow into unemployment with an average payment of £1,160 (Hughes and Perlman, 1984: 208). Redundancy payments were never intended to provide continuing financial support; indeed, they are not contingent on the recipient remaining unemployed for any particular period. Rather they are compensation payments, broadly intended to compensate for loss of security or seniority or other benefits which the worker might have expected but for redundancy. They tend to be used quickly and instrumentally rather than to provide an income from week to week (Sinfield, 1981; Melville, 1983).

Earnings
British social security was established primarily for those not in work at all, at a time when part-time employment was much rarer than today. Although benefits have been introduced to supplement low wages, the system remains firmly based on a distinction between working full-time and not working at all — a distinction which fails to recognise the enormous growth of part-time work as a normal source of income (Bradshaw, 1985). The embodiment of this rigid distinction is the very small amount that unemployed claimants are allowed to earn without loss of benefit (known as 'disregards'). Currently (June 1987) an unemployed person receiving unemployment benefit may earn up to £2 per day and one receiving supplementary benefit £4 a week without any benefit deductions.

The general conclusion of a review by the Social Security Advisory Committee (SSAC) of the effectiveness of these disregards in enabling claimants to supplement benefit income by part-time work was that very few claimants use them (SSAC, 1983). Consequently, earnings (at least those earnings that are declared to social security offices) seem to play little part in mitigating the impact of unemployment. In December 1982 only 2 per cent of the unemployed on supplementary benefit reported any earnings (Bradshaw, 1985: 207). This infrequent exploitation of such disregards as do exist may arise from lack of knowledge or misunderstanding about them. However, it may also be due to a mis-match between claimants' aspirations to work and increase their income, DHSS' aspirations to prevent claimants' earnings from boosting their income to the point where they are deterred from entering full-time work (DHSS, 1978: 64), and employers' unwillingness or inability to offer part-time work paying net wages at about the level of the disregards.

The meagreness of these disregarded earnings is thought to be one of the reasons why wives appear to withdraw from the labour force when husbands become unemployed (Moylan et al., 1984; Bradshaw et al., 1983; Smee and Stern, 1978), although it is still not entirely clear why this occurs and factors other than disregards may be equally important (Cooke, forthcoming).

Social Security
Although savings, borrowing, credit, disposal of assets, redundancy payments and earnings play some part, it is primarily social security benefits that mitigate the impact of unemployment on living standards. Nearly all of the unemployed have some social security income, but more important is the fact that for the vast majority it constitutes the major component of their out of work income (Bradshaw et al., 1983; Moylan et al., 1984).

Unemployment benefit normally lasts for twelve months and the unemployed are able to top up their income from unemployment benefit with supplementary benefit if it falls below the specified scale rate. In the past even those with maximum earnings-related supplement (ERS) were not always above the supplementary benefit level and in 1980 only 23 per cent of the unemployed received ERS (Burghes and Lister, 1981: 83). Since 1980, a number of measures have reduced the level of support provided by unemployment benefit. In November of that year a 5 per cent 'abatement' was introduced as an interim measure in lieu of the taxation of benefits which eventually came into force in July 1982. (The abatement was restored in November 1983, so both the abatement *and* taxation applied to unemployment benefit for sixteen months.) In January 1982 ERS was phased out (with average losses of £11.20 per week) and the taxation of benefits, introduced later in the year, had the main effect of eliminating the payment of tax refunds to those unemployed during a part of the tax year. Finally, from November 1980 the value of child dependency additions in unemployment benefit was eroded, and they disappeared completely in November 1984.

The failure to set the rates of unemployment benefit at an adequate level in relation to means-tested supplementary benefit, in conjunction with the erosion of the value of unemployment benefit and the increasing numbers of the unemployed who have exhausted whatever entitlement they ever had to it, have led to a massive and growing dependence of the unemployed on supplementary benefit. In 1983, 62 per cent of the registered unemployed were receiving supplementary benefit compared with 50 per cent who were receiving it ten years earlier (DHSS, 1986b: 214).

For the majority of the unemployed, therefore, it is the level not of unemployment benefit but of supplementary benefit which principally determines the cost of unemployment to them. They may perhaps be forgiven for wondering what was the purpose of compulsory deductions for national insurance while they were in work.

Despite its importance, supplementary benefit discriminates against the unemployed in the payment of two rates: an 'ordinary' rate and a higher 'long-term' rate which the unemployed are never allowed to receive, regardless of length of unemployment. Field (1977: 31) suggests that while the rationale for the long-term rate is sound — that after twelve months (previously two years) savings and stocks of household goods are likely to be depleted — the distinction between the unemployed, who are denied the long-term rate, and every other long-term group of beneficiaries who qualify automatically, is unjustified. Both the Supplementary Benefits Commission and more recently the Social Security Advisory Committee (SSAC, 1983) have called for the long-term rate to be made available to the unemployed. Despite this, the discrimination has been perpetuated in the latest review of social security, in that the unemployed will not, like other groups, qualify for any additional 'premium' in the income support system which replaces supplementary benefit (DHSS, 1986c).

Why Unemployment Costs What it Does

It is now possible to begin to see why unemployment costs what it does, and why the costs fall differently on different individuals and families. The costs of a spell of unemployment depend partly on who you are. Higher income earners lose more income than lower earners but families lose less than single people and childless couples. How much income is replaced depends on the level of previous earnings and on benefit entitlement. Benefit entitlement is largely determined by family composition (but also by housing costs), and for most families, who are most likely to experience hardship in unemployment, it is the level of supplementary benefit that determines their living standards. One of the reasons why families suffer most while having generally higher replacement ratios is that the dependent child additions to supplementary benefit which increase their replacement ratios do not adequately reflect the costs of children.

The costs of unemployment also depend to a lesser extent on what resources are brought into unemployment (redundancy payments, savings, a working spouse, saleable possessions) and what extra resources are accessible during unemployment (borrowing, credit, part-time earnings). But it is the level of social security benefits that is the principal determinant of the costs of unemployment for most people. This is partly because the people most likely to be unemployed are least likely to have access to other resources, and partly because social security policy actively prevents the unemployed from supplementing their benefit income with earnings by more than a small margin.

Conclusions — So What?

The importance of social security in determining the costs of unemployment makes these costs a matter of public rather than merely private interest; but to what extent is it a *problem* that unemployment imposes costs? Here a distinction has to be made between issues of principle and of practice. In principle, the costs of unemployment are a problem for at least four reasons.

First, unemployment is largely involuntary and in such circumstances the unemployed should not be unduly penalised. This does not make the costs of unemployment necessarily a special case: the disabled do not choose to be disabled. But unemployment is a special case to the extent that governments do have explicit manpower and labour market policies. Thus it might be argued that if the vagaries of international exchange rates, oil prices or the inexorable development of microtechnology frustrate attempts to reduce unemployment, or if the encouragement of industrial restructuring has job losses as its consequence, then those thrown out of work by these developments should not bear an unfair burden on their own shoulders.

Secondly, unemployment is largely unforeseeable and so the costs incurred are not something for which people can easily make special provision. Thirdly, unemployment has always tended to be more stigmatising than other contingencies giving eligibility to state benefits, and this, together with the public and political concern for the preservation of work incentives, has led to generally worse treatment in social security for the unemployed than for other groups. Fourthly, the heaviest incidence of unemployment falls on those with generally poorer access to resources other than social security benefits and this increases the importance of benefit adequacy.

It is this latter principle of benefit adequacy that essentially determines whether the costs of unemployment are a problem in *practice*. At present, it is largely a matter of opinion whether they are or not. On the one hand it is arguable that unemployment should not be devoid of costs, otherwise the incentive to return to work (or stay in work) will be undermined. On the other hand it can be argued that these costs ought not to be unreasonable. But as a recent review has suggested, the question: 'How much is enough?' is not easy to answer when social security benefits do not aspire to sustain any clearly defined standard of living (Cooke and Baldwin, 1984).

One exit from this impasse might be the creation of a British 'budget standard' (see Chapter 3) which would create some consensus about the costs of meeting a defined standard of living, against which benefit levels could be assessed. The evidence of surveys is that the unemployed themselves know that the costs of unemployment are unreasonable, but, in the absence of some generally agreed benchmark such as this, it remains impossible to say at what point the costs become unreasonable.

References

Alpren, L. (1977) *The Causes of Serious Rent Arrears*. London: Housing Centre Trust.

Atkinson, A.B. (1982) 'Unemployment, Wages and Government Policy', *Economic Journal*, 92: 45–50.

Berthoud, R. (1979) *Unemployed Professionals and Executives*. London: Policy Studies Institute.

Bradshaw, J. (1985) 'Social Security Policy and Assumptions about Patterns of Work', pp.204–15 in R. Klein and M. O'Higgins (eds), *The Future of Welfare*. Oxford: Basil Blackwell.

Bradshaw, J., K. Cooke and C. Godfrey (1983) 'The Impact of Unemployment on the Living Standards of Families', *Journal of Social Policy*, 12(4): 433–52.

Building Societies Association (BSA) (1985) *Mortgage Repayment Difficulties: Report of a Working Group*. London: BSA.

Burghes, L. (1980) *Living from Hand to Mouth*. London: Child Poverty Action Group.

Burghes, L. and R. Lister (1981) *Unemployment: Who Pays the Price?* London: Child Poverty Action Group.

Clark, M. (1978) 'The Unemployed on Supplementary Benefit: Living Standards and Making Ends Meet on a Low Income', *Journal of Social Policy*, 7(4): 385–410.

Cooke, K. (1987) 'The Living Standards of the Unemployed', in D. Fryer and P. Ullah (eds), *Unemployed People*. Milton Keynes: Open University Press.

Cooke, K. (forthcoming) 'The Withdrawal from Paid Work of the Wives of Unemployed Men: a Review of Research', *Journal of Social Policy*.

Cooke, K. and S. Baldwin (1984) *How Much is Enough?* London: Family Policy Studies Centre.

Culley, L. and P. Downey (1986) *Mortgage Arrears: Owner Occupiers at Risk.* London: Association of Metropolitan Authorities.

Daniel, W.W. (1974) *A National Survey of the Unemployed.* London: Political and Economic Planning.

Department of Health and Social Security (DHSS) (1978) *Social Assistance: A Review of the Supplementary Benefits Scheme in Great Britain.* London: DHSS.

Department of Health and Social Security (DHSS) (1986a) *Tax/Benefit Model Tables.* London: DHSS.

Department of Health and Social Security (DHSS) (1986b) *Social Security Statistics 1985.* London: HMSO.

Department of Health and Social Security (DHSS) (1986c) *The Reform of Social Security: Programme for Action,* Cmnd. 9691. London: HMSO.

Dilnot, A.W. and C.N. Morris (1983) 'Private Costs and Benefits of Unemployment: Measuring Replacement Rates', pp. 321–40 in C.L. Gilbert, C.A. Greenhalgh and A.J. Oswald (eds), *The Causes of Unemployment.* Oxford: Clarendon Press.

Doling, J., V. Karn and B. Stafford (1985) 'Unemployment and Mortgage Arrears', *Unemployment Unit Bulletin,* 18: 3–5.

Field, F. (1977) 'Unemployment and Poverty', pp. 28–42 in F. Field (ed.), *The Conscript Army.* London: Routledge and Kegan Paul.

Hartley, J.F. (1978) 'An Investigation of Psychological Aspects of Managerial Unemployment'. PhD dissertation. Manchester: University of Manchester.

Hill, M., R.M. Harrison, A.V. Sargeant and V. Talbot (1973) *Men Out of Work.* London: Cambridge University Press.

Hughes, J. and R. Perlman (1984) *The Economics of Unemployment.* Brighton: Wheatsheaf Books.

Layard, R., D. Piachaud and M. Stewart (1978) *The Causes of Poverty.* RCDIW, Background Paper No. 5. London: HMSO.

Manpower Services Commission (MSC) (1980) *A Study of the Long-Term Unemployed.* London: MSC.

Melville, J. (1983) 'Life after Redundancy', *New Society,* 63(1052): 51–3.

Moylan, S., J. Millar and R. Davies (1984) *For Richer, for Poorer? DHSS Cohort Study of Unemployed Men.* London: HMSO.

National Consumer Council (NCC) (1976a) *Behind with the Rent — a Study of Council Tenants in Arrears.* London: NCC.

National Consumer Council (NCC) (1976b) *Paying for Fuel.* London: HMSO.

Office of Population Censuses and Surveys (OPCS) (1985) *General Household Survey 1984.* London: HMSO.

Parker, G. (1983) 'Debt', pp. 58–68 in J. Bradshaw and T. Harris (eds), *Energy and Social Policy.* London: Routledge and Kegan Paul.

Parker, G. (1986) 'Unemployment, Low Income and Debt', pp. 27–49 in I. Ramsey (ed.), *Debtors and Creditors: Socio-legal Perspectives.* Abingdon: Professional Books.

Parker, S.R., C.G. Thomas, N.D. Ellis and W.E.J. McCarthy (1971) *Effects of the Redundancy Payments Act.* London: HMSO.

Piachaud, D. (1979) *The Cost of a Child.* London: Child Poverty Action Group.

Sinfield, A. (1976) 'Unemployment and Social Structure', pp. 221–46 in G.D.N. Worswick (ed.), *The Concept and Measurement of Involuntary Unemployment.* London: George Allen and Unwin.

Sinfield, A. (1981) *What Unemployment Means*. Oxford: Martin Robertson.

Smee, C. and J. Stern (1978) *The Unemployed in a Period of High Unemployment*. London: Government Economic Service.

Smith, D.J. (1980) 'How Unemployment Makes the Poor Poorer', *Policy Studies*, 1(1): 20–26.

Social Security Advisory Committee (SSAC) (1983) *Second Report of the Social Security Advisory Committee 1982/83*. London: HMSO.

7

The Costs of Marital Breakdown

Jane Millar

Financial needs and financial resources vary throughout life, with certain identifiable periods when they are very likely to be out of step. In general this life-cycle view of inequality has been based on observation of the *family* life cycle. Rowntree's vivid description (1902: 136) of the five periods of 'want and comparative plenty' covered childhood (want), single and in employment (plenty), married with children (want), children leave home (plenty) and old age (want). In Chapter 15 O'Higgins, Bradshaw and Walker describe the results of an analysis which uses the family life cycle in much the same way and shows that these periods of 'want' and 'plenty' can still be identified. Such an analysis of the changing relationship between income and needs over the life cycle is valuable in pinpointing those periods when state income support is particularly important. However, the concept of the family life cycle, defined in this way, has two major shortcomings as a tool for understanding life-cycle inequalities with the effect that the experience of women, in particular, may be excluded. First, the family is taken as a complete and self-contained unit in which all family members share in the same fortunes and misfortunes. This necessarily ignores evidence which demonstrates that there are inequalities in the distribution of resources within the family and that, where such inequalities exist, it is most likely to be the women who suffer (Land, 1983; Pahl, 1980). Secondly, this rather simple natural history of the family takes no account of the fact that for many families completely different patterns will apply. Specifically, many families will never complete this 'traditional' family life cycle because the family will be broken at an earlier stage. In the past the early death of one partner was probably the most common cause of this; today it is separation and divorce. Of those couples marrying now about one in three will eventually divorce. In 60 per cent of divorces there are dependent children in the family and when the family is broken in this way it is almost always the case that the children remain with the mother. Thus, for women and children a further potential life-cycle stage can be added, that of life as, or with, a lone parent. All the evidence points to the fact that this is a period characterised by financial hardship, when financial needs and financial resources are likely to be very far apart. In this chapter the financial circumstances of such families are examined, looking first at the type of resources available to them, and then at their financial situation relative to other groups in the population. But first the current pattern of separation and divorce is briefly described.

Marital Breakdown
A number of trends in recent years seem to have disturbed the traditional view of what families are like before, during and after marriage, although it is often difficult to judge to what extent these are real changes or whether they have simply become more visible. These changing family patterns include: more cohabitation before marriage; more abortions but at the same time more 'illegitimate' births and more single women bringing up children alone; later marriage; smaller families with childbearing compressed into a relatively short time-period; more married women (particularly mothers) in paid work and hence more two-earner families; and more marriages ending in the divorce courts.

In 1961 two out of every 1,000 married people divorced, but by 1980 this had risen to twelve and has stayed around that level since then. In 1984 144,501 couples divorced (Office of Population Censuses and Surveys [OPCS], 1986). However, this cannot be interpreted simply to mean that the likelihood of marital breakdown has increased. While this may be true, it is also the case that many families will have separated in the past without being able to obtain a divorce. The easier availability of divorce, following the 1969 Divorce Reform Act, means both that the divorce rates reflect the real extent of marital breakdown more accurately than they did in the past and that marital breakdown is more visible.

Those who marry young have the highest risk of divorce and the highest divorce rates occur three years after marriage (when one in thirty couples divorce). The risk declines the longer the marriage lasts, but the longer the marriage the more likely it is that the couple will have dependent children when they divorce. Among those divorcing in 1984 six in ten had dependent children (under sixteen), while among those divorcing after ten to fourteen years of marriage this proportion rose to eight in ten (OPCS, 1986). Every year since the mid-1970s about 150,000 children under sixteen have experienced the divorce of their parents. Many of the children affected are very young; in 1984 there were about 44,000 children under five and a further 57,000 aged between five and ten whose parents divorced. On current trends as many as one in five children will have parents who divorce before the child reaches the age of sixteen (Haskey, 1983a). The majority of these children stay with their mother following the divorce; most continue to have some contact with the father, although one estimate (Eekelaar, 1984: 68) suggests that as many as one-third do not.

Divorce is not the end of the story of changing family patterns as both partners, depending on their ages, are likely to remarry. A study by Leete and Anthony (1979) showed that about half of those who divorce when they are under thirty remarry within five years and at all ages men are more likely to remarry than women. Further, there is some evidence to suggest that second marriages (for one or both partners) are particularly likely to end in divorce again (Haskey, 1983b). Thus the family relationships that follow from divorce can be extremely complex, with emotional and financial commitments extending across a number of different families.

Marital breakdown is the major factor accounting for the increase in the number of lone-parent families. In Great Britain in 1984 there were estimated to be about 940,000 lone parents caring for about 1.5 million children (Haskey, 1986). Thus, of all families with dependent children about one in eight are headed by a lone parent, nearly always a woman. However, this is not a static group; each year newly formed lone-parent families will be added to the total while others will cease to be lone parents (primarily through marriage or remarriage). This means that the number of women and

TABLE 7.1 *One-parent families by sex and marital status, Great Britain, 1982–4*

Family type	%
Lone mothers	
Single	21
Separated	18
Divorced	40
Widowed	12
Lone fathers	
Single	—
Separated	3
Divorced	4
Widowed	2
All lone mothers	91
All lone fathers	9
All lone parents	100
Sample number	1,391

Source: Haskey, 1986: 5–13, Table 6; derived from the General Household Survey

children who have ever lived in a lone-parent family will be substantially higher than the cross-sectional total.

As Table 7.1 shows, lone mothers make up the majority (about nine in ten) of all lone parents and two-thirds of all lone mothers are women who are divorced and separated. Thus, to a large extent, the situation of lone mothers is the situation of separated and divorced women. Unmarried mothers — often thought of as 'typical' lone parents — make up only about a fifth of the total. However, except in the case of widows, the financial circumstances of lone mothers vary not so much according to the way in which they became lone parents as according to other factors, such as the ages of their children and hence their labour market status. Thus some of the evidence in this chapter refers to all non-widowed lone mothers and not only to divorced and separated women.

Financial Impact of Marital Breakdown

The financial impact of marital breakdown falls, as we shall see, mainly on the women and children. Couples with no children who divorce have usually been married for shorter periods than those with children, the median duration of marriage at divorce being 8.4 years and 11.0 years respectively (OPCS, 1986). Compared with those with children, childless couples who divorce are more easily able to settle their financial affairs (Eekelaar and Maclean, 1986). The women in such divorces are in a stronger position in the labour market because they are less likely to have had their employment interrupted, childbearing being the primary reason for married women's withdrawal from the labour market. While this withdrawal is usually only temporary it has long-term consequences for married women's pay and prospects (Joshi, 1984). For this reason, this chapter concentrates on divorced or separated families where there are children and, in particular, on the circumstances of lone mothers.[1]

The three main potential sources of income available to lone mothers are maintenance, earnings and state benefits. Each of these is now considered in turn.

Maintenance
As we have noted, the mother usually has the care of the children when a couple separate; however, the father (including the 'unmarried father') may have a legal obligation to provide financial support. The question of maintenance for divorced and separated families generates a great deal of controversy. The common view of maintenance is that men pay and women receive and therefore that

the costs of marital breakdown fall more heavily upon men than upon women. According to this view women do better out of divorce than men; they obtain a 'meal-ticket for life' while men struggle to make payments, often to the detriment of subsequent relationships, with little or no possibility of contact with their children. This line of thinking lay, in part, behind the changes to the divorce law introduced in the 1984 Matrimonial and Family Proceedings Act. This act requires the courts to give priority to the welfare of the children in determining the financial arrangements following divorce and emphasises that any maintenance for an adult should be rehabilitative — that is, limited in duration so that both parties can become 'self-sufficient' as far as possible. It is too early to judge the effects of these changes but the (admittedly rather limited) evidence available on the situation prior to 1984 suggests that, in the majority of cases, maintenance is neither a substantial contribution to the resources of women nor a substantial drain on the resources of men.

Maintenance does not contribute significantly to the resources of lone mothers for two reasons: first because they either receive nothing at all or else receive low and not always regular payments; secondly, because of the way maintenance is treated for social security purposes. Eekelaar and Maclean (1986), in their study of 276 divorced people, found that while 68 per cent of the divorced and separated mothers in their sample received some form of maintenance payments, half received less than £10 per week. In the Family Finances Survey (FFS), based on a study of about 3,000 low-income families carried out in 1978–9, only 32 per cent of the non-widowed lone mothers were receiving maintenance and the average weekly amount received was £12.25 per week.[2] More recent figures from the General Household Survey for 1982–3 showed that only 49 per cent of divorced and separated women with children were receiving maintenance; 32 per cent for the children only and 16 per cent for the women and the children.[3]

It is not surprising, therefore, that very few lone mothers are able to rely upon maintenance as their main source of income: overall maintenance is the main source of income for only 6 per cent of lone mothers (Popay et al., 1983). If the maintenance is being combined with earnings then it can provide a very useful, and perhaps essential, addition to the generally low earnings which these women are likely to obtain. However, if, as is often the case, it is combined with receipt of supplementary benefit then it will not increase the resources of the lone mother and her children at all. The amount of maintenance received is taken into account fully in assessment for supplementary benefit and the amount of benefit reduced accordingly. The majority of divorced and separated women will spend at least some time in receipt of supplementary benefit (see below) and in both the FFS sample and in the Eekelaar and Maclean study about two-thirds of the women with maintenance payments were also receiving supplementary benefit. Thus their total incomes were unchanged by the maintenance payments which were 'directed at replenishing the state not improving their own or their children's position' (Eekelaar and Maclean, 1986: 94). The FFS analysis also showed that maintenance is not necessarily a steady or regular source of income. Overall only 19 per cent of the lone mothers reported receipt of maintenance at both interviews (twelve months apart); 9 per cent were in receipt at the first interview only and 8 per cent at the second interview only. Thus, a third of those who had been in receipt when first interviewed were not in receipt twelve months later.[4]

What of the men? Is it the case that they cannot pay more or that they will not pay more? It is often assumed that men cannot pay — that those who are unemployed or on low, or even average, earnings cannot easily contribute financially to two households, and that this is particularly true if the man remarries. On the face of it this seems a reasonable view, but in fact there is very little information available on the financial circumstances of divorced men. What evidence there is suggests that the situation is a little more complicated than commonly believed. Eekelaar and Maclean found that of the twenty-nine divorced men in their sample nine were not paying maintenance, in five cases because the man was unemployed. Of those who were paying, two-thirds were paying only a very small proportion (less than 10 per cent) of their current incomes and this varied very little according to the level of their incomes. Thus Eekelaar and Maclean concluded that while unemployment, low incomes or the needs of second families meant that some men do find it difficult to pay maintenance, nevertheless for others (eight of their sample of twenty-nine) it would have been possible to pay more without a serious reduction in their living standards. Research from the USA has been more detailed on this question. Weitzman (1981), in a study of 228 divorced people, found that while divorce meant a rapid move downwards in living standards for women (on average a decline of 73 per cent in income relative to needs) divorced men actually improved their living standards (on average an increase of 42 per cent in income relative to needs). This led her to conclude that 'most fathers have the ability to comply with support orders while still maintaining a comfortable standard of living' (Weitzman, 1981: 1265; see also Chambers, 1979).

If it is indeed the case that men could pay more it does not necessarily follow that attempting to enforce this would be a

desirable policy objective. Divorced and separated women themselves do not necessarily welcome continuing dependence on their
ex-husbands. However, the nature of the debate about maintenance
and about the extent to which men should be expected to contribute
to the financial needs of their 'ex-families' is very revealing. While
the family income might be 'theirs' during marriage (and thus the
distribution of income within the family can be ignored), if the
marriage breaks down then it becomes clear that it was really 'his'
all along.

Earnings
The rising levels of unemployment in recent years have affected
lone mothers as well as other job-seekers, and perhaps more so than
married women who are more likely to be in part-time jobs.[5]
According to the General Household Survey (OPCS, 1985a) in
1980–82 48 per cent of all lone mothers were in employment, a
proportion which had remained fairly constant throughout the
1970s. In 1982–4, however, the proportion employed fell to only 39
per cent. Employment is more likely to be a financial necessity for
lone mothers than it is for married mothers. Forty-four per cent of
employed lone mothers are in full-time jobs compared with 29 per
cent of employed married mothers and, according to the Department of Employment's Women in Employment study (Martin and
Roberts, 1984), 85 per cent of employed lone mothers work to earn
money for basic essentials compared with 37 per cent of married
mothers. Divorced and separated lone mothers are more likely to
be employed than unmarried mothers but this is mainly because
they also tend to have older children. For all women — married or
not — having a child of under school age is a severe constraint on
labour market participation (Martin and Roberts, 1984). For many
lone mothers this is apparently not so much because mothers of very
young children prefer to care for their children full time as it is
because the lack of adequate child-care facilities gives them no
choice. In the FFS sample 49 per cent of the non-employed lone
mothers said they would prefer to be employed and this proportion
did not vary with the age of the youngest child (see also Evason,
1980).

However, even full-time employment cannot guarantee a lone
mother an adequate income to support herself and her children.
Low earnings (as women) and higher child-care costs (in comparison to those of couples) will often mean that the income from
employment does not raise the family much above supplementary
benefit levels. Among the non-employed lone mothers in the FFS
sample who took up full-time paid jobs between the first and second

interview, 37 per cent still had incomes below 140 per cent of the basic rates of supplementary benefit and thus had incomes little or no higher than their benefit incomes. Means-tested benefits for poor working families can be of some help — 39 per cent of FIS recipients are lone mothers — but there are two obvious problems with these benefits. First, there is the problem of non-take-up. The take-up rates for means-tested benefits are well known to be low (see, for example, Deacon and Bradshaw, 1983: 124) and from the FFS it has been calculated that as many as two-thirds of the lone mothers in the sample (excluding supplementary benefit recipients) had some entitlement to means-tested benefits. For some the amounts unclaimed were fairly low, but for a third of those who were not claiming benefits to which they were entitled, claiming would have increased their net incomes by at least 20 per cent.

The second problem with means-tested benefits is that of the 'poverty trap'. According to Department of Health and Social Security (DHSS) tax-benefit tables for July 1986 (DHSS, 1986a) the 'total income support'[6] from gross earnings of £60 per week, for a single person with a child aged three, would be £74.91 if all benefits were claimed. At double that level of earnings (£120 per week) the total income support is almost exactly the same at £76.58. This situation will be only marginally improved after the reforms to the social security system now proposed have been introduced (Cmnd. 9691, 1985). Parker (1986) has calculated that, under the new system, a lone mother with two children on gross earnings of £60 per week will have a disposable income (that is, net income less average rent and rates for local authority housing) of £85. On gross earnings of more than double that level (£140 per week) disposable income will be £100 per week, an increase of only £15.

Social Security

For the reasons reviewed above neither maintenance nor earnings is likely to provide an adequate standard of living for lone mothers and their children. It is not surprising, therefore, to find that dependence on social security benefits is very high. In 1984 there was a total of 491,000 lone mothers on supplementary benefit — of these 147,000 were women who were divorced and 161,000 were women who were separated (DHSS, 1986b). Of all children under sixteen living in families dependent on supplementary benefit 40 per cent (784,000 children) were children living with a lone mother. Many lone mothers are very long-term recipients: in 1984 three-quarters had been on benefit for at least one year and a quarter for at least five years. This has two effects. On the one hand it means that these families will be receiving the higher long-term rate of benefit and are therefore relatively better off than couples with children, most of whom receive the ordinary rate because the man is unemployed (Millar, 1985). On the other hand it also means that many children are spending several years of their childhood living on the 'official' poverty line as set by supplementary benefit levels. It should be remembered also that there is no long-term rate for children. Consequently, although the long-term rate for an adult householder is about 27 per cent higher than the ordinary rate, a lone parent with two children, aged five and eleven, would receive in total only about 15 per cent more on the long-term rate than on the ordinary rate.

Living on supplementary benefit at some time seems to be a situation that most divorced and separated women will face. In the FFS sample only 11 per cent of the non-widowed lone mothers never received supplementary benefit during the two years of the study. Over half (58 per cent) were in receipt continuously and 31 per cent moved on and off benefit, usually as they moved in and out of employment. Of the women who separated from their partners between the two interviews the vast majority (74 per cent) were living on supplementary benefit at the second interview.

Thus there are very high levels of dependence upon supplementary benefit, both in terms of continuing, long-term dependency and as a source of income which lone mothers are likely to need to rely on from time to time. On average as much as 45 per cent of the gross incomes of lone parents is derived from social security benefits. Even for those in employment, state benefits are an essential component of income — contributing, on average, as much as 21 per cent of the total gross amount (Cmnd. 9519, 1985). Child benefit is a very important element in this support. As has already been noted, means-tested benefits are very often not claimed by those who are eligible, but the take-up of child benefit is almost universal. (By contrast, only 75 per cent of those eligible claim the one-parent family addition to child benefit.) Thus, although it is not primarily intended as an income maintenance benefit, child benefit represents a substantial contribution to the income of these families, and is also one of the few sources of income available to them which is reliable, regular and has no stigma attached to its receipt. On average, 14 per cent of the net income of lone parents comes from child benefit, rising to almost 20 per cent for the poorest families — those with incomes below 140 per cent of the ordinary rates of supplementary benefit (Millar, 1984).

Inequalities in Income

In this section inequalities in income as they affect lone mothers are considered from two perspectives. First, lone mothers' position in the overall income distribution (as a measure of vertical inequality) is examined. Secondly, lone mothers are compared with other families with children (as a measure of horizontal inequality).

The analysis carried out by the DHSS as background information for the recent review of social security (Cmnd. 9519, 1985) provides the most up-to-date figures on the overall distribution of income (capital assets and other measures of wealth not being included). The figures are based on equivalent gross income, that is income calculated to take into account family size. Table 7.2 shows the results. Most lone parents are crowded into the lowest quintiles. Just over two-fifths are in the bottom quintile — much of the highest proportion of any family type — and only 5 per cent are in the top quintile. Thus, while lone parents make up only 4 per cent of all households, 7 per cent of the households in the bottom quintile and 6 per cent in the second quintile are headed by a lone parent.

TABLE 7.2   *The distribution of equivalent income in quintiles by family type, 1982*

		Non-pensioners			
Quintiles	Pensioners (%)	Single Persons (%)	Couples (%)	Couples with children (%)	Lone parents (%)	All (%)
Bottom	23	24	9	18	41	20
2nd	42	11	9	17	32	20
3rd	19	15	17	27	15	20
4th	10	24	26	23	6	20
Top	6	26	38	15	5	20
All	100	100	100	100	100	100
Bottom (%)	27	34	9	23	7	100
2nd (%)	49	15	9	22	6	100
3rd (%)	23	21	16	37	3	100
4th (%)	12	33	24	30	1	100
Top (%)	7	36	36	20	1	100
All (%)	24	28	19	26	4	100

Source: DHSS, 1985b: Tables 1.7 and 1.9

Many studies of poverty[7] have shown that lone mothers have a very high risk of poverty and there is also evidence to suggest that such a situation is long-term rather than temporary. In the FFS 34 per cent of the two-parent families but only 17 per cent of the lone mothers were no longer poor (as measured by comparing net family income with a poverty line of 140 per cent of supplementary benefit) when they were re-interviewed twelve months after the initial contact. The difference between lone mothers and two-parent families in the likelihood of escaping from poverty was in fact even greater than this. In about half the cases where the income of the lone mother had gone above the poverty line this was associated with ceasing to be a lone parent. Of the women who remained lone mothers only a very small minority — 11 per cent — crossed this poverty line.[8] Thus, long-term poverty is very likely for lone mothers, with only the prospect of marriage or remarriage likely to alleviate this or at least render it invisible. The extent to which remarriage *actually* means that the living standards of lone mothers improve is unknown. We know little about the distribution of resources in families in general, and even less about the distribution within reconstituted families. Thus, although the incomes of such families are likely to be above what the lone mother could expect on her own (but nevertheless below those of families in general), whether or not this means a significant improvement in living standards is unclear. There are clearly economic pressures on divorced and separated women to remarry, but despite their financial difficulties at least some lone mothers value their financial independence as lone parents. Some even say that they are better off financially than they were when married because they are no longer dependent on the husband sharing 'his' income with them (Evason, 1980; Pahl, 1985).

As regards the comparison between lone parents and other families with children there have been two opposing trends in recent years. On the one hand, rising unemployment has meant that many more couples with children have joined the ranks of the poor. In 1971 16.7 per cent of those in the lowest quintile of equivalent income were couples with children, but by 1982 this had risen to 23.3 per cent (Cmnd. 9519, 1985). On the other hand, the fact that about half of all two-parent families have two earners, while the proportion of lone mothers in employment has fallen, has tended to increase the gap in income between the two groups. As Table 7.3 (derived from the Family Expenditure Survey) shows, in 1985 the average gross weekly income for a two-parent family with two dependent children was £270.95; for lone parents the equivalent figure was only £112.81. Furthermore, in 1979 the average gross income of lone parents was just over half (51.1 per cent) that of couples with two children but by 1985 it had fallen to just over two-fifths (41.6 per cent). Thus, while the gross incomes of two-parent families with two dependent children rose by about 80 per cent between 1979 and 1985, those of lone parents rose by only about 48 per cent. The Retail Price Index rose by some 67 per cent over the same period, which means that the incomes of lone parents have, in real terms, fallen.

One possible objection to these comparisons is that they are not actually comparing like with like. In two-parent families the income must meet the needs of four people (two adults and two children) whereas in lone-parent families there are, on average, 1.8 children and only one adult. Therefore the fact that the latter have lower incomes does not necessarily mean that they have a lower standard of living. One way of attempting to control for this is to calculate income and expenditure per 'adult equivalent' from the information given in the Family Expenditure Survey. This is shown in the lower half of Table 7.3, using the equivalences implied in the supplementary benefit scale rates (although without taking into account the ages of the children because there is insufficient information in the published Family Expenditure Survey data to do this). As the table shows, if income and expenditure are recalculated in this way the position of lone parents relative to couples does improve, but

TABLE 7.3   *Income and expenditure, 1979 and 1985*

	Lone parents (£ p.w.)	Couples with two children (£ p.w.)	Lone parent income and expenditure as a % of those of couples
Gross normal weekly household income			
1979	76.09	148.91	51.1
1985	112.81	270.95	41.6
Normal weekly net household income			
1979	70.46	123.30	57.1
1985	102.81	216.04	47.6
Average weekly household expenditure			
1979	73.87	118.56	62.3
1985	105.89	199.11	53.2
Per equivalent adult 1985[1]			
Gross income	60.65	104.21	58.2
Net income	55.27	83.09	66.5
Expenditure	56.93	76.58	74.3

[1] Calculated by giving couples a weight of 1.62, lone parents a weight of 1.00 and children a weight of 0.49. Thus, for example, the 1985 calculation for lone parents was the number of adults (265) × 1.00 plus the number of children (468) × 0.49 = 229, in total 494. This was then divided by the number of households (265) to give an average figure of 1.86 adult equivalents per household.

Sources: DE, 1980: Tables 18, 20 and 46; DE, 1986: Tables 11 and 22

nevertheless a large gap remains between them. Expenditure — which is perhaps a better indicator of living standards than income — per adult equivalent in lone-parent households is shown to be about three-quarters of the level in two-parent households. Even after controlling for family size, then, lone-parent families are still significantly worse off than two-parent families.

Other indicators of living standards confirm the picture: lone parents are less likely to have access to consumer assets, particularly a car, which is available to only 32 per cent of lone parents but to 79 per cent of two-parent families (Department of Employment [DE], 1986). They are less likely to be living in owner-occupied housing (29 per cent compared with 67 per cent) and more likely to live in a flat or maisonette rather than a house (24 per cent compared with 7 per cent) (OPCS, 1985b). Expenditure on 'social' activities such as holidays, hobbies and entertainment is very restricted: in 1983 couples with one or two children spent on average £26.08 per week (or 15.3 per cent of total expenditure) on leisure activities, while lone parents spent only £8.78 or 9.5 per cent of total expenditure (Central Statistical Office [CSO], 1985).

Conclusions

Marital breakdown has major financial consequences for the individuals involved over both the short and long term. For divorced and separated women with children neither public nor private sources of income support are adequate to ensure such families a standard of living comparable to that of other families with children. The reality of 'self-sufficiency' through employment is limited by the lack of jobs, the low level of earnings available to women, and by the fact that the day-to-day care of children is left almost entirely to the 'family' with the state providing little or no assistance by way of child-care facilities. Although we have little hard information on this, the extent to which men directly bear the financial costs of marital breakdown is probably limited and mainly short-term. Over the long term other commitments may intervene and thus the longer ago the separation the less likely it is that the man will be able or willing to provide financial support (see, for example, Robins and Dickinson, 1984, who found this to be the case in the USA). The recent changes in divorce law are likely to reinforce this pattern. For women, on the other hand, the consequences may be very long-term. Even when her children become independent, a divorced or separated woman is unlikely to be able to return easily to the labour market and her age and lack of employment experience will put her at a severe disadvantage. The consequences may still be felt in old age, when the woman has been unable to build up an adequate pension in her own right but has lost any entitlement she might have had through her husband to an occupational pension or widow's pension (see Chapter 4). For the children also there may be long-term implications, with the economic deprivation suffered in childhood affecting educational attainment and hence future earnings (McLanahan, 1985; Fogelman, 1983).

The financially precarious situation of lone mothers does not, however, spring from nowhere, newly created at the point of marital breakdown. Rather, it is the case that these financial implications are not so much the consequence of *marital breakdown* as they are the consequence of gender inequalities *within marriage*. Because women are assumed to be (and are) financially dependent on men within marriage, their earnings and their earning capacity are assumed to be of secondary importance. Because women are assumed to have (and do have) the major responsibility for child-care, their position in the labour market — where the demands of such responsibility are ignored — is weak. If women are treated as financially dependent within marriage, and their access to the labour market and to social security benefits is structured by this, then it is hardly surprising to find that they cannot immediately become financially independent if the marriage breaks down.

Notes

1. The financial consequences of divorce for older women are not therefore discussed. However, for such women, who have often been out of the labour market caring for children, the financial consequences can be quite severe, including the loss of their rights to occupational pensions and survivors' benefits (Groves, 1987).

2. The analysis of the Family Finances Survey was carried out with financial support from the ESRC (grant no. G00232074). For a more detailed description of the results see Millar and Bradshaw (forthcoming).

3. For details of other studies on maintenance see Eekelaar (1984), Family Policy Studies Centre (1983) and Smart (1984: 194–7).

4. The women included here are those who were lone parents at both interviews. Of the original lone mothers, 16 per cent were no longer lone parents at the second interview (13 per cent were living with a man and 3 per cent no longer had dependent children). Unfortunately we do not have the information necessary to determine what happened to their maintenance payments.

5. Tarpey (1985), seeking to explain the dependency rates of lone mothers on supplementary benefit, found that while the level of female unemployment is an important factor in this, it is also the case that many lone mothers, because of their child-care responsibilities, are unable to enter the labour market. He estimated that, even in a situation of 'full employment' about 35 to 40 per cent of lone mothers would still be dependent on supplementary benefit (compared with the current figure of almost 50 per cent).

6. 'Total income support' refers to gross earnings *minus* tax, NI contributions, fares to work and gross housing costs *plus* child benefit, family income supplement, housing benefits and the value of free school meals and free welfare milk.

7. For example, see Cmnd. 5629 (1974); Layard et al. (1978); Townsend (1979); and Mack and Lansley (1985).

8. See also Eekelaar and Maclean (1986: 100), who found that the divorced women in their sample who were lone parents when they were interviewed had substantially lower incomes than those in 'reconstituted' families.

References

Central Statistical Office (CSO) (1985) *Social Trends 15, 1985*. London: HMSO.

Chambers, A. (1979) *Making Fathers Pay: the Enforcement of Child Support*. Chicago: University of Chicago Press.

Cmnd. 5629 (1974) *Report of the Committee on One-Parent Families* (Finer Report). London: HMSO.

Cmnd. 9519 (1985) *The Reform of Social Security: Volume 3, Background Papers*. DHSS. London: HMSO.

Cmnd. 9691 (1985) *The Reform of Social Security: Programme for Action*. DHSS. London: HMSO.

Deacon, A. and J. Bradshaw (1983) *Reserved for the Poor: the Means-Test in British Social Policy*. Oxford: Blackwell/Martin Robertson.

Department of Employment (DE) (1980) *Family Expenditure Survey 1979*. London: HMSO.

Department of Employment (DE) (1986) *Family Expenditure Survey 1985*. London: HMSO.

Department of Health and Social Security (DHSS) (1986a) *Tax/Benefit Model Tables*. London: DHSS.

Department of Health and Social Security (DHSS) (1986b) *Social Security Statistics 1986*. London: HMSO.

Eekelaar, J. (1984) *Family Law and Social Policy* 2nd ed. London: Weidenfeld and Nicolson (1st edition, 1978).

Eekelaar, J. and M. Maclean (1986) *Maintenance After Divorce*. Oxford: Clarendon Press.

Evason, E. (1980) *Just Me and the kids*. Belfast: Equal Opportunities Commission.

Family Policy Studies Centre (1983) *Divorce: 1983 Matrimonial and Family Proceedings Bill Briefing Paper*. London: Family Policy Studies Centre.

Fogelman, K. (1983) *Growing Up in Great Britain*. London: Macmillan.

Groves, D. (1987) 'Occupational Pension Provision and Women's Poverty in Old Age' in C. Glendinning and J. Millar (eds), *Women and Poverty in Britain*. Brighton: Wheatsheaf Books.

Haskey, J. (1983a) 'Children of Divorcing Couples', *Population Trends*, 31: 20–26.

Haskey, J. (1983b) 'Marital Status Before Divorce and Age at Divorce: Their Influence on the Chance of Divorce', *Population Trends*, 32: 4–14.

Haskey, J. (1986) 'One-Parent Families in Britain', *Population Trends*, 45: 5–11.

Joshi, H. (1984) *Women's Participation in Paid Work: Further Analysis of the Women and Employment Survey*. London Department of Employment, Research Paper No. 45.

Land, H. (1983) 'Poverty and Gender: the Distribution of Resources Within the Family', pp. 49–71 in M. Brown (ed.), *The Structure of Disadvantage*. London: Heinemann.

Layard, R., D. Piachaud and M. Stewart (1978) *The Causes of Poverty*. RCDIW, Background Paper No. 5. London: HMSO.

Leete, R. and S. Anthony (1979) 'Divorce and Remarriage: a Record Linkage Study', *Population Trends*, 16: 5–11.

Mack, J. and S. Lansley (1985) *Poor Britain*. London: George Allen and Unwin.

Martin, J. and C. Roberts (1984) *Women and Employment: a Lifetime Perspective*. London: HMSO.

McLanahan, S. (1985) 'Family Stucture and the Reproduction of Poverty', *American Journal of Sociology*, 90(4): 873–901.

Millar, J. (1984) *The Contribution of Child Benefit to Family Income*. Social Policy Research Unit Working Paper No. 202. York: University of York.

Millar, J. (1985) 'The Incomes and Expenditure of Supplementary Benefit Recipients', *Poverty*, 60: 41–4.

Millar, J. and J. Bradshaw (forthcoming) 'The Living Standards of Lone-Parent Families', *Social Affairs*.

Office of Population Censuses and Surveys (OPCS) (1985a) *OPCS Monitor: General Household Survey, preliminary results for 1984*. London: Government Statistical Services.

Office of Population Censuses and Surveys (OPCS) (1985b) *General Household Survey 1983*. London: HMSO.

Office of Population Censuses and Surveys (OPCS) (1986) *Marriage and Divorce Statistics, England and Wales 1984*. London: HMSO.

Pahl, J. (1980) 'Patterns of Money Management within Marriage', *Journal of Social Policy*, 9(3): 313–35.

Pahl, J. (1985) 'Violent Husbands and Abused Wives: a Longitudinal Study' in J. Pahl (ed.), *Private Violence and Public Policy: the Needs of Battered Women and the Response of the Public Services*. London: Routledge and Kegan Paul.

Parker, H. (1986) 'Off Target', *New Society*, 75 (1206): 232.

Popay, J., L. Rimmer and C. Rossiter (1983) *One-parent Families: Parents, Children and Public Policy*. London: Study Commission on the Family.

Robins, P. and K. Dickinson (1984) 'Receipt of Child Support by Single Parent Families', *Social Service Review*, 58(4): 622–41.

Rowntree, S. (1902) *Poverty: a Study of Town Life* 2nd edn. London: Macmillan (1st edn, 1901).

Smart, C. (1984) *The Ties That Bind: Law, Marriage and the Reproduction of Patriarchal Relations*. London: Routledge and Kegan Paul.

Tarpey, T. (1985) *Explaining the Increasing Dependence of Lone Parent Families on Supplementary Benefit*. Unpublished MA thesis. York: University of York.

Townsend, P. (1979) *Poverty in the United Kingdom*. Harmondsworth: Penguin Books.

Weitzman, L. (1981) 'The Economics of Divorce: Social and Economic Consequences of Property, Alimony and Child Support Awards', *UCLA Law Review*, 28(6): 1181–268.

FINANCIAL RESOURCES

8
Wages and Salaries

Chris Pond and Robin Smail

For most families and individuals, wages and salaries are still the main source of income. They determine their position in the structure of incomes, not only at a given point in time, but over the whole life cycle. Rich rewards from work can provide security from want during retirement or periods of ill-health, as well as a good standard of living during periods of labour market activity. Low wages can cast their shadow into retirement (see Chapter 4).

This chapter examines the pattern of wage inequalities as they exist today, and the ways in which that pattern has changed in the recent past. It also considers the effects of taxation in helping to reshape the distribution of real net pay, and therefore living standards.

The Importance of Pay

The share of wages and salaries as a proportion of household incomes has fallen in recent years, from 69 per cent in 1975 to 60 per cent ten years later (Central Statistical Office [CSO], 1987; Table 5.1). The main reason for this change has been the substantial increase in the numbers of people dependent on social security benefits. This in turn was the result of demographic changes (such as the increase in single-parent families and in the number of pensioner households) and of the sharp increase in unemployment. There has also been some increase in personal property incomes (rent, dividends and interest) and in private pensions (see Chapter 10). Nevertheless, income from employment remains the single most important determinant of living standards, especially when fringe benefits are included (see Chapter 9).

It is not only material living standards that are affected by the level of a person's earnings. An individual's position in the hierarchy of pay very often also determines his or her status and access to non-financial resources. The phrase in the loan advertisement 'according to status' means little more than an assessment of an individual's credit-worthiness according to current and likely future earnings.

This association between pay and status manifests itself in public and political assessments of 'worth'. Articles reporting the 'excessive' earnings of individual manual workers ('the £10,000-a-year gardener') are a mainstay of popular journalism, even though the pay levels cited are often commonplace among white-collar occupations. So, in terms of pay, manual workers are assumed to be 'worth' less than non-manual workers, women less than men, blacks less than whites. The National Federation of the Self-Employed (NFSE), for instance, recently warned that:

> When minimum wage rates are imposed and employers are (or believe they are) paying more for staff than they otherwise would, they are less likely to be tolerant of foibles and allow less flexibility. They are that much more likely to be prejudiced against employing women. (NFSE, 1985: 17)

Similarly, the Institute of Directors (IoD) asserted that: 'A statutory minimum wage discourages employers from taking on blacks, who for a number of socio-economic reasons have a lower marginal productivity than whites' (IoD, 1984).

Such beliefs are implicitly justified by orthodox economic theory which states that, in a competitive market, pay will be determined by the marginal revenue product of labour — the amount that an employer could add to his total revenue by taking on an additional worker. It follows from this that employers will only take on workers whose 'productivity' exceeds or equals their wage, and that less productive workers will only be employed at below average wage levels.

However, as is argued below, the competitive market conditions which might validate this theory rarely operate. Some groups of workers find themselves in a 'buyers' market' in which employers can pay wages below the productivity of the workers, simply because the workers concerned lack the bargaining power necessary to get a fairer return for their labour. Unemployment reduces the bargaining power of those workers who have the fewest opportunities of employment, especially if they are not well represented by trade unions (for a fuller explanation see Pond and Winyard, 1983).

While the market is often used to legitimise inequalities in pay, social and institutional factors are more important determinants of wage levels than economic forces. When the Royal Commission on the Distribution of Income and Wealth (RCDIW) considered the determination of top salaries, it concluded that pay levels for directors and managers bore little relation to the economic success of their companies (RCDIW, 1976). A more important influence appeared to be the corporate image that the company wished to portray, high executive salaries being considered an outward sign, sometimes of success, sometimes of irresponsibility.

And so, while an individual's level of pay serves to influence his or her status and position in society, so too his or her status can help to determine the level of financial reward. The links between status and pay are circular and self-reinforcing.

The Distribution of Income

The distribution of income generated by the market is far from equal. Analysis of the Family Expenditure Survey shows that in 1985 the top quintile — the richest 20 per cent of households — shared between them nearly half of all 'original' income, derived from work, occupational pension schemes, rent, interest and dividends. This was before the effects of taxes or public spending were taken into account. The poorest quintile shared less than one-third of one per cent of original income (see Table 8.1).

TABLE 8.1 *Distribution of original, disposable, and final household income (UK)*

	Quintile groups of households (%)					
	Bottom	2nd	3rd	4th	Top	Total
Original income[1]						
1976	0.8	9.4	18.8	26.6	44.4	100.0
1981	0.6	8.1	18.0	26.9	46.4	100.0
1984	0.3	6.1	17.5	27.5	48.6	100.0
1985[4]	0.3	6.0	17.0	27.0	49.0	
Disposable income[2]						
1976	7.0	12.6	18.2	24.1	38.1	100.0
1981	6.7	12.1	17.7	24.1	39.4	100.0
1984	6.7	11.7	17.5	24.4	39.7	100.0
1985[4]	6.5	11.0	17.0	24.0	41.0	
Final income[3]						
1976	7.4	12.7	18.0	24.0	37.9	100.0
1981	7.1	12.4	17.9	24.0	38.6	100.0
1984	7.1	12.1	17.5	24.3	39.0	100.0
1985[4]	6.7	12.0	17.0	24.0	40.0	

[1] Households ranked by original income.
[2] Households ranked by disposable income.
[3] Households ranked by final income.
[4] Figures for 1985 are rounded, taken from *Economic Trends*, November 1986: 97.

Source: CSO, 1987: Table 5.19

This income distribution among households is modified by government intervention through the tax and benefit systems (Table 8.1). However, this still leaves the richest fifth with about 41 per cent, and the poorest fifth with only 6.5 per cent of all disposable income. Redistribution brought about by direct taxes and benefits amounts to taking 11 per cent of the total income share from the top 40 per cent and giving it to the bottom 40 per cent. The share of those in the middle is unchanged.

Accounting for the effects of other public spending — on the health service and education, for instance — barely alters the redistributive effect. The top fifth share 40 per cent of the income — proportionately twice as much as would be the case if incomes were equally shared. The bottom fifth have half as much income as they would in an equal distribution (only one-tenth of the total). The last section of Table 8.1 gives the details.

Tables 8.1 and 8.2 reveal that, together, the welfare state, a tax system intended to shift resources from the rich to the poor, and a social security system designed to eliminate poverty, do not greatly alter the overall distribution of income. The social services, including the NHS and education, actually provide more benefits to the better-off than they do to the poor. The social security system fails often to meet the real needs of claimants and provides barely a subsistence level of income (see Chapter 11). The tax system (see below) remains far from progressive.

TABLE 8.2   *Percentage shares of income, before and after income tax, received by given quintile groups*

	1949	1959	1970–71	1976–7 (old basis)	1976–7 (new basis)	1977–8	1978–9	1981–2
Before income tax								
Top 1 per cent	11.2	8.4	6.6	5.4	5.5	5.5	5.3	6.0
Top 10 per cent	33.2	29.4	27.5	25.8	26.2	26.2	26.1	28.3
Next 40 per cent	43.1	47.5	49.0	49.7	49.7	49.8	50.4	49.0
Bottom 50 per cent	27.3	23.0	23.5	24.5	24.1	23.9	23.5	22.7
Bottom 10 per cent	—	—	2.5	2.5	2.5	2.5	2.4	2.0
After income tax								
Top 1 per cent	6.4	5.3	4.5	3.5	3.9	3.9	3.9	4.6
Top 10 per cent	27.1	25.2	23.9	22.4	23.2	23.3	23.4	25.6
Next 40 per cent	46.4	49.7	49.9	50.0	49.9	50.2	50.4	49.2
Bottom 50 per cent	26.5	25.0	26.1	27.6	26.9	26.5	26.2	25.2
Bottom 10 per cent	—	—	—	3.1	3.0	3.0	2.9	2.4

Source: CSO, various years, *Economic Trends*

The Post-war Trend

Throughout the post-war period, redistribution of income has been limited, as Table 8.2 shows. Although the inequality of the pre-tax distribution of income has been reduced, the gap between pre- and post-tax shares has actually fallen. The tax system appears to have become less redistributive in its effects. In recent years, moreover, there has been a redistribution which has shifted resources away from the poor towards the rich. Most significant has been the effect of policies in both the labour market and the tax system. The recent impact of these policies is examined below.

The Pay Structure

Since the end of the 1970s there has been a significant change in the structure of earnings. The most comprehensive source of data on the level and distribution of earnings is the Department of Employment's *New Earnings Survey* (*NES*) (Department of Employment, annual). The survey is carried out in April each year, based on a one per cent sample taken from national insurance records. As with most official surveys, the *NES* tends to under-record the extremes of the distribution (for a fuller discussion see Low Pay Unit, 1980).

According to the *NES*, average (mean) weekly earnings for all full-time workers in April 1986 stood at £184.70. However, no less than 60 per cent of full-time workers earned below this average and over 90 per cent of part-timers earned less than the hourly equivalent. The figure also hides enormous disparities between manual and non-manual workers, between men and women, between different occupations, industries and regions and, of course, between the high paid and low paid. Some of these disparities are illustrated in more detail below.

Manual and Non-manual Work

Manual workers tend to work longer hours than those in white-collar jobs, but earn less for each hour they work. So full-time manual workers, working an average of nearly forty-four hours a week, received gross earnings amounting to £163.20 in 1986. Full-time non-manual workers — working under thirty-eight hours a week — earned £200. Those in manual jobs therefore earned on average 30 per cent less for each hour worked than did those in non-manual jobs.

However, even this comparison does not give a true indication of the actual difference between pay in manual and non-manual occupations. This is because some — mainly female — low-paid jobs, such as shopwork, are classified as non-manual. If the earnings of men are considered alone, the average gross hourly earnings of manual males are 37 per cent less than those of white-collar men.

Men and Women
The weekly earnings gap between men and women is even greater than that between manual and non-manual workers. While adult men working full time earned an average of £207.50 in 1986, adult women averaged weekly earnings of only £137.20. Part of this difference is due to the fact that women work, on average, fewer hours than men. However, even when hours of work are standardised, women earn only three-quarters as much as men for every hour they work.

Part-time Work
Since the early 1970s there has been a substantial growth in the number of part-time employees. The number of female part-time workers has increased by about 1.5 million to 4 million, while the number of male part-timers has doubled to more than 800,000. The majority of these jobs are low-paid. Unfortunately, about one-third of all part-time workers are excluded from the *New Earnings Survey* because their weekly earnings fall below the national insurance contribution floor (£38 in 1986–7). However, even though the lowest paid part-timers are excluded, the 1986 survey gives a figure for average hourly earnings of female part-time workers of only £2.77. The figure for all full-time workers (including overtime pay and hours) was £4.51. An alternative way of illustrating the gap between full-timers and part-timers is to express the latter's average hourly figure for part-timers as a weekly equivalent. This yields gross wages of just under £112 a week, compared with £185 for full-time employees.

Region
Pay disparities between regions have once again become a highly topical subject. The government and some employers have been calling for regional pay differences and decentralised pay bargaining which is capable of adapting to local economic conditions. The debate has virtually restricted itself to the pay divide which exists between the south-east of England and the rest of Britain. Average full-time earnings for non-manual workers in Greater London in April 1986 stood at £242 a week, compared to figures of between £180 and £190 in most other regions. For all full-time manual workers the corresponding figures were £186 in London and between £155 and £165 elsewhere.

Regional disparities also reflect themselves in differences in the size of the low-pay problem in different parts of the country. Throughout most of England, Wales and Scotland, a little over a third of full-timers are paid less than £125 a week, the Council of Europe's 'decency threshold', when overtime earnings are excluded. In Scotland, the proportion is about 36 per cent, in the West Midlands a little over 34 per cent. In the south-east as a whole, however, the figure is 24 per cent, and in Greater London only 17 per cent of full-time workers are paid less than the 'decency threshold'. In Greater London, the proportion of part-time working women who are low paid is 58 per cent. Almost everywhere else in the country it is four-fifths. However, these regional averages themselves disguise very real pay inequalities, even within the most prosperous regions.

High Pay and Low Pay
The earnings statistics reveal a yawning gap between the high paid and the low paid. In 1986 an estimated 8.8 million adult workers — 43.2 per cent of the adult workforce — are being paid less than the Council of Europe's 'decency threshold' (£125.60 a week or £3.25 an hour) for the basic hours they work. Two-thirds of these workers are women, and around 40 per cent are in part-time jobs. At the lowest levels of pay, women and part-time workers are even more heavily represented. Nearly one in three (1.5 million) manual women workers earned less than £100 for a basic week. Nearly 2 million female part-time workers (one half of the total) earned below £2.40 an hour in April 1986.

Windfalls to the High Paid
The pay divide has widened sharply in recent years. The NES shows that the top fifth of male full-time workers received average earnings increases of 120 per cent between 1979 and 1986. Meanwhile, the relative earnings of low-paid workers have fallen sharply. In the seven years to 1986 average (mean) earnings of full-time men rose by 108 per cent. By contrast, average earnings for the lowest-paid fifth of men rose by only 87 per cent, barely enough to keep pace with inflation. Although the Retail Price Index increased by 80 per cent between 1979 and 1986, the Low-Paid Price Index — which measures price increases facing low income groups — increased by 86 per cent.

Explaining Pay Inequalities

The orthodox wage theories referred to above suggest that differences in earnings reflect differences in productivity or ability.

However, an analysis of the distribution of pay by industry and occupation throws doubt on this over-simple explanation.

The highest paid jobs (in which the average full-time wages of men and women exceed £200 a week) are in higher education, banking and finance, telecommunications, the police force, airways and aerospace equipment production, printing and publishing, drink and tobacco, motor vehicle production, chemicals, parts of electronic engineering, iron and steel, and the energy supply industries.

By contrast, the lowest paying industries, where average full-time wages fall below £150 a week, are agriculture, textiles, footwear and clothing, retailing, hotel and catering, and various public and personal services, such as social security and hairdressing. In hotel and catering, for example, which employs around a million workers (full-time and part-time) average full-time earnings in April 1986

TABLE 8.3   *The ten worst paying jobs, full-time employees, April 1986*

	Percentage of workers earning under £123 (excluding any overtime pay)[1]	Average earnings (including any overtime pay) (£ p.w.)
Women		
Shop check-out	96.9	90.30
Hairdressers	95.6	78.10
Shop assistants, etc.	91.3	93.10
Barmaids	89.5	89.30
Waitresses	89.2	—
Other cleaners	87.6	98.20
Sewing machinists (textiles)	86.2	96.40
Receptionists	83.2	100.60
Chefs/cooks	81.7	106.80
Packers, canners, etc.	79.3	111.80
Men		
General farmworkers	88.0	121.00
Barmen	74.4	123.50
Hospital porters	73.9	125.70
Caretakers	67.6	136.20
Butchers, etc.	66.0	129.00
Salesmen/shop assistants	65.5	126.30
Bakers, etc.	58.9	149.60
Goods porters	58.8	146.20
Craftsmen's mates	57.8	140.90
General labourers	57.7	145.00

[1] The figure of £123 represents the Low Pay Unit threshold for low pay.

Source: New Earnings Survey, 1986, Parts A and C (unpublished data)

were just £126 a week. Around 700,000 catering workers are considered to be low-paid.

Table 8.3 lists the worst low-paying occupations. Most farm-workers are poorly paid, particularly when overtime hours are excluded. More generally, male shopworkers, barmen, caretakers, security guards and building labourers are often working for low wages. Average wages (including overtime) for barmen, for example, amounted to just £123.50 a week in 1986.

Low wages for women are commonplace, not just in the low-paying industrial sectors, but also in the relatively better paid manufacturing or engineering industries, and throughout much of the public sector. In education, for example, virtually all part-time cleaning and catering jobs are low paid. As noted above, even in the relatively prosperous industrial sectors of banking, insurance and other finance there are concentrations of low-paid women — cleaners and some clerical workers tend to be poorly paid regardless of where the office or workshop is.

The reason is that certain occupations draw their labour force from groups within the population who are in a weak bargaining position: young people starting off in work with little experience, unlikely to unionised, and with few other employment opportunities; married women seeking part-time employment that is consistent with the demands of looking after children; ethnic minorities facing discrimination and high rates of unemployment. These groups are often poorly paid, not because of low levels of productivity or ability, but because employers find themselves in a 'buyers' market'. In these circumstances, low pay and high profits can coexist.

However, this is not a universal explanation for low pay. In many industrial sectors where low pay is prevalent, profitability tends also to be low. Such industries are typically comprised of small, scattered establishments, where unionisation is difficult. Individual firms often operate with older, labour-intensive technology and, like the UK clothing and textiles industries, face fierce competition for a declining market. They are characterised by low efficiency and by low levels of investment. Their low profitability reduces the ability of firms to pay higher wages, even if they wished to do so. In such cases low wages are a reflection not of the low productivity of the individual employees, but of individual firms and entire industries (see Craig et al., 1982).

A different explanation applies in the case of low pay in the public sector. Here the persistence of low pay is related not to the ability of the employer to pay, but to political judgements about the appropriate level of earnings for employees and the amount of public expenditure that should be allocated to providing that level of earnings. Concentrations of low-paid employees are found in manual and many clerical grades in local government and as cleaners, messengers and security guards in DHSS and Inland Revenue offices. In the National Health Service, ancillary workers, such as hospital porters (with 1986 average earnings of £125.70), domestics, cleaners, and even auxiliary nurses, are often forced to survive on inadequate wages (see, for example, Low Pay Unit, 1985; Rahman, 1985).

How are the highest earnings to be explained? It is often asserted that, at the top end of the labour market, salary rises have generally been tied to 'performance' (or productivity) and company profits. A shortage of highly skilled executives and professional staff restricts supply in the face of unremitting demand. Consequently, high salaries are necessary as incentives and to ensure the efficient operation of the market.

Despite the high levels of unemployment in the economy as a whole, it is true that a number of occupations at the upper end of the labour market do not experience excess supply. In these occupations it is easy to maintain high wage levels. In other fields of work, however, where there are more able people than jobs available, the price of well-paid labour still tends not to fall, as would be expected in a freely competitive market characterised temporarily by excess labour supply. Why should the upper end of the labour market operate in these ways?

The primary reason is because the upward mobility of labour is, at all levels, carefully determined within an arena of organisational structures and hierarchies and institutional restrictions. In short, companies and other organisations (with their 'internal labour markets') provide a limited number of highly paid jobs and restrict access to them.

The relatively small number of highly paid jobs which exist (for example, journalists, City of London stockbrokers, business executives, senior university academics, top civil servants) may be justified to some degree by organisational efficiency or even on the grounds of limitations on physical space within offices. The exclusiveness of these jobs cannot, however, be explained away on the grounds of ability alone. Many more people are capable of doing these sorts of jobs and would do them if the openings were created. Moreover, it should not be overlooked that it is in the interests of people in senior positions to maintain the controlled hierarchies at the top of which they sit. Thus, conveniently, there will frequently appear to be a 'shortage of talent' and a subsequent rise in high wages in order to 'attract' and retain that valuable commodity.

The Widening Pay Divide

Recent years have seen the gap between the high paid and the low paid widen. Government policy has played a large part in bringing this about.

Deregulating the Labour Market

The post–1979 Thatcher governments attributed much of the blame for unemployment to 'market rigidities'. In particular, Ministers believed that 'artificial' constraints on the labour market had prevented wages falling so as to adjust to changed conditions, and that for many groups wages were being held at above their true market level, thereby 'pricing out' workers from jobs.

A number of measures designed to reduce wages and enable the 'market to work more freely' were implemented. Employment rights (such as unfair dismissal protection and maternity provisions) were weakened; public services were contracted out to private firms, often at wages and conditions much poorer than in the public sector itself; wage reduction schemes such as the New Workers Scheme, Job-start, and the Job Training Scheme were introduced; wage protection conventions such as the Fair Wages Resolution were abandoned; and the minimum wage setting bodies, the Wages Councils, were given reduced powers.

These policies have had three effects. First, the number of employees earning low wages has risen by about a million between 1979 and 1986. The increase would have been bigger still had it not been for the fact that many low-paid workers were removed from the labour market altogether by unemployment.

Secondly, the decline in the relative earnings of the low paid has been so severe that the poorest workers now find themselves worse off than they were one hundred years ago when earnings data were first collected. In 1886, when the average (median) male manual wage was £1.21 a week, the workers within the bottom fifth of the pay ladder earned an average wage worth 69 per cent of this. In 1986, wages in the bottom fifth were worth only 65 per cent of the overall average (£163). Compared with one hundred years ago, the highest-paid fifth, by contrast, have seen a marked improvement in their relative wages. In 1886 they earned 43 per cent more than the overall average; today, the figure is 55 per cent.

The third major effect of government policies has been to intensify domestic hardship as many low-paid workers suffer real and nominal pay *cuts*. Department of Health and Social Security (DHSS) figures reveal that in 1983 about 700,000 people were living in households which contained at least one full-time wage-earner and yet still had incomes below the equivalent of the supplementary benefit level. In addition, there were many low-paid single parents in part-time jobs. Moreover, large numbers of working households now survive on incomes only marginally greater than the supplementary benefit (SB) level. Thus, of the 10.7 million people in all non-pensioner households living on or below SB, or up to 40 per cent above SB, nearly 40 per cent (4.1 million) were dependent on a full-time wage (DHSS, 1986).

According to the Breadline Britain Survey, carried out by MORI/LWT in 1983, an estimated 7.5 million people were living in poverty — unable to afford three or more 'necessities', as defined by public opinion. Around 1.75 million adults, more than one-third (35 per cent) of all those in poverty, were in families where the head of the household worked full-time. And of the 2.5 million children in poverty, one million were living in these conditions as a result of their parents' low wages (Mack and Lansley, 1985). Clearly, although many low-paid workers do not live in poor households, low wages are a major and growing cause of poverty.

The Shifting Tax Burden

It has long been accepted that the British tax system should be *progressive*: that as income rises, so too should the proportion of income paid in tax. The arguments for such a structure are essentially twofold. First, there is the objective of redistribution, where taxes collected will enable the provision of adequate public services and state welfare benefits, and this facilitates a reduction in the gap between the rich and the poor. Secondly, given that the state needs to raise a certain amount of revenue, the sacrifice is more evenly shared if tax rates rise with income. Simply put, it may be expected to impose a smaller sacrifice on the rich to give up a proportion of their income than would be imposed on the poor if they were to give up the same proportion of their income. The sacrifice can be equalised if a larger proportion of the incomes of the rich are taken in tax (for a fuller explanation see Field et al., 1977).

By either criterion, the British system of taxation is only mildly progressive, and much less progressive now than used to be the case. Since the Second World War, as Table 8.2 shows, the level of redistribution (between before and after tax incomes) has gradually declined. One reason for this trend is that more wage-earners have become subject to tax, at lower levels of income. While in 1950 the married man without any children started paying tax at a level of earnings equivalent to 60 per cent of average full-time manual male earnings, by 1986–7 tax was payable at only 38 per cent of average manual pay. The other reason is that fewer and fewer people are being taxed at the higher rates. In 1987–8, only 5 per cent of tax payers will be subject to income tax at above the standard rate.

Since 1979, the relative burden of taxes on different groups has changed significantly. Although income tax has been cut by £2 billion since 1978–9, 15 per cent of this reduction has gone to the wealthiest 0.7 per cent of households — those with incomes over £50,000 per annum — amounting to an average reduction of £219 per week, for each tax unit. Overall more than 43 per cent of the cuts have gone to the richest 11 per cent of households. The low paid, on the other hand, have received an estimated 7 per cent of the cuts in income tax, worth around £2 a week to each tax-unit (House of Commons, 1987).

Moreover, the reduction in income tax paid by the low paid has been more than outweighed by greatly increased national insurance contributions (raised from 6.5 to 9 per cent between 1979 and 1985). For instance, a married couple with two children earning about £115 a week now pay, proportionately, nearly three times more in direct taxes than they did in 1978–9. By contrast, those on £50,000 a year

TABLE 8.4   *Incidence of direct and indirect taxes on all households, 1985*

Income band[2] (decile group)	Taxes as a proportion of gross incomes[1]		
	Direct[3]	Indirect[4]	All taxes
Bottom	−0.4	23.2	22.8
2nd	−0.1	23.9	23.8
3rd	2.9	27.5	30.4
4th	9.4	26.3	35.7
5th	14.9	23.1	37.9
6th	17.3	22.5	39.8
7th	18.7	20.4	39.1
8th	20.1	19.7	39.8
9th	21.4	18.2	39.6
Top	24.1	15.7	39.8
All households	18.0	19.9	37.9

[1] Gross income includes gross earnings, investment incomes and welfare benefits.
[2] Households are ranked according to original income, before the effect of taxes and benefits.
[3] Direct tax is income tax and national insurance contributions, less tax reliefs at source.
[4] Indirect taxes include VAT, excise duties, rates, TV licences and intermediate taxes (including commercial rates).

Source: Economic Trends, November 1986: 107, Table 5

are paying 12 per cent less (representing a cut in their direct tax burden from around 52 per cent to 46 per cent) (Low Pay Unit, 1987).

What is not shown on Table 8.2 is the impact that taxes on *spending* have on the redistributive efficacy of the tax system as a whole. Over the past forty years indirect taxes such as rates, excise duties and various other taxes on purchased goods have become a major resource of revenue for the Exchequer. This trend has had a disproportionate effect on the living standards of the poor, since spending taxes are not levied according to ability to pay. Hence they are at best neutral in their distributive effects. At worst they can be highly regressive. What is more, since 1978–9 indirect taxes have been increased by £19 billion.

Table 8.4 shows that the effect of expenditure taxes is to erode much of the small amount of progressivity evident in the income tax system. While the poorest households pay almost a quarter (23 per cent) of their income in indirect taxes, the richest households pay only 16 per cent of theirs. Taking all taxes together, progressivity is limited to the lowest incomes. A household in the middle of the income range (£150 in 1985) pays just under 40 per cent of their income in tax; so too do the richest tenth of households (CSO, 1986).

Conclusions and Policy

Earnings are still the major source of household income in Britain. But although the spread of gross earnings has narrowed in the past forty years, massive inequalities still exist in the distribution of pay. The tax system, moreover, not only seems to be limited historically in its powers of income redistribution, but has recently been modified so as to enable a shift in income away from the poor towards the wealthy.

Like the welfare state, the tax system seems unable to challenge the maldistribution of resources; it merely reflects, and perhaps even reinforces, the underlying inequalities which exist in household welfare. The reason for this is that the post-war strategy of redistribution was based on the implicit assumption that intervention in the operation of market forces would be damaging. Market forces, themselves influenced and determined by the initial distribution of resources, were thereby allowed in turn to distribute economic rewards unequally, with only the worst excesses of this maldistribution being mitigated through fiscal policy and the social services. This *after-the-event* redistribution has, naturally, had disappointing results. It follows that if damaging inequalities in the distribution of household income are to be challenged at their source, then policies are required which are designed directly to intervene in the processes that generate those inequalities.

A Fair Wage Structure

Trade union action, though necessary to tackle low pay, is not on its own sufficient. Even in well unionised sectors, such as the NHS, local authorities and other parts of the public sector, low pay remains a problem. There is also a real danger that collective bargaining unaccompanied by legally enforceable rights at work could lead to a widening of certain inequalities, especially between men and women, part-timers and full-timers, young people and adults, blacks and whites. Those groups for which the level of unionisation or bargaining strength remains relatively poor may find themselves falling further behind in the general advance.

Dealing with the problem of low pay — as with health and safety and equal pay — requires a partnership between trade union action and the law. Thus, an across-the-board statutory national minimum wage should be introduced, not as an alternative to, but as an instrument of, collective bargaining. This means that unions would be involved at every stage in establishing, operating and enforcing the minimum wage, with the level of the minimum being determined by negotiations between individual trade unions, employers and the government at a national level (see Low Pay Unit, 1986). A minimum wage cannot be 'imposed' by a government, however sympathetic, nor should it be a covert form of pay restraint policy.

A minimum wage would tend to truncate the lower tail of the earnings distribution and compress, to some extent, the dispersion. The case for a maximum wage ceiling also deserves careful consideration. In present conditions inequalities tend to be legitimated and perpetuated through dominant social values which explain high incomes in terms of high productivity, a proposition for which little evidence exists. A maximum wage, set at perhaps £40,000 a year, would fulfil two important functions. First, it would represent a public statement that excessive incomes were not considered to be justified by the contributions of recipients to society. Secondly, it would help to reinforce the effectiveness of a progressive tax system in redistributing rewards. At present, high-income recipients are able to award themselves gross salaries at a level which neutralises the effect of taxation, leaving them with a target net income. A maximum wage would help to prevent this circumvention of progressive taxation, illustrating the partnership needed between direct interventions and fiscal policy.

Tax Reform

Improving the social wage and eliminating excessive disparities in the distribution of earnings could have only a limited impact if unsupported by reform of the tax and social security system.

The possibilities for tax reform have been well illustrated since 1979, though an essential first step towards a progressive tax system would be the broad reversal of those policies. Creating a highly efficient and fair tax system should go much further. We would advocate a widening of the tax base, through the phasing out of most tax allowances and reliefs, and the rebuilding of a more progressive structure of average and marginal tax rates. Fewer people should pay tax at the basic rate: the lowest paid at a reduced rate and a significant proportion at a new higher rate. A unified personal allowance should be created which could be converted into a cash payment worth the same to every worker. National insurance contributions should eventually be incorporated into the income tax system.

To complement such changes in direct taxation, full taxation of company perks must be legislated and unearned income taxed at higher rates than earned income. Mortgage interest tax relief should, in the short run, be provided only at the basic rate of income and, in the long run, should be phased out and replaced with a unified housing subsidy. The erosion of capital tax revenues should be arrested and reversed rapidly.

These radical tax reforms, together with an overhaul of social security — whereby universal benefits replace means-tested benefits where possible — are essential if family poverty and the undesirable inequalities in household finances are to be eliminated.

References

Central Statistical Office (CSO) (1986) 'The Effects of Taxes and Benefits on Household Income 1985', *Economic Trends*, 397: 96–109.

Central Statistical Office (CSO) (1987) *Social Trends 17, 1987*. London: HMSO.

Craig, C. et al. (1982) *Labour Market Structure, Industrial Organisation and Low Pay*. Cambridge: Cambridge University Press.

Department of Employment (annual) *New Earnings Survey (NES)*. London: HMSO.

Department of Health and Social Security (DHSS) (1986) 'Low Income Families', mimeo.

Field, F., M. Meacher and C. Pond (1977) *To Him Who Hath*. Harmondsworth: Penguin Books.

House of Commons (1987) *Hansard*, 23 March, col. 34.

Institute of Directors (IoD) (1984) 'Wages Councils: the Case for Abolition', December. London: IoD.

Low Pay Unit (1980) 'Profile of the Low Paid in Britain', in A. Atkinson (ed.), *Wealth, Income and Inequality*, 2nd ed. Oxford: Oxford University Press.

Low Pay Unit (1985) *Low Pay: What Can Local Authorities Do?*, Low Pay Pamphlet No. 27, 3rd ed. London: LPU.

Low Pay Unit (1986) 'The TUC Fair Wages Strategy: A National Minimum Wage — A Low Pay Unit Commentary'. London: LPU, mimeo.

Low Pay Unit (1987) 'Two Nations — Double Standards: The 1987 Budget and the Poor', *Low Pay Unit Briefing*, March. London: LPU.

Mack, J. and S. Lansley (1985) *Poor Britain*. London: George Allen and Unwin.

National Federation of Self-Employed and Small Businesses (NFSE) (1985) *Still Priced Out*, London: NFSE.

Pond, C. and S. Winyard (1983) *The Case for a National Minimum Wage*, Low Pay Unit Pamphlet No. 23. London: LPU.

Rahman, N. (1985) *Pricing into Poverty: Council Manual Workers' Pay*, Low Pay Unit Pamphlet No. 38. London: LPU.

Royal Commisson on the Distribution of Income and Wealth (RCDIW) (1976) *Higher Incomes from Employment*, RCDIW Report No. 3, Cmnd. 6383. London: HMSO.

9

Non-wage Benefits from Employment

Robin Smail

When considering the distribution of rewards from employment it is no longer sufficient just to examine wages and salaries. Non-wage benefits at work, in the form of fringe benefits such as occupational pension schemes and company cars, have become so important for many employees that they now constitute a distinct 'company welfare system'. The self-employed, for their part, are able to claim substantial 'business expenses' against their gross earnings. Often the boundary between legal tax avoidance and illegal tax evasion is blurred and constitutes a sort of 'grey economy'. More clearly illicit, and therefore part of the 'black economy', are falsified and extravagant expense accounts of PAYE employees and tax evasion by 'moonlighters'.

Most workers now benefit from some sort of addition to their salary or wage — legitimate or otherwise — which can add considerably to their living standards. However, these additions are not equally available and there is evidence that those with the highest basic wages and salaries are likely to receive most in non-wage benefits. Moreover, as the number of workers in part-time, temporary and casual employment (those in the so-called 'secondary' labour market) rise, this inequality increases.

The first part of this chapter examines the nature and distribution of company welfare, the second investigates incomes from the grey and black economies. But, first, some definitions are in order.

Locating Non-wage Benefits

Fringe Benefits
Fringe benefits or 'perks' make up a substantial proportion of total remuneration. They constitute a form of company welfare in the sense that, in the words of the British Institute of Management, they 'increase the well-being or wealth of employees at some cost to the employer' (Murlis, 1974). A typical middle-manager on £18,000 per annum, for instance, can expect at least five weeks paid holiday per annum, the security of a good sick-pay scheme, an occupational

pension worth as much as 20 or 30 per cent of salary, the private use of a company car, and a host of other smaller benefits besides, including subsidised meals and subscriptions for medical insurance.

It is not always a straightforward task to locate the fringe benefit element of total reward from work. Normally, perks will consist of items 'over and above' the basic remuneration of wages or salaries. Part of the value of being in an occupational pension scheme, for example, is that employers will contribute a sum to the employees' superannuation fund. This contribution is treated as a normal business expense for the employer, and for the employee it is not treated as taxable income.

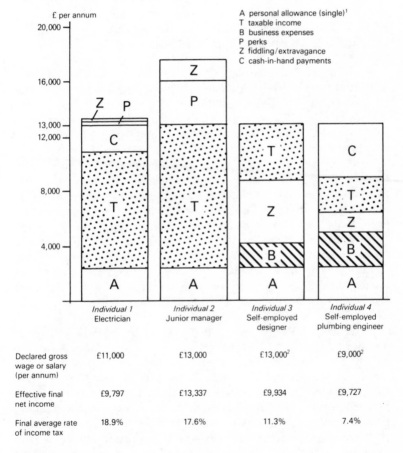

	Individual 1 Electrician	Individual 2 Junior manager	Individual 3 Self-employed designer	Individual 4 Self-employed plumbing engineer
Declared gross wage or salary (per annum)	£11,000	£13,000	£13,000[2]	£9,000[2]
Effective final net income	£9,797	£13,337	£9,934	£9,727
Final average rate of income tax	18.9%	17.6%	11.3%	7.4%

[1] £2,335 per annum in 1986-7.   [2] Before deductions for business expenses.

FIGURE 9.1   *Locating 'non-wage' benefits*

Yet this is only part of the story. A further benefit to the employee is that the portion of their gross earnings paid into the scheme is tax deductible. Figure 9.1 illustrates the point. For individual 2, the junior manager earning £13,000 per annum, the value of most fringe benefits could be added to the basic wage, as indicated by area P. This could be denoted in terms of the cash in hand (the net value) or in terms of the equivalent gross salary. Alternatively, some portion of fringe benefits — such as the employee's superannuation contribution — might be represented as a tax deduction, added to area A, which represents statutory tax-free income. Either way, the proportion of income subject to tax (T) is reduced. For simplicity, in Figure 9.1 all employee fringe benefits or perks are added, as a net cash value, on to the basic wage. Figure 9.1 does this for both a manual employee (individual 1) and a junior manager, with the areas labelled P.

Tax Avoidance and Evasion
Although the self-employed — those in businesses and the professions paying tax on Schedule D — cannot add to their gross earnings in the same way as employees can through the company welfare system, they can enjoy substantial benefits in the form of additional tax allowances over and above the basic personal allowance. The self-employed person who runs a car or works from home is likely to increase their tax-free income by setting the costs of running a car and heating the home against tax. Many business-expenses, denoted by area B in Figure 9.1 for the two self-employed individuals 3 and 4, may be legitimate: some may not be. Legal tax avoidance can become illegal tax evasion. Though strictly locating a fiddle, in practice there is likely to be a grey area, usually labelled 'avoision'. This may take the form of overlapping living costs and business expenses, or just sheer extravagance in the name of business. Avoision and pure evasion are located together, as area Z in Figure 9.1.

Returning to PAYE employees (on tax Schedule E), there is another fiddle: the falsified expense account. Any claimed expense which does not constitute a genuine business expense for the employee is represented by area Z and can be added to the gross salaries of individuals 1 and 2. The effect of incorporating these fiddles is always to reduce the amount of tax paid on each pound of gross income. In other words, the fiddle will reduce a worker's tax burden or average rate of tax — the proportion of income paid in tax.

Beyond these fiddles there is the popular view of the black economy, the moonlighting or cash in hand work done by the self-employed or company employees. Though not exactly the sort of illegal 'non-wage benefit' represented by area Z, undeclared earnings are most easily come by from positions of employment rather than unemployment. Moreover, any discussion of personal tax evasion in the context of the distribution of financial resources should consider the black economy in its widest possible form.

In Figure 9.1 undeclared earnings are denoted by area C and, for the purposes of illustration, are restricted to the skilled manual employee (an electrician) and the self-employed manual worker (a plumbing engineer). This income represents significant additions to the declared earnings of these individuals, raising their overall gross earnings to £13,000 in our examples. But since no tax is paid on the undeclared element of income, their average rate of tax will fall.

Company Welfare

In order to assess the value of company fringe payments, it is useful to begin by defining them as far as is practicable. All legal and quantifiable benefits from work are included over and above earned income. Thus, all traditional perks are covered: private use of company cars, meal vouchers or subsidised meals, occupational pension schemes, free or cheap goods, tied accommodation, time off work with pay, crèche facilities, social, medical and sports facilities, travel and removal expenses, private health insurance, cheap loans, insurance cover and the payment of educational fees. In addition, it is usual to include other benefits which arguably should be provided as 'rights at work' — namely, paid holidays and sick-pay schemes. Extra earned income such as overtime or bonuses are excluded from our definition, as are any statutory payments such as employers' national insurance contributions. Other types of non-wage reward, such as the informal expectation of tips or inflated expense accounts, are considered later.

Growing Perks
Previous studies have revealed enormous increases in fringe benefits paid out to employees (Smail et al., 1984; Green et al., 1984, 1985). In the manufacturing industries, for example, average fringe payments — excluding company cars — have risen from 11 per cent of total remuneration in 1964 to nearly 20 per cent in 1981. Similarly, in finance and in the gas, electricity and water industries the proportion of remuneration attributable to fringe benefits varied from about a quarter to a third and from 18 per cent to 30 per cent respectively between the early 1960s and the 1980s.

Tax Exemptions

Why has there been such a growth in the provision of perks? One of the major reasons has undoubtedly been a favourable tax environment. Private pensions, for example, have been encouraged for over sixty years through a series of fiscal measures and now cover about 11 million employees in Britain. Tax exemptions are currently allowed up to certain limits on both the employer's and the employee's contributions. The income and capital gains from pension funds and most lump sums on retirement are also exempt so that the only tax is on the benefits paid out later to pensioners.

A whole host of other non-wage benefits attract no tax liability at all for employees. These include provision of sports and social facilities, most gifts and cheap goods, reasonable removal expenses, employers' sickness insurance premiums, life insurance premiums taken out prior to 1984, the first 15p of luncheon vouchers, canteen subsidies (where meals are available to all grades of employees), share option schemes, and cheap mortgage subsidies.

The annual value of these perks can be enormous, particularly for the high paid. The Review Body of Top Salaries (1982) found that senior executives in the private sector could expect superannuation benefits worth 15 to 40 per cent of salary each year, and chief executives in the largest companies might receive an amount equivalent to 50 or 60 per cent of salary or upwards of £50,000 per annum. For the average full-time employee, the perk value of superannuation contributions amounts to an estimated £1,500 per annum.

Cheap mortgage loans are frequently available to employees in the financial sectors of the economy. The clearing banks, for example, typically will lend an employee up to £30,000 at a rate of interest equal to the standard home mortgage rate less 5 per cent. Such a benefit, worth as much as £1,065 per annum in cash, or £1,500 in terms of the equivalent gross salary, attracts no tax liability as long as the interest on the loan ordinarily qualifies for tax relief. The highest paid, and employees of merchant banks, can enjoy even more favourable terms. A 5 per cent flat rate of interest on a mortgage loan of £40,000 to £50,000 is not uncommon. Reduced interest payments increase employees' disposable income and facilitate bigger mortgages which in turn generate larger, untaxable, capital gains from their house purchase.

Life insurance and sick-pay schemes are increasingly popular methods of boosting employees' remuneration packages. Together these perks will usually amount to about £150 a year, although life insurance premiums have attracted tax since 14 March 1984. Cheap meals in company dining-rooms or canteens are often worth about

£300 a year to the basic rate taxpayer, or over £400 in gross wage terms. For the high paid, they may be worth up to £800 a year in terms of the equivalent gross salary.

Taxable Perks
Besides these tax-free items, a number of other perks are taxable if, and only if, an employee is classed as 'higher-paid' by the Inland Revenue. This category covers most directors, and all employees with gross earnings of over £8,500, or those with effective gross earnings of over £8,500 when all fringe benefit items are added to basic salary. Benefits in this bracket include cheap loans, staff education and training fees, fees for the education of children, medical insurance premiums, and the private use of a company car.

Some employees, most frequently in financial industries, enjoy the benefit of cheap loans from their employer, perhaps for the purposes of buying a car or paying private school fees. Although tax may be payable on the difference between the amount of interest paid to the employer and the amount of interest which would have been paid under normal market conditions, benefits to the employee could amount to £500 a year for a basic rate taxpayer. Similarly, over 625,000 employees have their full medical insurance premiums paid for by their employers (House of Commons, 1985). Even after paying tax on this benefit, as two-thirds of recipients' employees do, the net benefit to basic rate taxpayers can amount to over £300 per annum. Where employers do not actually pay the insurance premium for private medical treatment, many will subsidise this cost to employees by organising a group discount on premiums.

One of the most important and conspicuous perks provided by employers is a company car. Often, though certainly not always, directors and employees genuinely do have a requirement for a car for work purposes. The fringe benefit is generated through the private use of that car. For some, it accrues in the form of saved standing charges, such as vehicle depreciation, car tax, repair costs, insurance and interest on the capital which would otherwise have been spent on car purchase; for others, it includes these savings *plus* free petrol for private use.

About 73 per cent of the 1.5 million directors and employees with company cars pay tax on the imputed value of the car in accordance with the special 'scale charges' laid down by the Inland Revenue (House of Commons, 1985; Board of the Inland Revenue, 1986a). These charges are based on taxable cash sums tied to engine size, car value and car age. Successive chancellors have increased the taxation of company cars since the introduction of the charges in

1977–8, but they still do not cover the full value of the benefit. Indeed, managers and junior executives, with the full private use of a 1,600cc car, in effect receive an addition to their gross salary of between £2,500 and £4,500 even after paying tax based on the scale charges. For senior executives and directors, the benefits are staggering and may be worth anything between £5,000 and £15,000 per annum in terms of the equivalent gross salary.

Finally, there are a number of fringe benefits which do not attract any tax advantage. Some gifts (outside special occasions), non-work clothing, travel season tickets and subsidised rent for accommodation outside the needs of work are all taxable, regardless of employees' earnings. Likewise, earnings during spells of illness and holidays are taxed as normal. What is interesting here, however, is the relative quality of sick-pay schemes and holiday entitlements. These discrepancies between employee benefits are examined next.

Unequal Perks

Perks add considerably to the unequal distribution of rewards from work. 'Rich people do not simply receive more fringes than the poor: they get more in relation to already high incomes' (Green et al., 1984: 11).

Sectoral Inequalities

One aspect of this inequality concerns differences in the prevalence of fringe benefits between various sectors of British industry. These differences are considerable and may exceed the differentials in basic wage rates which they tend to support. In the distributive sector, characterised generally by low wage rates, the average value of perks is less than 18 per cent of total remuneration. By way of contrast, in the finance sector, where in 1985 wages were on average 76 per cent higher, perks make up about a third of total remuneration. Substantial differences are also evident within the main sectors of industry. For example, perks constitute about 20 per cent of total remuneration in manufacturing industry as a whole but the proportion ranges from nearly one-third in chemicals to only 15 per cent in clothing and footwear where average wages are just 58 per cent of those in chemicals.

There is also some evidence that the differences between sectors are increasing although published statistics are far from comprehensive. In 1981 the average package of fringe benefits received by workers in the construction and water industries was worth £960 and £2,800 per annum respectively. By 1984 the comparable figures were £1,000 and £3,800.

Inequality between Households

These are enormous differences and have far-reaching implications for the financial resources of different households. *Within* each industry, however, discrepancies between different grades of workers are even greater. The 1983 General Household Survey revealed that while 72 per cent of employers and managers belonged to an occupational pension scheme, just 58 per cent of skilled manual workers and 48 per cent of unskilled manual workers did so. For sick-pay schemes in 1976 (the latest year for which information is available) the proportions were 91 per cent, 57 per cent and 50 per cent respectively (Green et al., 1984). Moreover, many schemes — particularly pension schemes — offer relatively better benefits to the higher paid while part-timers are likely to be excluded altogether.

Many non-wage benefits are enjoyed primarily by executives. Ninety-two per cent have their life assurance premium paid by their company, one-third are members of share option schemes, 74 per cent receive free medical insurance, and nearly 80 per cent enjoy the full use of a company car. Executives also tend to have longer paid holidays and better meal allowances than lower-paid workers.

A survey carried out by Charterhouse Management Consultants in 1983, for instance, found that a typical director of a medium-sized company receiving a basic salary of £25,000 per annum (including the holiday element) usually costs the employer a further £12,500 per annum in bonuses and fringe benefits (Incomes Data Services, 1983). A well-paid executive or manager will now expect at least one-third of their total remuneration in the form of fringe benefits.

In sharp contrast, low-paid workers receive few, if any, perks. Most receive four weeks or less paid holiday per annum and, even if covered by an occupational sick-pay scheme, workers can often find themselves little better-off during sickness than they would be with minimum statutory sick-pay. Many, especially those working in small firms, are forced on to the statutory minimum when ill. Only a small proportion belong to occupational pension schemes and these tend to be worth very little. Most have to rely on the state pension. Some receive subsidised meals either in a canteen or with luncheon vouchers, but this is also less likely in smaller companies (Green et al., 1984).

Part-time, women, and manual workers generally receive fewer fringe benefits than their full-time, male, and white-collar counterparts (Green et al., 1984). And in the wake of the Conservative government's labour market 'deregulation' policies this relative disadvantage is increasing steadily. In those government and health board sectors, for example, where work has recently been contracted-out to private companies, many workers have lost all entitlement to occupational sick-pay and paid holidays. When the new Wages Act is fully effective in 1987, nearly 3 million workers in shops, catering, hairdressing and clothing manufacturing will lose the legal right to paid holiday (Low Pay Unit, 1985).

Increasing Inequality

As far back as 1969, Townsend calculated that fringe benefits (excluding paid holidays) represented over 13 per cent of the household income of the wealthiest fifth of the population. For the second poorest fifth of households they represented just 7 per cent of income and for the poorest fifth, just 2.6 per cent of income (Townsend, 1979). For those in work, it would appear that the inequality of payment of the most valuable perks — such as pensions, cars, medical insurance — has increased. For example, the proportion of executives receiving medical insurance cover increased fourfold between 1970 and 1986 while the proportion with company cars rose from a half to four-fifths (Inbucon Management Consultants, annual). Added to this, the number of unemployed — who receive no perks — has trebled since the late 1960s. Perks cannot be considered in isolation from the impact both of the recession and of the government's policies designed to deregulate the labour market. When these three factors are taken into account it is evident that statistics on wages and salaries mask the full extent of inequality in the distribution of rewards from the labour market.

This inequality is illustrated within the confines of Figure 9.1. The junior manager with a basic salary of £13,000 per annum can probably add over £3,000 to his net salary, in the form of fringe benefits (excluding paid holidays) provided by the company. The perks will include an occupational pension scheme, cheap loans, subsidised meals, life insurance and the payment of medical insurance premiums. If a company car is included, the addition to salary would probably exceed £4,500 in cash, or around £6,500 in terms of the equivalent gross income. As a consequence the amount of income tax paid by the junior manager — as a proportion of total legal remuneration — would fall from around 24 per cent to just over 19 per cent.

By contrast, the skilled manual worker earning a relatively good wage of £11,000 per annum (average male manual earnings are £8,300), will probably accumulate only a few hundred pounds to his net salary by way of perks. Moreover, his tax liability will fall only very slightly, from 22.8 per cent to 22.3 per cent.

Beyond Tax Avoidance

So far the discussion in this chapter has concerned the provision of perks, those non-wage benefits which are quantifiable and which represent opportunities for employees and employers to avoid tax legally. These fringe benefits are usually viewed as an addition to the wage and have the effect of reducing average tax rates.

But there are other ways in which non-wage benefits may be accrued. Employee expense accounts and the business expenses of the self-employed can boost net remuneration substantially. This can be done either by fiddling or through extravagance, in the sense that not all expenses claimed are entirely genuine or necessary. Represented by area Z in Figure 9.1, both these elements of remuneration have the effect of reducing the proportion of gross reward subject to income tax.

Tax evasion of this nature, where remuneration is effectively provided for *work not done*, is a part of the black economy, and should be considered alongside the undeclared earnings produced by *work done* (area C in Figure 9.1). The impact on the financial well-being of individuals or groups, and the implications of tax evasion for the economy as a whole, are such that both these elements of the black economy must be evaluated.

All Expenses Paid — and More

Employees' expense accounts are often thought of as perks. However, they should not be treated in this way. Modest business lunches, it is true, can be of substantial personal value to an employee since all the costs — which an employee would otherwise have made — will be covered by the employer. However, these costs are likely to be offset by the requirement of working through lunch breaks. The more important non-wage benefit is likely to accrue in the form of grossly inflated or mythical expenses which — in the words of the Inland Revenue — are not 'wholly, exclusively and necessarily in the performance of' an employee's duties.

Although it is hard to evaluate the 'fiddles' and the extravagance, anecdotal evidence of this form of tax evasion (or avoision) abounds. When Clive Thornton headed the Mirror Group of Newspapers he discovered that the expenses bill for Mirror Group employees entertaining *each other* (for business purposes) exceeded the total profits of the whole Mirror Group. The top slice of expenses, revealed Thornton, ranged from £8,000 to £20,000 per annum, and consisted of, 'a list of names covering several sheets of single-spaced typing' (Diverse Productions, 1984). Much of the expenses bill may have been legitimate. However, it is not unknown for journalists and media executives to entertain each other for less-than-essential business reasons.

Similar abuses occur throughout British industry in the areas of telephone and stationery usage, overnight subsistence, meals and car mileage allowances. Many non-manual workers are able regularly to use telephones for private calls, while it is quite common for company employees to overestimate business miles travelled in order to subsidise private mileage.

But how important are such fiddles? One recent study conducted by Business Decisions Ltd (BDL) reported that in 1985 the private company travel and entertainment expenses bill in Britain amounted to £17.4 billion (BDL, 1985). And yet, as the survey concluded:

> Surprisingly, given the massive scale of business travel and entertain-ment costs in Britain, less than four in ten companies actually have a written policy to control spending. Moreover, two-thirds of all companies surveyed have not reviewed their business travel and entertainment expenses policy — written or otherwise — for at least twelve months.

Although fiddling on air fares, rail fares and car hire would be difficult, there is scope for such activity within the £10.6 billion entertainment, petrol, accommodation and subsistence bill. Indeed, if just 5 per cent of this bill, or £530 million, constituted fiddles or extravagance, the loss of revenue to the Exchequer could be as high as £200 million.

While such a 'guesstimate' does not produce an overwhelming sum, the bulk of these benefits will accrue to restricted groups of employees, notably managers and professionals, but including some lower-grade sales staff. Manual and clerical employees are unlikely to enjoy such opportunities. The BDL survey also found that small firms are less inclined to let high proportions of workers carry out expense-incurring business activity.

On the basis of this evidence, Figure 9.1 depicts an area Z which is significantly greater for the junior manager (£1,500) than it is for the electrician (£50). The effect of these additions is to reduce average tax rates still further for both employees, but by a greater amount for the white-collar worker. His (or, unusually, her) final average tax rate is only 17.6 per cent, leaving an effective net income of £13,337.

Schedule D — the Self-Employed

Just as employees may overestimate business expenses and under-estimate effective income, the self-employed can evade tax, either by paying less tax on their fully declared gross earnings, or by failing to declare all gross earnings. Evading tax by exaggerating business expenses is common, although it is not always easy to decide what should count as a legitimate business expense. Take, for example, a freelance journalist working from home. When are heating and lighting costs business expenses and when are they costs of living? Likewise, the actress or singer-dancer: which haircut, taxi fare, item of clothing or exercise class and what portion of video-rental cost is business and which is an everyday living expense? For the business partner, what portion of car-running expenses, meal costs and phone bills are business costs? In the event, so difficult are such costs to attribute to work activities that tax avoision is often achieved by reaching agreement with the Inland Revenue.

Many of the expenses claimed by the self-employed are legitimate and are represented by area B in Figure 9.1. Anything over and above a true expense is represented by area Z for individuals 3 and 4. Quantifying these areas amounts to guesswork and one is left with items of anecdotal evidence such as the case of a person with average gross earnings of £19,000 per annum — over five years — and an average tax bill of just £1.34 each year.

The areas in Figure 9.1, though purely illustrative, are designed to reflect this casual evidence. For the self-employed designer with gross earnings of £13,000, effective net income is £9,934 after paying income tax and any true business expenses. Her (his) average tax rate falls from about 19 per cent to just over 11 per cent as a result of the fiddled expenses.

Perhaps just as important to many of the self-employed, and to the Inland Revenue, is undeclared legal income — cash handed over for work done (area C for individual 4 in Figure 9.1). As the general secretary of the Inland Revenue Staff Federation remarked in 1976: 'The low incomes to which the self-employed admit defy belief. Only 70,000 of them declare the average wage of £60 or more. Only 250,000 of them admit to more than £30 a week' (O'Higgins, 1980).

Under-declaration of true gross earnings could explain why, in the occupations where there are significant numbers of self-employed people, the average earnings of employees almost always exceed those not on PAYE. What is not clear is whether the extent of under-declaration has increased in the past decade or so, when the numbers of self-employed have risen from 1.9 million to 2.5 million. The Survey of Personal Incomes indicates that the distribution of declared self-employed earnings now matches that of employees more closely than it did in the early 1970s. However, this need not be the result of more honesty or greater Inland Revenue success in detecting under-declaration. It may be that the self-employed — particularly at the upper end of the earnings scale —

are actually earning, relatively, even more and continue to declare the same proportion of their income.

For some occupations the scope for making undeclared earnings undoubtedly exists: painters and decorators, electricians, musicians, hoteliers, retailers, lawyers and construction workers are well placed to receive cash in hand payments. Other jobs would seem to provide little scope: actors, caterers and launderette owners are unlikely to be able to work 'off the books' to any large degree.

Where additional undeclared earnings can be made, the costs of doing so may be great. The Labour Research Department (1986) recently reported that 45 per cent of the self-employed said that they worked over sixty hours a week. Many are not covered by maternity leave, sick-pay schemes and pension schemes (although they can enjoy greater tax relief on superannuation) and taking holidays may be difficult. On top of the absence of such benefits, there is the additional risk of business failure.

Working Out of Hours
Some employees are in a position to earn income which is not declared to the tax authorities. Such income could come from overtime worked 'on the side', 'hidden' second jobs, tips or even income from stolen property. Tips, though, are increasingly being brought into the tax net: hotel and catering workers, taxi drivers and postmen are often unable to evade tax.

Most tax evasion by employees probably arises from moonlighting (area C for individual 1 in Figure 9.1). According to one recent MSC survey, more than 750,000 people (over 3 per cent of the workforce) were double-jobbing or moonlighting (*Guardian*, 27 November 1985). While this estimate probably covers those discrete second jobs, such as barwork, taxiwork and so on, it will certainly underestimate the extras many employees make illegally. Through workmates and colleagues, employees are continually in a position to hear of odd jobs needing doing. One study of a shop-floor plant stressed the availability of goods and hidden services — such as betting, haircuts, repairs — among their workmates (quoted in Pahl, 1984: 94). The employed are also meeting customers and prospective customers all the time. Moreover, dealings at work may provide the goodwill needed to cement financial transactions out of work. Hairdressers, joiners, car mechanics, electricians, decorators and even architects are, for example, all easily placed to sell their skills informally.

The self-employed plumbing engineer illustrated in Figure 9.1 earns £4,000 per annum cash in hand. After paying income tax and genuine business expenses (which exclude raw materials of work), this income raises his (her) effective net income to £9,727, and lowers his (her) average tax rate from 15.5 per cent to 7.4 per cent. Our moonlighting electrician earns less 'illegal' income (£2,000) and can only lower his (her) average tax rate to 18.9 per cent under our assumptions. His (her) net effective income is higher, however, at £9,797.

How Much Tax Evasion?
Estimates of the size of the black economy vary from the cautious to the generous. The Institute of Fiscal Studies, on the one hand, by examining both discrepancies between household income and household expenditure and the activities of the self-employed and moonlighters, measure the black economy at between 2.5 and 5 per cent of Gross Domestic Product. This would imply illegal activity at around £14 billion per annum, and a possible loss of revenue to the Exchequer of £3 billion (Dilnot and Morris, 1981; Smith, 1986). At the other extreme, economists at Liverpool University have suggested that 14.5 per cent of national income, or £52 billion, represents black economy activity. This could imply a revenue loss of as much as £13 billion (Matthews, 1985). The Inland Revenue themselves, through various chairmen since Sir William Pile in 1979, regularly come up with a figure of 6 to 8 per cent of GDP.

While there is little agreement about the size of the black economy, there is a growing body of evidence which suggests that it is the already employed and *not* the unemployed who are dominating the cash in hand economy, and thereby 'fiddling the dole'. Intuitively, this makes sense: 'Unemployed people lack the transport, tools, and the network of social contacts necessary to participate in the black economy' (Miles, 1985). The relative success of DHSS and Inland Revenue inspection and fraud teams lends some support to this argument. The most recent Inland Revenue report reveals that investigations from ordinary tax offices yield £1.68 for every £1 spent on the work. Inquiry offices are much more cost-effective, yielding £17.60 for every £1 spent. Inland Revenue special offices, meanwhile, are dramatically successful: in 1984 every £1 spent on investigations and back-up yielded £17; by 1985 £27 was recouped for every £1 spent (Board of Inland Revenue, 1986b). Such yields stand in stark contrast to those of DHSS teams, who recover only 30p for every £1 which is spent on their operations (Christopher, 1986).

Conclusions

The provision of fringe benefits is now very widespread for

employees. However, it is grossly inequitable. While the relatively high paid can enjoy perks worth over one-third of all remuneration — often with a value in excess of £10,000 per annum — the low paid rarely enjoy even a small fraction of such largesse. The effect of providing perks is to widen the distribution of reward beyond that created by wages and salaries alone.

But non-wage benefits for employees are not confined to perks. Salespeople and higher-grade white-collar staffs often have access to expense accounts and the legal and illegal benefits derived from these. At the same time many self-employed workers are expert at evading tax and others manage to confuse business expenses and costs of living. Large numbers of both employees and the self-employed also have easy access to work rewarded by cash in hand.

Contrary to the message of media 'scrounger' campaigns, the black economy provides opportunities for the employed to cheat and evade tax. Even if the unemployed do take the great risk of working while claiming benefits, it is likely to be a less lucrative business. Beyond the cash in hand economy, the unemployed of course enjoy no perks and no opportunity to fiddle expenses. Within employment itself, the low paid — often working for small firms, in high labour turnover service industries, and in the public service — have little opportunity to evade tax.

The policy implications of this analysis go far beyond issues relating to income distribution, inequality and equity. Perks are a source of economic inefficiency which distort the labour market price mechanism and hinder labour mobility by tying employees to company specific welfare. Tax avoidance schemes have eroded the tax base and altered the balance of tax burdens with the result that taxes on the low paid have risen disproportionately. Tax incentives have caused the pension industry to amass excessive funds and distorted actuarial comparisons between private occupational pensions and the state earnings related pension scheme (SERPS) since national insurance contributions are not tax deductible. At the same time, company-provided medical insurance schemes have had a significant and detrimental impact on the development of the National Health Service.

In the interests of economic justice and economic sense there is a need to move towards more comprehensive taxation. In the pension field this would emphasise the relative strengths of SERPS in efficiently protecting the rights of mobile workers and meeting the needs of the unemployed, many low-paid workers and married women. Alongside the tax reforms there is the need for greater clarity as to what constitutes an appropriate 'right' at work and what should be seen as a perk. As perks have grown, certain rights have been eroded. The new Wages Act makes Britain the only European country where all workers are without a legal entitlement to paid holiday. Nurseries have recently been brought into tax as a 'perk'. The statutory sick-pay scheme is in need of improvement, most notably for the low paid and less healthy who are entitled to low rates and are penalised by unfair qualifying periods.

In sum, the non-wage benefits from work that have been the focus of this chapter have little discernible basis either in terms of economic efficiency or social justice.

References

Board of Inland Revenue (1986a) *Notes on Expenses Payments and Benefits for Directors and Certain Employees*, Document No. 480. London: HMSO.

Board of Inland Revenue (1986b) *Report for the Year Ended 31.12.85*, 128th Report. London: HMSO.

Business Decisions Ltd (BDL) (1985) *Travel and Entertainment Expenses in British Business*. London: American Express Europe.

Christopher, T. (1986) Contribution, IFS Conference 'Britain's Shadow Economy', 19 October.

Dilnot, A. and C.N. Morris (1981), 'What Do We Know About the Black Economy', *Fiscal Studies*, 2(1). London: IFS.

Diverse Productions (1984) *Diverse Reports*, Channel 4, 10 November. London: Diverse Productions.

Green, F., G. Hadjimatheou and R. Smail (1984) *Unequal Fringes*, LSE Occasional Papers on Social Administration, 75. London: Bedford Square Press.

Green, F., G. Hadjimatheou and R. Smail (1985) 'Fringe Benefit Distribution in Britain', *British Journal of Industrial Relations*, 23(2). London: LSE.

House of Commons (1985) *Hansard*, 26 February, cols. 149–50.

Inbucon Management Consultants (annual) *Surveys of Executive Salaries and Fringe Benefits*. London: Inbucon/AIC.

Incomes Data Services (1983) 'Charterhouse's 1983 Study', *IDS Top Pay Unit, Review* 32, October. London: IDS.

Labour Research Department (1986) 'The Growing Army of Self-Employed', *Labour Research*, February. London: Labour Research Department.

Low Pay Unit (1985) *Low Pay Review*, No.23, Autumn. London: Low Pay Unit.

Matthews, K. (1985) 'Little Mo and the Moonlighters: Another Look at the Black Economy', *Quarterly Economic Bulletin*, 6(2). Liverpool: Liverpool Research Group in Macroeconomics.

Miles, I. (1983) *Adaptation to Unemployment*, Science Policy Research Unit Occasional Paper, 20. Brighton: SPRU.

Murlis, H. (1974) *Employee Benefits Today*, British Institute of Management Survey, Report No.19. London: BIM.

O'Higgins, M., 1980, *Measuring the Hidden Economy: A Review of Evidence and Methodologies*, Outer Circle Policy Unit. London.

Pahl, R.E. (1984) *Divisions of Labour*. Oxford: Basil Blackwell.

Review Body of Top Salaries (Chair: Lord Plowden) (1982) *Fifth Report on Top Salaries*, Appendix F. Cmnd. 8552. London: HMSO.

Smail, R., F. Green and G. Hadjimatheou (1984) *Unequal Fringes*, Low Pay Report No. 15. London: Low Pay Unit.

Smith, S. (1986) *Britain's Shadow Economy*. Oxford: Clarendon Press.

Townsend, P. (1979) *Poverty in the United Kingdom*. Harmondsworth: Penguin Books.

10
New Patterns of Wealth:
The Growth of Owner Occupation

Stuart Lowe

Over the last twenty-five years the value of personal wealth has approximately doubled in real terms. This substantial increase has been caused by major changes in the composition of assets and in their relative value. Of particular importance has been the rapid and continuous growth of home ownership and, from the mid–1970s, the development of occupational and other private pension funds as a primary form of long-term financial savings. Together, owner-occupied houses and private pension funds account for over 60 per cent of total personal sector wealth compared to less than a third twenty years ago.

The main reason for the accumulation of wealth in these forms is that access to them has been massively subsidised by the state, normally in the form of special tax concessions.

The 'new wealth' is more evenly distributed than the 'old' forms which were held mainly in land and company stocks. However, the holders of old forms of wealth are in no way threatened because their assets continue to be inaccessible to most people and their future ownership is assured through the system of inheritance (Harbury and Hitchens, 1979). The most important feature of the new wealth is its *vertical* distribution which cuts across the occupational class structure. Major divisions of material interests exist between, for example, home owners and tenants, or between solely public and mainly private pensioners, which are at least as important as income derived from occupation.

Attention is drawn in this chapter to the way in which access to welfare services of a good standard is becoming increasingly dependent on people's ability to accumulate and trade against personal assets, primarily housing, in order to release cash. Pensions are much less amenable to being used in this way. Entitlement to draw a pension on retirement is dependent on a gradual level of uninterrupted payments into the pension fund. Housing, however, is a much more 'liquid' investment from which cash can be extracted by a variety of means. The rapid growth of owner occupation over the last twenty years is helping to sustain a major social and welfare cleavage between owners and tenants. Cash leakage from the private housing market is also underwriting differential access to public and private forms of service provision and, in part, explains the degree of mobility users have within them.

This chapter first describes changes in the value and composition of personal assets over the last twenty years and, secondly, briefly summarises the evidence concerning the distribution of privately held wealth. However, the main focus of the chapter is on owner occupation: the reasons for its growth, the complex process of equity creation, the withdrawal of cash from the housing market and the transfer of housing wealth from one generation to the next.

Personal Sector Assets: an Overview

In 1983 the gross value of personal sector assets held by individuals as opposed to institutions was £1,070 billion. Of this total £597 billion was held in the form of physical assets (mainly dwellings) and £473 billion in financial form (occupational pensions, building society investments, stocks and shares, British Government Equities, etcetera). Outstanding mortgage debts and other liabilities reduced the figure to a combined net value of £922 billion. Because these forms of wealth are different and owned for a variety of purposes, there are a number of difficulties in interpreting the crude figures. Not all assets are equally disposable in a cash sale or exchange. Cashing in a building society investment account is easy, but realising the equity stored in a private house is normally possible only in specific situations, typically when an owner moves house. In the case of pensions it is not normally possible to sell the fund at all, certainly not without jeopardising the retirement income. But private pensions are treated as part of personal sector wealth because the funds belong to the individual contributor and have become an integral part of the network of financial assets.

A second problem of interpretation is that while the value of some assets is relatively stable (such as National Savings Certificates) others fluctuate very considerably from year to year. Figure 10.1 shows that in the last twenty-five years the value of net personal wealth has approximately doubled in real terms. But when the figures are controlled for inflation, using the 1980 Retail Price Index, it can be seen that this growth has been very uneven. A peak was reached in 1972, mainly due to rapid house price inflation, and was not exceeded again for over a decade.

Over the last twenty years or so the balance between physical and financial assets has fluctuated, with people switching their holdings

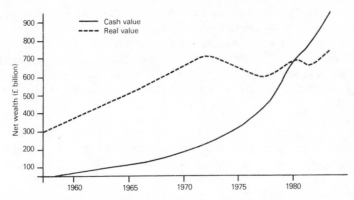

FIGURE 10.1 *Net wealth, real and cash value, 1957–83*

Data for Figures 10.1–10.3 come from Central Statistical Office (CSO) (1985: Table 52) for the period 1976 to the present and from Cmnd. 7937 (1980: Appendices, Table 10) for the period 1957 to 1962.

in the hope of maintaining their value. In the 1960s and 1970s physical assets grew rapidly mainly due to the increasing numbers of owner-occupiers and the rapid increase in house prices. By the same token financial assets slumped, reflecting high inflation and negative real interest rates. Those who did not switch from the financial sector in the late 1960s and early 1970s saw the value of their investments decline. Building society investors, for example, received negative returns for fourteen consecutive years between 1968 and 1982.

Housing
Figure 10.2 shows the increasing proportion of physical assets held

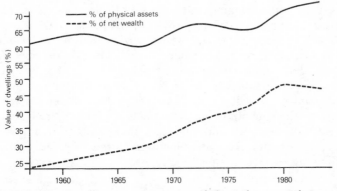

FIGURE 10.2 *Dwellings as a proportion of physical assets and net wealth, 1957–83*

as housing and the value as a percentage of net wealth. From only 30 per cent of dwellings in 1950, owner occupation became the majority tenure in 1970 and since then has grown at about one per cent per year, reaching 66 per cent of dwellings in 1986. Privately owned houses now account for approaching half of all personal disposable assets compared with less than a quarter in the early 1960s.

Stocks and Shares

The value of stocks and shares declined rapidly from a peak in 1972 when they constituted 23 per cent of net personal wealth to only 7 per cent in 1974. They rose again in 1975 to 10 per cent and have subsequently sustained their share of the asset market.

Since 1980 the financial sector has recovered some of the lost ground. The virtual abolition of Capital Gains Tax which applies to profits from the sale of shares, but not houses, has removed some of the relative advantage of investment in housing. With inflation falling and the return of positive interest rates the financial sector is again an attractive and competitive form of investment. By 1981 the average value of the *Financial Times* 30 Share Index was back to its 1972 level and between 1980 and 1983 house prices rose by only 32 per cent, compared with increases of 55 per cent in the value of ordinary shares and 53 per cent in government stocks. As a result, in the early 1980s the proportion of net wealth held as housing fell slightly (Figure 10.2). But falling interest rates in 1986 and average earnings running ahead of inflation suggest that house prices may grow more rapidly in future. An additional change in the last few years is the rapid growth of the number of private shareholders. This has mainly been due to the programme of privatisation pursued by Conservative governments since 1979. The sale of shares to employees is also an important feature of this development. There are, for example, 20,000 employee shareholders of the National Freight Corporation, most of whom participated in the buyout of the company from the government in 1982. Overall, the number of private shareholders has about trebled during the 1980s and following the sale of British Gas is in excess of 20 per cent of the adult population in the UK. Most of the new shareholders hold relatively small quantities of shares and this trend is more significant for the spread of the idea of share ownership than any major financial restructuring. It often involves a straightforward switch of existing investments from a building society to a company.

Pensions and Life Assurances

Apart from the escalation of home ownership, the most important feature in the restructuring of asset composition in the last twenty-five years has been the rapid increase in the level of life assurances and particularly of private and occupational pensions. As Figure 10.3 shows, insurances and pension funds are now the dominant forms of financial assets.

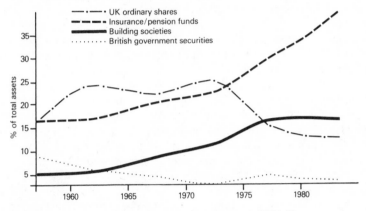

FIGURE 10.3   *Trends in selected financial assets, 1957–83*

This sustained increase reflects the very favourable fiscal and financial environment within which these funds can be accumulated compared to other financial assets. Occupational pensions, for example, are a good form of long-term saving because the contributions attract tax relief at the highest marginal tax rate. A major boom in their value occurred after the 1975 Social Security Pensions Act, which allowed occupational schemes to 'contract out' of the directly state-managed system, so long as they could guarantee at least an equivalent performance. This situation has created, therefore, a system of state regulated purchase of private assets. As with the national insurance scheme, pension scheme contributions are normally deducted directly from people's salaries. In 1982–3 the contributions to and investment earnings from occupational pension funds amounted to over £25 billion. This huge sum totally outdistanced the £15.5 billion paid out under the direct state national insurance pension (Reddin, 1984). Moreover, in that year alone the occupational schemes received an effective subsidy from the Exchequer through tax forgone on the contributions of over £5 billion.

Building Societies
Building society funds now constitute the second largest type of

financial asset. They grew rapidly in the 1950s and 1960s and have stabilised at between 16 and 17 per cent of total financial assets. These funds characteristically comprise large numbers of small accounts, mainly attracting short-term, easy-access investment. Most mortgagors are bound to be investors as a condition of being given a mortgage. There were some 36 million shareholders in building societies in 1983 and these were disproportionately people on average and below average incomes.

The composition of personal wealth, comparing the mid–1960s to the mid–1980s, shows some remarkable and significant changes. In real terms there has been a substantial growth in wealth. A large part of this increase has been due to the expansion of owner-occupied housing and the increasing value of the dwelling stock. On the other hand, there has been no major change in the relative positions of other physical assets such as land and consumer durables. Private pensions, which in the mid–1960s were a smaller proportion of financial assets than company stocks, have now completely outstripped their rivals to stand at nearly 40 per cent of financial assets. Between them housing and pensions (including life insurances) currently account for over 60 per cent of total personal sector wealth, nearly twice their share of total assets compared to twenty years ago.

The Distribution of Wealth

The changes in the volume and composition of privately owned assets have had a significant effect on the distribution of wealth. Although the distribution across the social strata has changed, the main feature of the new wealth is to bring many people into the range of substantial asset holders for the first time. A brief description of the distributive pattern also indicates the importance of the types of asset which combine to differentiate the very wealthy from the rest.

Detailed analysis of the trends over the last ten years is not possible because the relevant Inland Revenue statistics are not publicly available. However, the final reports of the Diamond Commission (Royal Commission on the Distribution of Income and Wealth [RCDIW], 1977), reveal the gathering momentum of the redistributive impact of private housing assets. First, there was a narrowing of the gap between the very wealthy and those who are less well off but who own a house. This was due to the very rapid house price inflation of the early 1970s, and the fact that the very wealthy hold a relatively small proportion of their assets in the form of dwellings, compared to the middle band of asset holders. Above that level the proportion of assets held in the form of company shares and land relative to dwellings gradually increases. People with assets worth £200,000 had nearly 60 per cent in shares and land but under 11 per cent in housing, whereas for those in the middle tier, who owned assets of between £5,000 and £20,000, housing accounted for over 50 per cent of their assets.

Secondly, the Diamond Commission revealed a widening gap between disposable assets held by tenants and those held by the growing ranks of home owners during the 1970s. Owner-occupiers moved out of the category of wealth holders with few assets, whereas tenanted households had little opportunity to acquire assets on the same scale as owner-occupiers. These trends will certainly have been continued into the 1980s. With 65 per cent owner-occupied households in the population in 1986, there will be more people acquiring a place in the middle tier of asset holders than ever before.

The surge in the growth of occupational and other private pension and life insurance funds, which mainly dates from after 1975, does not show up in the Diamond Commission reports. Data published by the Central Statistical Office indicate, however, that the private pensions market is having its own impact on wealth distribution. For example, in 1983, the richest 10 per cent of the population owned 54 per cent of marketable wealth excluding pensions, but with the inclusion of occupational pensions this share fell to 46 per cent. Again there is evidence of a levelling down between the very wealthy and the middle-range asset holders but unresolved interpretative problems make a precise assessment of the true position difficult. It can be inferred that those people with reasonably substantial assets — mainly, of course, housing — are the same groups who are acquiring occupational pensions. This trend underpins, and very probably extends, the gap between the middle band asset holders and those with few assets of any sort. British society is differentiated not only by income or by the 'old' forms of wealth but increasingly by people's access to house ownership and private pensions, which are not inherently related to stratified social class.

Owner Occupation

The rapid growth in owner occupation is frequently said to reflect the preferred option of the British people. Mrs Thatcher even talks of the moral superiority of home owning and its importance in sustaining the 'property-owning democracy'. But this is a spurious argument. Were we less democratic or less morally worthwhile as a nation in 1950? Moreover, the highest levels of owner occupation in Europe occur in the socialist states of the Eastern bloc: Hungary at 75 per cent and Bulgaria at over 80 per cent are the highest. The escalation of owner occupation in Britain is a specific policy arising from a series of unique tax concessions and investment advantages.

Subsidies
Owner-occupiers enjoy the benefit of being subsidised both for the purchase of the house and in its treatment as an investment. Mortgagors receive tax relief (MIR) at their highest marginal tax rate, on the interest payments on the first £30,000 of the loan. House purchase and improvements alone continue to attract this concession which was abolished for other personal borrowing in 1969. The cost to the Exchequer of tax revenues foregone rose from £20 million in the 1950s to nearly £5 billion in 1985. Figure 10.4 shows the trend from the mid–1960s onwards.

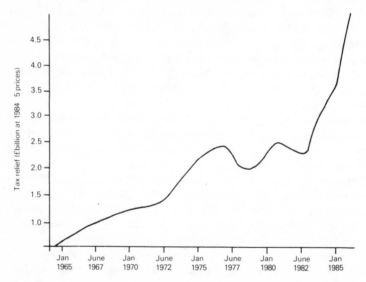

FIGURE 10.4   *Growth of mortgage interest tax relief (NFHA, 1985)*

Moreover, the subsidy is regressive. In 1982–3 people whose income exceeded £20,000 per annum, paying higher rates of tax, comprised 8.5 per cent of mortgagors in receipt of MIR but received 19 per cent of the total tax relief. The hostile reception given to the suggestion made in the Duke of Edinburgh's Inquiry into British Housing (NFHA, 1985), that MIR should be phased out, is indicative of the sensitive political status of this subsidy. Parties openly advocating this sort of reform stand to lose millions of votes.

As an investment asset, owner-occupied housing enjoys a range of additional tax-linked privileges. Until 1963 all owners of dwellings, whether owner-occupiers or landlords, were taxed on the annual investment value of their property. Landlords' rental income was taxed and owner-occupiers were taxed on the imputed rental income arising from their occupation of the house. Schedule A taxation of owner-occupiers was surrounded with anomalies, but its abolition in effect created a subsidy because owners continued to receive MIR on the loan but paid no tax on their imputed rental income. Landlords continued to pay tax on their rental income and on capital gains when they sold a property. The cost to the Exchequer in 1963 of abolishing Schedule A taxation of owner-occupiers was a relatively modest £48 million. But Shelter estimate that taxation from this source in 1982–3 would have been nearly £7 billion. The exemption of owner-occupiers from payment of Capital Gains Tax (despite MIR) cost the Exchequer, in uncollected revenue, £3 billion in 1982–3 (Shelter, 1982).

Although not specifically a housing tax exemption, people's estates when they die are nil-rated for Capital Transfer Tax (the old 'death duties') up to a value of £65,000. Because of the importance of housing in the composition of assets the effect is of an additional large-scale subsidy. Owner-occupiers, having been subsidised to purchase their house, can pass on all or a substantial proportion of the resultant equity to their beneficiaries. The cost to the Exchequer of this tax exemption, estimated on a 1981 figure and calculated at basic rate taxation, would have been £2 billion (net).

Other direct state subsidies to owner occupation include the down-rating of stamp duty on house sales in 1971, and in 1973 new houses were zero-rated for VAT. Owner-occupiers were made eligible for improvement and standard or intermediate grants for specified work on the house in the Housing Acts of 1969 and 1974. More recently, under the 'right to buy' clauses of the 1980 Housing Act, council tenants are offered discounts of between 35 and 60 per cent on the market value of their rented home if they buy it. These discounts have subsequently been further extended by reducing the qualifying period for the higher levels of discount, and in the case of high-rise flats the maximum discount is being raised to 70 per cent of their market value. Since 1980, one million council houses with a value in excess of £7 billion have been sold into the private sector under this scheme.

None of the advantages of owner occupation is available to council tenants. Moreover, between 1979–80 and 1985–6, council house rents increased by 109 per cent (against a 70 per cent increase in earnings over the same period) while the means-tested rent rebates became less generous. Indeed, for many years owner-occupiers have enjoyed a very considerable financial advantage compared with council tenants. In 1982–3 78 per cent more by way of state subsidy went to home owners. Furthermore, mortgage payments diminish in real terms (see below) and ultimately end when the loan is paid off; rents, on the other hand, increase at least in line with inflation year by year, payments never finish and there is no question of tenants retaining the equity value of the dwelling or even of 'passing on' the tenancy to their children or relatives when they die.

Capital Accumulation
Not only do the subsidies disproportionately favour owner-occupiers compared with tenants but the escalating capital value of private housing, and the chance to trade against this value for cash borrowing, is of growing significance. The capital accumulation potential of owner-occupied housing can usefully be measured by the rate of house price increase compared to price increases as a whole. Since the early 1960s house prices have consistently risen faster than the Retail Price Index (RPI), although the rate of increase of the house price/RPI ratio has been uneven. This is attributable to a range of factors including the rate of increase of incomes, credit availability, the rate of house construction and government policy on the forms of subsidies and tax reliefs which underpin the housing market. In the latter context it is noticeable, for example, that house prices began to accelerate away from the RPI following the abolition of Schedule A taxation of owner-occupiers in 1963 which increased demand and, therefore, prices. Owner-occupiers who bought an average price new house in 1970 saw the value of their property increase from a little over £5,000 to between £35–40,000 in 1986. In London and the south-east the increase in the value of the house has been significantly higher: the average house price in the Greater London area rose from £6,882 in 1970 to £43,689 in mid–1986, compared with an increase from £3,634 to £23,401 in Yorkshire and Humberside (Building Societies Association [BSA], 1986). These large regional disparities illustrate the dangers of treating owner occupation as a single, homogeneous tenure. It is not. But for most owners their house accrues in value ahead of inflation.

Historically this has not always been the case. In the decades when owner occupation was still a minority tenure — the 1930s to the 1960s — the investment potential of home ownership was less assured and lacked the current ideological and institutional support systems. Whether the trends of the last twenty-five years will be maintained is also debatable. But without very dramatic, and at the present time, politically unacceptable, reforms, particularly the phasing out of MIR, the housing market in the foreseeable future is likely to remain buoyant. The probability is that, as owner occupation reaches saturation levels, the housing market will fragment into more or less desirable fractions, but short of a catastrophic collapse of the economy as a whole, it is not unreasonable to suppose that the investment potential of private housing will remain attractive — if more differentiated by region, location and type of dwelling. Prophets of doom, such as Beckman (Shelter, 1986) who predicts an 80 per cent fall in house prices, underestimate the political and institutional forces which shore up the housing market.

Assuming that house prices stay in line with inflation, the mortgage debt also diminishes in real terms. This can be illustrated by the reduction in costs for owners who bought an average price house in 1970. By now they will have repaid some, but not much of, the original capital cost of £5,000. This is because on an ordinary annuity mortgage over twenty-five years the repayments are interest-weighted at the beginning with the capital element paid off only in the last few years of the term. But with house-price inflation at record levels in the early 1970s, the 'gearing' ratio (the relationship between a dwelling's current value and the outstanding mortgage debt) was very considerably reduced. With a mortgage covering 80 per cent of the purchase price, the debt/value ratio of the house in the example fell to less than 15 per cent within a decade. Even if house prices were not running ahead of the RPI most mortgagors experience decreases in costs as the repayment term expires.

Moreover, mortgages, compared to other forms of credit facility, are offered at very much lower rates of interest. In mid–1985 the gross mortgage rate was 15.5 per cent, bank overdrafts 17 per cent, personal loans 22 per cent, and interest on credit card payments 27 per cent. Net of tax relief the gap between mortgages and other borrowing was very substantial: at a net rate of 10.8 per cent, mortgage interest was two and a half times cheaper than borrowing against a credit card.

Linking the net cost of mortgage borrowing to the rate of increase in house prices, the picture of the real costs of access to home ownership becomes clear. For example, in 1983–4 the average net mortgage interest rate was 8.2 per cent while house prices rose by an average of 9.6 per cent. With the value of the house increasing faster than the outlay on the mortgage, there was in real terms a negative rate of interest. This was not an exceptional year. For someone paying off a twenty-five-year mortgage between 1960 and 1985 there were only five years when the net mortgage rate/house price inflation ratio was positive. At its 'worst' point, in 1981, mortgagors were paying a positive interest rate of 6.9 per cent, but during the period of the house price boom in the early 1970s (between 1970 and 1974 house prices increased on average by 124 per cent) the ratio reached minus 29.6 per cent.

Cash Withdrawal

The financial position described above is based on an average — some owners will do better and others significantly worse. And, of course, the analysis does not apply to outright owners who have already paid off their mortgage except that the value of their property will be increasing at a rate dependent on its location, type and condition. Equity held in owner-occupied housing need not be dormant but can be released to enhance further people's standard of living. There is evidence of very large-scale borrowing and/or profit taking from the equity stored in owner-occupied houses. Estimates of the amounts being withdrawn (or 'leaking') from the housing market are very complex (Kemeny and Thomas, 1984; Bank of England, 1985). It is apparent, however, that the sums involved are very substantial indeed.

One method of estimating the leakage is to calculate the gap between the annual increase in loans for house purchase and improvement, and net expenditure on the supply of housing. Using figures produced by the Bank of England, Figure 10.5 shows that since the late 1960s loans have increasingly exceeded the amount of money being spent on buying or improving owner-occupied housing, and that this pattern of excess lending has accelerated rapidly since 1980. From a relatively modest £240 million in 1970 excess lending has reached over £7 billion, equivalent to 3.5 per cent of total consumer expenditure in 1984 (Bank of England, 1985).

There are two main ways in which this apparently uncontainable leakage of cash occurs. First, existing mortgagors can increase their debt by applying for a further advance to undertake house improvements but 'cream off' some or all of this money for other things (which do not, of course, legitimately qualify for tax relief). Mortgage finance is by far the cheapest form of credit available, and particularly if a mortgagor's gearing ratio has fallen over a period of years, they may feel able to increase or even restore the debt/house price ratio. In December 1986 the House of Commons Committee

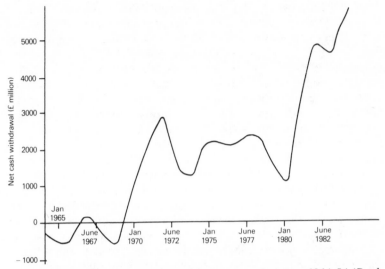

FIGURE 10.5   *Net cash withdrawal from private housing, 1964–84 (Bank of England Quarterly Review, March 1985)*

on Public Accounts reported a calculation made by the Inland Revenue that home improvement loans could have attracted between £250 million and £500 million tax relief in 1985–6 without any checks to see if the loan was in fact used for a home improvement. Further advances on existing mortgages have increased tenfold since the late 1960s, reflecting both the cheapness of this form of credit and falling gearing ratios caused by rapid house price inflation in the 1970s. From a level of about £1 million during the 1960s, further advances have soared to nearly £1.2 billion in 1983 (at 1980 prices) which is 7.5 per cent of total gross mortgage advances.

Secondly, owner-occupiers can move house to release cash by taking out bigger mortgages than they need and retaining some of the profits from the sale of their previous house. The surge in 'leakage' between 1980 and 1984 occurred at a time when an increasing proportion of the purchase price of houses was being covered by mortgage advances; building society mortgages rose from about 45 per cent of purchase prices in 1980 to nearly 60 per cent in 1984. Of the £18.7 billion net cash withdrawal from the housing market between 1982 and 1984 most appears to have been derived from this source.

Inherited Wealth from Housing
In addition to the fluctuating pattern of leakage described above

there is a third major source of cash withdrawal from the housing market. When an elderly owner-occupier dies there often occurs what is called a 'last time sale'. The equity value of the house is finally realised and passed on to the beneficiaries of the will. As noted above, these bequests are nil rated for Capital Transfer Tax on estates valued at up to £65,000. With smaller families (and therefore fewer beneficiaries) and average house prices currently at £30,000 to £65,000 (depending on region) very large capital sums are transferred. Because life expectancy has increased significantly, inheritances are not normally received until the beneficiaries themselves are well into middle age. It may be that grandchildren will borrow or be given a share of this money to finance first-time buying in the housing market. This gives them a very great competitive advantage over people with few savings. The scale of inter-generational wealth transfers involved is very substantial. Last-time sales were reported by the building societies to involve equity valued at over £4 billion in 1979 alone. Not all these sales will, of course, be due to the death of the owner. But the scale of cash released is very substantial.

With an increasing number of owner-occupiers in the population, the trend in leakage through inheritance can only grow. Indeed, there has been an increase in inherited housing wealth in recent years because the first generation of mass owner occupancy, dating from the late 1920s and 1930s, has been dying out in the 1970s and 1980s.

Welfare Issues
Given the massive level of state subsidies, the capital accumulation potential of owner-occupied housing, the nature of the gearing ratio and the ease of cash withdrawal, the escalation of home ownership over the last twenty years is not surprising. There are, however, problems and uncertainties. Not the least of these is that the accumulation potential of private housing is not an historically assured process (Thorns, 1981). The home ownership 'bubble' may in time burst (or more likely slow-puncture) although the institutional, ideological and political support is so strong that a dramatic collapse of the market seems unlikely. Of more immediate concern are the huge sums of private investment circulating round the housing market. This money helps existing owner-occupiers to accrue personal wealth and to move within the owner-occupied sector. It does not, however, help to expand the existing housing stock because most money is used for exchanges of second-hand houses. Moreover, this reservoir of savings does not find its way into the key manufacturing sector of the economy (Kilroy, 1980). In 1986 alone it seemed probable that building societies loaned in

excess of £30 billion, all of which represented investment sucked away from the primary circuit of capital.

Largely due to unemployment in manufacturing industry, the rate of repossessions of houses by building societies has risen from 2,500 in 1979 to 16,500 in 1985 (Karn et al., 1986). The number of mortgagors between six and twelve months in arrears on their loan has quadrupled in the same period to 49,000. In some parts of the country badly affected by industrial contraction, particularly in inner city areas, the housing market is prone to collapse. These problems are indicative of the over-extension and disproportionate application of state subsidies to support owner occupation over the last twenty years. Many contradictions are emerging and for those people irresistibly drawn into home ownership, only to find themselves unemployed, divorced or ill, the apparent benefits of owner occupation can become major liabilities.

Evidence is emerging that 'right to buy' owners in particular are adversely affected by such changes of circumstance and also by the costs of the repair and maintenance of their house. Neither is it at all clear whether former council houses, especially those bought with large discounts, have a resale value which will allow the owners to move.

There are problems, too, for elderly owners who have paid off the mortgage but are faced with repair and maintenance bills at a time of life when income may have diminished (see Chapter 4). The asset value of the dwelling is of little use to them if they cannot in some way unlock it while they are still alive. There are a growing number of schemes of Home Equity Conversion and remortgaging which may, in time, become significant. But the financing of these schemes is complicated and currently 'passing on' the home remains a strong social convention. At the other end of the age spectrum, first-time buyers face a range of problems including high prices and large repayments.

Conclusions

The rate of change in the composition and distribution of personal assets over the last twenty years has been dramatic. The absolute and relative growth of home ownership and of private pensions are the central pillars of this process. Both these forms of asset are irresistibly attractive in financial terms, largely because they have been, and remain, uniquely state subsidised. Moreover, home ownership, unlike the relatively inflexible form of savings represented by pensions, offers very considerable potential for accessible capital gains and cash withdrawal. The extent of the 'leakage' from the housing market has reached multi-billion pound proportions. Whether through trading against the equity, excess borrowing, profit taking or inheritance, there is a massive source of relatively uncontained cash. The sums involved over the last three or four years are conservatively estimated to be between £10 and £12 billion annually. This money is effectively state subsidised 'cheap' credit. Although evidence of the uses to which this money is put is at the moment fragmentary, the destinations of much of it is predictable. Much of it will certainly find its way back into housing to sponsor 'up market' moves. But some of the 'new' wealth will sponsor people's flexible use of the public and private sectors of service provision. Examples include the purchase of private health care at a certain stage in treatment; the increased use of private geriatric care for the elderly; the rapid growth of the second-hand car market in recent years reflecting the curtailment and increasing expense of public transport; and the purchase of private education — both individual tuition as a state pupil or wholly private schooling.

The shift to owner occupation and the partial 'privatisation' of pensions during the 1970s have generated major long-term changes in the patterns of welfare in British society. The public/private division has long been a feature of the British welfare state but there is currently a very strong impulse to switch into private solutions in order to avoid declining standards of state welfare. Access across the sectoral divide is available only to those people able to purchase entrance to private services. One of the major factors in the ability to maximise welfare choices in this way is the potential of owner-occupiers to release the equity stored in their houses. For those excluded from the 'new housing wealth' the range of possibilities is very much narrower.

References

Bank of England (1985) *Quarterly Review*, April.
Building Societies Association (BSA) (1985) *BSA Bulletin*, 44 (October).
Central Statistical Office (CSO) (1985) *Financial Statistics*. London: HMSO.
Cmnd. 7937 (1980) *Report of the Committee to Review the Functioning of Financial Institutions*. London: HMSO.
Harbury, D. and M.W.N. Hitchens (1979) *Inheritance and Wealth Inequality in Britain*. London: George Allen and Unwin.
NFHA (1985) Inquiry into British Housing (Chaired by H.R.H. the Duke of Edinburgh). London: National Federation of Housing Associations.
Karn, V., J. Doling and B. Stafford (1986) 'Growing Crisis and Contradiction in Home Ownership' in P. Malpass (ed.), *The Housing Crisis*. London: Croom Helm.
Kemeny, J. and A. Thomas (1984) 'Capital Leakage from Owner-Occupied Housing', *Policy and Politics*, 12: 13–30.

Kilroy, B. (1980) 'The Finance Implications of Government Policies on Home Ownership', *SHAC*.

Reddin, M. (1984) *Can We Afford Our Future?* London: London School of Economics.

Royal Commission on the Distribution of Income and Wealth (RCDIW) (1978) *The Causes of Poverty*, RCDIW Background Paper No. 5. London: HMSO. Also Cmnd. 6999, 1977.

Shelter (1982) *Housing and the Economy — a Priority for Reform*.

Shelter (1986) Press release as reported in the *Sunday Times*, 27 July.

Thorns, D.C. (1981) 'Owner Occupation: its Significance for Wealth Transfer and Class Formation', *Sociological Review*, 29(4).

11
Welfare Benefits

Jonathan Bradshaw

Welfare benefits matter a great deal. Unless an individual is very rich, benefits will contribute a major source of income at some part of her or his life. Benefits determine the living standards of a growing proportion of the population for long periods of their life and are the most important source of money for the most vulnerable people in society. On average, social security benefits contribute 31 per cent of the net income of all households and only 25 per cent of households at any one time receive no social security income. One person in seven in the UK population is now dependent for all or part of their income on one benefit — supplementary benefit.

As well as mattering to individuals and families, benefits are a very important element in the social and economic structure of the country. Benefits will cost £46,000 million in 1987–8 — nearly a third of all public expenditure and three times as much as is spent on education, the health service or defence. Benefits are the most important mechanism for distributing and redistributing resources: horizontally, from the single and childless to families with children; vertically, from the better off to the worse off; over the life cycle, from the working population to pensioners; and even spatially or geographically, from the richer areas of the country to the more depressed.

Benefits are also inextricably linked with human behaviour — literally from birth to death. There is, of course, controversy about the extent to which they do or should influence behaviour but they are undoubtedly *a* factor in determining whether *some* people marry, whether they have children and how many they have, whether they work, whether a couple remains together, separates or divorces, whether children stay on at school after the statutory school-leaving age, whether older children leave home, whether people retire, where they are living when they die and how they are buried.

The level of benefits paid to individuals and families determines their living standards — including the amount of food they purchase and the adequacy of their diet, the fuel they consume and their level

TABLE 11.1 *The contribution of welfare benefits to the gross incomes of selected household types, 1985*

Household and benefit type	Percentage of gross income					
	Quintiles of original income					
	Bottom	2nd	3rd	4th	Top	Average
One adult retired						
Retirement pension	66		69	59	28	51
Other contributory	4		3	2	2	3
Supplementary benefit	6		2	1	0	2
Other non-contributory	23		13	6	1	11
Total benefits	99		88	68	31	67
Two adults retired						
Retirement pension	64	61	60	41	19	42
Other contributory	7	10	6	5	2	5
Supplementary benefit	8	4	2	1	0	2
Other non-contributory	20	14	6	4	1	6
Total benefits	99	89	74	50	23	55
Two adults non-retired						
Contributory	30	8	2	2	1	5
Non-contributory	20	2	1	0	0	2
Total benefits	50	10	3	2	1	7
One adult with children						
Contributory	4		9	8	2	5
Supplementary benefit	54		32	5	1	22
Child benefit	19		18	15	5	14
Other non-contributory	22		19	11	1	12
Total benefits	99		78	40	9	53
Two adults, two children						
Unemployment benefit	4	1	0	0	0	1
Other contributory	4	1	0	0	0	1
Supplementary benefit	18	1	0	0	0	2
Child benefit	12	8	6	5	3	5
Other non-contributory	10	0	0	0	0	1
Total benefits	48	11	7	5	3	10

	Deciles of original income										
	Bottom	2nd	3rd	4th	5th	6th	7th	8th	9th	Top	Average
All households											
Contributory	60	46	36	19	12	7	5	3	3	1	9
Non-contributory	26	27	25	15	10	7	5	4	3	2	7
Total benefits	86	73	61	34	22	14	10	7	6	3	16

Note: Columns may not sum due to rounding.

Source: CSO, 1986

of warmth, the range and variety of their clothing, the quality and quantity of their furnishing and household equipment, and the extent to which they and their children can read, listen, watch, play and participate generally in social and recreational activity.

Table 11.1 presents data from the Central Statistical Office (CSO) analysis of the contribution of welfare benefits to incomes. Benefits contribute 67 per cent of the incomes of single retirement pensioners and 53 per cent of the incomes of one-parent families. They form 86 per cent of the gross incomes of the lowest decile and only 3 per cent of the gross incomes of the highest.

So benefits matter a great deal. However, the basis of eligibility and level of benefit payable vary markedly from one benefit to another. Many of these variations can be justified on the basis of variations in need — thus, for example, households of different sizes have different needs. However, in addition there are variations that have little to do with meeting needs. There are administratively determined variations due to the type of benefit — whether it is contributory or non-contributory. There are also variations due to value judgements about the worth of certain categories of claimant. The purpose of this chapter is to explore these variations and the assumptions underlying them.

Variation by Size

Benefits vary according to an evaluation of the needs of different sizes and types of household. Thus most benefits take account of assumed economies of scale in paying a lower benefit for a spouse or second adult in the household and all benefits assume that children do not need the same amount as adults. Each of these variations will be reviewed in turn.

Adults
In Table 11.2 it is evident that the single householder rate is about 62 per cent of the couple's rate for both types of supplementary benefit and both long- and short-term national insurance benefits. The housing benefit needs allowance has a slightly different but still very similar ratio of 68 per cent. This ratio between the single householder and couples has remained more or less unchanged throughout the whole period since the war. When insurance and assistance benefits first became payable in 1948 the ratio between single people and couples was 62 per cent. This is also very close to the ratio in pre-war unemployment benefit — for unemployment insurance it was 65 per cent and for unemployment assistance it was 66 per cent. However, it was not true of pre-war pensions where a

TABLE 11.2 *Scales of benefit payable, April 1987 (£ per week)*

	Supplementary benefit		NI retirement and invalidity pension (£ p.w.)	Unemployment benefit (£ p.w.)	Housing benefit needs allowance (£ p.w.)	FIS prescribed limits (£ p.w.)
	Ordinary (£ p.w.)	Long-term (£ p.w.)				
Single person	30.40	38.65	39.50	31.45	48.90 ⎫	88.80
Couple	49.35	61.85	63.25	50.85	72.15 ⎭	
Child aged:						
under 11	10.40	10.40	15.25[1]	7.25[2]	14.75	18.15[1]
11–15	15.60	15.60	15.25[1]	7.25[2]	14.75	20.20[1]
16–17	18.75	18.75	15.25[1]	7.25[2]	14.75	27.45[1]
18+	24.35	24.35	15.25[1]	7.25[2]	14.75	27.45[1]
Implied equivalence scale, couple = 100						
Single person	62	62	62	62	68	100[3]
Couple	100	100	100	100	100	100
Couple + child under 11	121	117	124	114	120	120

[1] Including child benefit.
[2] Child benefit only.
[3] Single *parent*.

single pensioner warranted only half the amount paid to a couple (Bradshaw and Deacon, 1986).

During the whole of the post-war period there has been no attempt to base the ratio on some empirical assessment of relative needs — since 1948 social security benefits have been upgraded from time to time in line with earnings or prices and existing relativities have just been maintained. Why? Was the pre-war assessment of the relative needs of a single householder and a couple reliable enough to justify such an immutable policy? For an answer to this question it is necessary to turn first to the Beveridge Report (Cmnd. 6404, 1942). Beveridge sought to provide rates of benefit or pension 'such as to secure for all normal cases an income adequate for subsistence' (para. 193). He acknowledged 'that any estimate of subsistence income for the population as a whole . . . is to some extent a matter of judgement' (para. 196) and in reaching his judgement he was advised by a subcommittee which included Seebohm Rowntree. He also made considerable use of a 1937–8 Ministry of Labour Family Budget Inquiry. Using these sources he drew up the schedule of requirements for adults of working age at 1938 prices which is reproduced in Table 11.3 below.

TABLE 11.3   *Beveridge's requirements for adults of working age at 1938 prices (weekly, in shillings and pence)*

	Man and wife (s/d p.w.)	Man (s/d p.w.)	Women (s/d p.w.)
Food	13/–	7/–	6/–
Clothing	3/–	1/6	1/6
Fuel, light and sundries	4/–	2/6	2/6
Margin	2/–	1/6	1/6
Rent	10/–	6/6	6/6
Total	32/–	19/–	18/–

He drew up a similar schedule for pensioners giving requirements of 29s 8d for a pensioner couple, 17s 8d for a pensioner man and 17s 4d for a pensioner woman. He then argued that the difference between men and women was not worth maintaining and that the distinction between pensioners and others need not be maintained because

> there is strong public opinion in favour of securing for the aged something more than bare subsistence, and apart from this there is convenience in keeping pensions at least equal to working age benefits in order to avoid stepping down from benefit to pension on reaching a particular birthday. (para. 251)

The benefits he ended up proposing were 40s a week for a man and wife and 24s for a single person. These were the figures given in Table 11.3 uprated by inflation between 1938 and 1942. Thus the ratio that Beveridge derived was 60 per cent — very close to the 62 per cent ratio that was eventually introduced.

However, the justification for it is very difficult to discern from the published report. Thus, for example, the rent element of 10s for a household was derived from the average weekly rent paid by all industrial households in the Family Budget Inquiry but, without further explanation, 'For solitary individuals a figure of 6s 6d is taken' (para. 201). The food component was derived from dietaries and again without further explanation, 'The 13s may reasonably be divided as 7s for a single man and 6s for a single woman'. The allowance for fuel for a couple was also based on the Family Budget Inquiry but it is not at all clear how Beveridge fixed the relativities allowed for fuel for single people and couples or for the margin element. Certainly there is no explicit justification in the report. It is suspected that he was much influenced by the work of Rowntree.

The Beveridge Report was published in 1942 the year after Rowntree's 1936 study of poverty in York appeared (Rowntree, 1941). In this study Rowntree derived equivalence scales on the basis of what he described as 'a careful examination of the families' real needs' (p. 31). His actual methods were set out more fully in *The Human Needs of Labour* (Rowntree, 1937). His determination of food requirements were explicitly based on nutritional studies of the relative food requirements of men and women — an adult female needed only 83 per cent of an adult male's requirements. A single figure for housing requirements (9s 6d) was based on rents charged by local authorities. For clothing, 'I made enquiries among a number of men and women who knew from first-hand experience at how low a cost it was possible to clothe a family' (p. 94) and derived a figure of 3s for men and 1s 9d for women. For fuel he allowed 4s 4d without commenting in any way on any variation due to household size, and the same applied to household sundries.

It is rather difficult to discern in this how the differential in the needs of adults actually emerged. Nevertheless, in *Poverty and Progress*, Rowntree published quite an elaborate equivalence scale which varied according to whether the adult was employed, unemployed or a pensioner and by sex. It is summarised in Table 11.4 below.

If the Rowntree equivalences are valid, then it would appear that the ratio Beveridge took is somewhat on the low side.

While the equivalence scales inherent in social security benefits were fixed early — as a result, it appears, of some fairly rough-and-

TABLE 11.4   *Rowntree's equivalence scale*

	Employed	Unemployed	Pensioner
Single man	0.81	0.82	0.69
Single woman	0.67	0.63	0.56
Couple	1.00	1.00	1.00

Source: Rowntree, 1941: 30

ready pre-war budgetary analysis — there has since been a consider-able body of scientific effort devoted to deriving equivalence scales (see Chapters 3 and 15). These studies have used a variety of methods. Some have employed elaborate budget studies. Others have fixed equivalence on the basis of the proportion of expenditure devoted to food or savings or essentials. Other studies have employed economic consumption theory, deriving equivalence scales from expenditure data using econometric techniques. Others have used attitudes — what people think is a fair or reasonable differential. Whiteford (1985) concluded from a review of this work that there was no one valid method for deriving equivalence scales. He found that the adult equivalence found in all these studies fell within a range of values between 0.59 and 0.68 with a geometric mean of 0.64, which perhaps suggests that Beveridge and the UK benefit relativities for an adult are not that far from the mark.

Children

The same conclusion cannot be derived in the case of the benefits payable to children. It can be seen in Table 11.2 that supplementary benefit and family income supplement child additions vary with the age of the child, paying more for older children. The other benefits pay a standard addition for each child. Additions vary from £7.25 per week child benefit, which is all that families with children now receive on top of unemployment benefit, to £24.35 for a child aged over eighteen on supplementary benefit (the FIS prescribed benefits are not actually paid). The implied equivalence scale (couple = 100) for a child thus varies by age and benefit from 114 to 149 and for a child aged under eleven years from 114 to 124. These variations are supposed to reflect variations in the needs of children of different ages. However, the extent to which they do is a moot and controversial point (see Chapter 3).

Like the relativities in the rates payable to adults, the relativity between the children's rate and the rates payable for adults (at least in national assistance/supplementary benefit) have remained extra-ordinarily stable since 1948. In 1948 a child under five received 19 per cent of the rate for a married couple and in 1987 a child up to ten received 17 or 21 per cent of the rate for a couple depending on whether they were on the ordinary or long-term rates. Once again scales have been uprated, without fundamental review, by an index and in order to maintain existing relativities. So it is their origins that have to be examined for a justification of the existing relativities. Field (1985) has already undertaken a review of the origins of the children's scales which shows that they have their roots both in the pre-war Unemployment Assistance Board (UAB) scales and also in the work on budgets of Rowntree and Beveridge. Drawing on the work of Lynes (1977) he found that the UAB scales were determined rather more by anxiety about maintaining differentials between income in work and out of work than by the relative needs of families of different sizes — the UAB were anxious to avoid paying benefits to families which were higher than the wages paid to unskilled labourers. They were also concerned to pay lower benefits than the unemployment insurance scheme.

Rowntree's determination of the relative needs of children were very largely based on nutritional evidence — evidence which led him to reduce substantially the relative allowances for children from 31 per cent of a couple's allowance in his 1899 survey (Rowntree, 1902) to 24 per cent for the first child and 11 per cent for a second child in the 1936 survey (Rowntree, 1941). Beveridge's calculations for children were more generous than Rowntree's 1936 figures. He drew on a League of Nations dietary for the food element, and the Ministry of Labour Family Budgets data for clothing, fuel and sundries and arrived at an annual subsistence allowance at 1938 prices of 7s per week, or 32 per cent of his allowance for a couple (excluding rent). Family allowances eventually were introduced at 5s for the second and subsequent child with the promise (never fulfilled) of free dinners for all. The child additions introduced into the insurance scheme in 1946 and the assistance scheme in 1948 have never met the Beveridge relativities. In 1948 the children's rates in national assistance varied from 19 per cent for a child under five to 26 per cent for a child aged thirteen to fifteen.

Since then there has been considerable discussion about whether the relative value of the rates paid to children is adequate. Equivalence scales based on the econometric analysis of consumption data have tended to suggest that they are. Thus Whiteford (1985) in his review found that the mean equivalence scale for couples with one child was 1.20 with a range between 1.16 and 1.24. The implied equivalence scales in SB for a couple with one child under 10 is 1.17 or 1.21. Nevertheless, a number of studies (Cooke and Baldwin, 1984) have concluded that life on benefit for families with children is particularly bleak. Wynn (1970) concluded that the benefits payable for older children and teenagers were grossly inadequate. Piachaud (1979) concluded that the child scale rates needed to be increased by as much as 50 per cent to meet his 'modern minimum set of requirements'. Bradshaw and Morgan (1987) described the restricted and dreary range of choices open to families living on supplementary benefit. The government recognised the special needs of families with children in the Social Security White Paper (Cmnd. 9691, 1985).

> Low income families with children are among those with the greatest needs today. (para. 1.22)
>
> We believe that resources must be directed more effectively to areas of greatest need, notably low income families with children. (para. 1.5)

Only time will tell whether the level of income support and premiums that become payable in April 1988 will achieve this objective.

So far variations in the level of benefits paid to different types of claimant due to the implied evaluation of their relative needs have been considered. There are other important variations within the structure of supplementary benefit in particular which have not been discussed. These include the distinction in the level of benefits paid to householders and non-householders which in April 1987 was £7.70. This is justified on the ground that non-householders do not have to pay housing maintenance expenses out of their budgets. Also there are the 'additional requirements' paid to claimants in a variety of circumstances to meet assumed extra needs. The most common of these are the extra heating payments which vary from £8.80 per week payable to tenants of a hard-to-heat estate, to £2.20 per week for pensioners and children under five. There are also additions for the over eighties, people requiring baths, for blind people and for diet and laundry. This array of differential payments has been introduced and developed over time for a variety of reasons and their level and coverage has often proved difficult to justify in terms of the needs of individual claimants (see for example Hutton et al., 1987). This fact, together with the complexity involved in their administration were factors that led the government to propose a simplified system of benefit scales and premiums in the new Income Support scheme.

Short Term/Long Term

Perhaps the most important and interesting distinction within the benefit system is the differential payments that are made for short-term and long-term claimants. They are important because they are now quite substantial. A single householder on supplementary benefit receiving the long-term rate receives £8.25 more than an ordinary rate claimant, and a couple receive £12.50 more on the long-term rate. These differentials between long-term and short-term benefit rates do not apply just to supplementary benefit. Thus, the main contributory benefits vary: retirement and widows' pensions and invalidity pension are paid at higher rates than unemployment benefit and sickness benefit. An unemployed single person receives £8.05 per week less than a single pensioner and a couple receives £12.00 less. For families with children the differences are even greater because child additions are payable on top of widows', retirement and invalidity pension, but not unemployment or sickness benefit. Thus, for example, a couple with three children on invalidity benefit would receive £34.55 more per week than the same family receiving unemployment benefit.

The differentials are interesting because they are based on the arguments that new claimants may have a cushion of resources to protect them, but the longer they are on benefit their needs increase and at the same time things such as bedding and household equipment run out or need replacing. An alternative argument is that benefits should be higher initially to cushion the impact of a sudden fall in income and that as time on benefit persists claimants learn to adjust their consumption patterns to living on a low income. There is little empirical evidence to support either argument. The Supplementary Benefit Commission in its 1976 annual report (Cmnd. 6910, 1977) said that 'the work of the Department's Economic Advisor's Office suggests that for households with children it is difficult to justify a differential in excess of about 6 per cent' (para. 9.8). White (1982) found that living standards stabilise as unemployment progresses but an analysis by Bradshaw et al. (1983) of the living standards of the unemployed found that they deteriorate as unemployment progresses. A study by Berthoud (1985) suggests that the claimants of supplementary benefit do not have a cushion to protect them in the early weeks of claiming and do suffer most while still adjusting to a lower standard of living.

The differentials between long- and short-term benefits did not exist when they were first introduced. Pensions, unemployment benefit and sickness benefit were paid at a single rate with standard additions for children and there was only one rate of supplementary benefit. There was no difference in the level of insurance benefits until the uprating in October 1973 when pensions and invalidity benefit were increased in line with movements in earnings and unemployment and sickness benefit in line with movements in prices. This distinction was later established in legislation in the Social Security Act 1975 which laid a duty on the government to increase the 'long-term' insurance benefits in line with earnings and the 'short-term benefits' are least in line with prices. By 1979 a substantial gap had already opened up between the two sets of benefits and though since 1980 all benefits have been increased in line with prices, each percentage increase has widened the gap between the rates of benefits.

The distinction between the ordinary and long-term rates of supplementary benefit did not exist until 1966. However, the Ministry of Social Security Act 1966 introduced for certain classes of claimants a standard sum known as the long-term addition (initially of 45p) to the scales for supplementary pensioners and claimants under pensionable age (except the unemployed) who had been on benefit for more than two years. The objective of the long-term addition was to incorporate into the scales standard discretionary payments which at that time had become payable to a much larger number of claimants. From 1973 the long-term addition was incorporated into a long-term rate which was applicable under the same conditions. Then the long-term rate began to be uprated in line with earnings while the ordinary rate kept pace only with prices and the gap between the rates has continued to grow since 1980 as both rates have been increased in line with prices.

The distinction in the rates of benefit in supplementary benefit have been questioned on a number of grounds: why are higher rates only paid for adult claimants and not also in respect of children who have been on benefit for a long time? Why should retirement pensioners receive the long-term rates as soon as they claim, whereas single parents and others have to wait one year? Does the fact that the qualifying period has to be continuous discourage claimants from going off benefit even for a temporary period because they would lose their entitlement to the long-term rate? Above all, why should the unemployed, however long they have been on benefit, never qualify for the long-term rate?

The reason for the unemployed being excluded from the long-term rate is partly to do with successive governments' evaluation of their priority, and partly to do with the cost of extending the long-term rate to an increasing number of long-term claimants — over half the unemployed have been on benefit for over a year. But most important of all has been the anxiety that paying the long-term rate of benefit to the unemployed would increase the unemployment trap — the differential between income in unemployment and net income in work — and undermine work incentives. These factors have sustained the resolution of successive governments against extending to the long-term unemployed the long-term rates despite considerable lobbying effort and evidence of the hardship of living on the ordinary rate for long periods of time. This discrimination against the unemployed will continue into the Income Support scheme because while the distinction between the ordinary and long-term rate of benefit is to be abolished, premiums on top of the scales will be paid to pensioners, the disabled, lone parents and families, but not the long-term unemployed. Thus, families with children with an unemployed head can expect to receive an increase in their benefit but not the single and childless — however long they have been on benefit.

Contributory/Non-contributory/Means Tested

It was Beveridge's intention that insurance benefits for which citizens had contributed throughout their lives should be paid at higher rates than the means-tested assistance scheme which would be available 'for the limited number of cases of need not covered by social insurance' (para. 19). However, partly because of the 'problem of housing costs', partly because insurance benefits were introduced without a transitional period, and partly because successive governments have found it cheaper to rely on means-tested benefits than enhance insurance benefits, the difference in the levels of benefit have never been very great. Insurance beneficiaries without other resources have in very large numbers been able to claim assistance benefits renamed significantly *supplementary* benefit after 1966 to top up their incomes. Only when earnings-related contributory benefits began to be introduced after 1965 did the gap between the benefits payable to contributory beneficiaries move ahead of supplementary benefits, but short-term, earnings-related benefits were abolished and the build up to full entitlement to the state earnings related pension scheme only began in 1978. So the gap between contributory benefits and assistance benefits that was envisaged by Beveridge has not emerged.

Nevertheless, there has developed a new class of benefit — non-contributory, non-means tested benefits — notably the severe disablement allowance (SDA) and the invalid care allowance (ICA) which from the time they were introduced in the mid-1970s have been paid at a rate lower than other comparable earnings-related benefits. Thus SDA and invalid care allowance are paid at rates of only 60 per cent of invalidity pension. This means that someone who becomes an invalidity beneficiary after having established a contributory entitlement will receive £15.85 per week more than someone with identical disability who through no fault of her or his own has been disabled from birth or before establishing a contributory record. A person who leaves the labour force to care for a dependent relative and claims invalid care allowance will receive £7.70 per week less than she would have received if she had become unemployed without caring for a dependent person. These differentials are really quite absurd. When introduced they were justified as a way of ensuring that the contributory system was not undermined by introducing non-contributory benefits paid at the same rate. However, this argument is not very convincing as the vast majority of contributors cannot choose whether to contribute or not and those eligible for SDA — mostly people disabled from birth — have little choice about their condition. The effect of paying these benefits at lower levels is that most of those eligible for them who have no other resources will need to claim supplementary benefit. Or put another way — only those with other resources who are ineligible for supplementary benefit will derive any net benefit from ICA and SDA.

Single Parents and the Disabled

There are other ways that the social security system discriminates between different types of claimant. Thus, there are benefits that discriminate in favour of one-parent families: they are entitled to one-parent benefit — a sum of £4.70 on top of the child benefit for the first child; they are treated as two-parent families with respect to housing benefit and FIS; they are entitled to the long-term rate of supplementary benefit after a year; they can remain on supplementary benefit without registering for work until their eldest child is sixteen and they have more generous earnings disregards than other claimants (see Chapter 3). All this represents a judgement about the special needs of parents bringing up children alone; the fact that not more is done for them, reflects an anxiety that if single parents were treated more generously than couples, then the status of marriage would be undermined or that, in equity, it would be unfair to married couples (see also Chapter 7).

Perhaps the best developed (though not necessarily therefore coherent) discriminatory system of benefits is that for people with disabilities. The variation in the level of two of the income replacement benefits for the disabled, invalidity pensions and severe disablement allowance, has already been discussed. There is another distinction between the earnings replacement benefits for the disabled. Those entitled to industrial disablement benefit or war disablement pensions are entitled to considerably higher levels of benefit than the 'civilian' disabled with equal handicaps. Thus, a man injured as a result of an accident at work assessed as 100 per cent disabled will receive £64.50 disablement benefit and may also qualify for the unemployability supplement of £39.50 and special hardship allowance of £25.80. Thus, he would receive £129.80 per week in comparison with £47.80 which includes the higher rate invalidity allowance payable to a man similarly disabled by, for example, an accident while playing football. In this case the different rates of benefits are expressing varying evaluations of the origins of the disability and these evaluations have their origins in the Beveridge Report.

The other main distinctions in the benefit system for the disabled are those benefits designed to provide extra help over and above the income replacement benefits for the *severely* disabled; these distinctions have developed since Beveridge. Attendance allowance is payable at one of two rates depending on the degree of helplessness of the disabled person and mobility allowance is also available for those who are unable or virtually unable to walk. Despite its name, attendance allowance was never intended as a benefit for paying for attendance. It was rather intended as a general contribution to the extra expenses associated with severe disablement. The mobility allowance likewise was intended to help with the extra costs of the immobile (and to be a replacement for the invalid tricycle). The problem is that the criteria for eligibility for both benefits are only a rough indication of need for help with extra expenses. Many with extra expenses arising out of their disablement do not qualify for attendance or mobility allowance because they do not require constant or repeated attention during the day or night and are not completely immobile.

As a result of these new disablement benefits the incomes of the disabled can now vary considerably. A 'civilian' disabled single person could receive weekly as much as: invalidity pension (£39.50), invalidity allowance (£8.30), higher rate attendance allowance (£31.60), mobility allowance (£22.10) — total £102.30; or as little as: severe disablement allowance (£23.75) which could be supplemented by SB (£6.65) — total £30.40. Which level of living they would have depends on whether or not they contributed before becoming disabled and whether or not their disablement meets the criteria of the two extra expenses benefit. It may have very little to do with their actual needs.

Conclusions

This chapter has argued that welfare benefits are of great importance to the living standards of most of us at some time in our lives and for many people for quite long periods. However, the level of living provided by welfare benefits varies a good deal and the equity of these variations is not always easy to discern. Some of them are without doubt a reflection of judgements about the relative needs of different people within a household. It was suggested that the equivalence scales in the benefit systems are based on pre-war budget standards as well as the structure of benefits that had developed. These relativities have never been reassessed though they may change in the new structure of benefits being introduced into Income Support. Then there are differences between the level of payments to short-term and long-term claimants, though the unemployed are excluded from entitlement to the higher long-term rates of benefit. Beveridge envisaged that there would be a distinction between the level of benefits paid on a means test and that paid in return for contributions. However, although it never developed, the new range of non-contributory benefits have tended to be paid below the level of contributory benefits. Finally, the extra benefits paid to one-parent families and the disabled have been examined.

In all these distinctions the operation of conflicting objectives typical in social policy is observed. There is an aspiration to meet need and maintain fairness between one claimant and another but at the same time a concern that work incentives or traditional family patterns should not be undermined, that the benefit system should be reasonably simple to administer and that expenditure should be minimised. As the Social Security Advisory Committee (1985) argued:

> The present supplementary benefit scale rates are not the result of considered thought about the finance required to maintain a claimant at an objectively established standard of living. They represent, rather, the outcome of a number of different pressures and methods of approach, and of generations of political bargaining. (para. 4.24)

References

Berthoud, R. (1985) *The Examination of Social Security*. London: Policy Studies Institute.

Bradshaw, J., K. Cooke and C. Godfrey (1983) 'The Impact of Unemployment on the Living Standards of Families', *Journal of Social Policy*, 12(4): 433–52.

Bradshaw, J.R. and A. Deacon (1986) 'Social Security', in P. Wilding (ed.), *In Defence of the Welfare State*. Manchester: Manchester University Press.

Bradshaw, J.R. and J. Morgan (1987) *Budgeting on Benefit: the Consumption of Families on Social Security*. London: Family Policy Studies Centre.

Cmd. 6404 (1942) *Report on Social Insurance and Allied Services*. (The Beveridge Report). London: HMSO.

Cmnd. 6910 (1977) *Supplementary Benefits Commission Annual Report 1976*. London: HMSO.

Cmnd. 9691 (1985) *Reform of Social Security: Programme for Action*. London: HMSO.

Cooke, K. and S. Baldwin (1984) *How Much is Enough?* London: Family Policy Studies Centre.

Central Statistical Office (CSO) (1986) 'The Effects of Taxes and Benefits on Household Income 1985', *Economic Trends*, 397: 96–109.

Field, F. (1985) *What Price a Child: a Historical Review of the Relative Cost of Dependants*. London: Policy Studies Institute.

Hutton, S., J.R. Bradshaw and G. Hardman (1987) 'Domestic Fuel Expenditure and Payment of Fuel Allowances', *Consumer Studies and Home Economics*, 11: 1–20.

Lynes, T. (1977) 'Making of the Unemployment Assistance Scale', in *Low Income, Supplementary Benefit Administration Paper 6*. London: HMSO.

Piachaud, D. (1979) *The Cost of a Child*. London: Child Poverty Action Group.

Rowntree, B.S. (1902) *Poverty: a Study of Town Life* (2nd ed.). London: Macmillan.

Rowntree, B.S. (1937) *The Human Needs of Labour*. London: Longman.

Rowntree, B.S. (1941) *Poverty and Progress: a Second Social Survey of York*. London: Longman.

Social Security Advisory Committee (SSAC) (1985) *Third Report of the Social Security Advisory Committee 1984*. London: HMSO.

White, M. (1982) *The Significance of Material and Financial Problems in Long-term Unemployment*. Policy Studies Institute, mimeo.

Whiteford, P. (1985) *A Family's Needs: Equivalence Scales, Poverty and Social Security*; Research Paper No. 27. Australian Department of Social Security.

Wynn, M. (1970) *Family Policy*. London: Michael Joseph.

12
Credit

Gillian Parker

Money-lending, pawnbrokerage and payment for tradesmen's goods by periodic account have all played a part in consumer buying for centuries. However, it was not until the mid-nineteenth century, with the introduction of hire-purchase as a mechanism to expand the market for sewing machines and pianos, that credit was first advanced in the UK for the purchase of specific consumer goods. Since then the use of consumer credit has grown substantially, particularly since the Second World War.

Given this expansion in credit use and its undoubted importance as a resource by which people gain access to consumer goods and services, it is puzzling that the topic has attracted relatively little interest from social scientists. While education, health, housing and income replacement have long been recognised as social goods, the full recognition that consumer credit might also be a social good has yet to take place.

On initial examination, of course, the state appears to perform only an adjudicative function in the relationship between creditor and consumer. However, this is not the whole case. The state is also closely involved in the regulation of credit transactions and, thereby, influences the nature of the credit market. Moreover, the state has the power to adjust the balance between creditor and debtor when the former brings the latter to court for non-payment. Further, policies in other areas of the state's activity have a direct effect on the consumers' access to credit; income, tenure and the minimum lending rate are three of the variables which might affect whether or not a consumer is able to obtain credit and what he or she might pay for it.

The aim of this chapter is to demonstrate the importance of consumer credit as a resource, to analyse the unequal distribution of this resource, and, thereby, to argue for a re-evaluation of credit as a social good.

The Size of the Consumer Credit Market

The proportion of consumer expenditure which is financed by credit has grown in the past two decades. Since 1976 particularly, the rate of growth of hire-purchase (HP) and other retail credit use has been greater than that of expenditure on consumer goods generally, and since 1981 this process has accelerated sharply (see Table 12.1). The ratio of new HP and other retail credit (excluding bank lending) to expenditure on consumer goods has risen and the amount of new HP and retail credit extended annually has been running well above the Retail Price Index since 1977 (1974 = 100) (*Annual Abstract of Statistics*, 1966, 1976, 1985, 1987).

Some £12,996 million of new HP and other retail credit were extended to consumers in 1985; in addition, at the end of 1985 £20,103 million were owed by individuals, for purposes other than house purchase, to UK banks (*Annual Abstract of Statistics*, 1987). This last figure includes advances of £4,052 million on bank credit cards in that year. In total, around £38,000 million was owed by UK residents at the end of 1985 for predominantly consumer purchases. This amount represents an average commitment of £883 for every adult in the country.

TABLE 12.1 *Expenditure on 'consumer goods', new HP and retail credit extended and credit outstanding at the end of the year, 1974–85*

(1974 = 100)	Expenditure on 'consumer goods'[1]		New HP and retail credit		Credit outstanding at end of year	
1974	100	(= £9750m)	100	(= £2517m)	100	(= £2330m)
1975	120		119		100	
1976	139		138		141	
1977	156		190		180	
1978	195		245		236	
1979	238		292		296	
1980	254		311		337	
1981	263		312		364	
1982	282		362		416	
1983	326		418		524	
1984	328		457		655	
1985	368	(= £35,910m)	516	(= £12,996m)	772	(= £17,997m)

[1] 'Consumer goods': clothing, footwear, household durable goods, cars and motor bikes.

Sources: Annual Abstract of Statistics (1976, 1985, 1987)

Further, the amount of consumer credit which remains outstanding at the end of any year, as a proportion of total new credit extended, has started to increase. Between 1967 and 1979 credit outstanding at the end of the year was always lower than the amount of new credit extended in that year. This indicated that while the amount of credit was growing from year to year the level of 'indebtedness' was not. Since 1979 this balance has radically changed to the extent that in 1985 some £5,001 million more were outstanding than had been newly extended in that year (see Table 12.1). This change appears to reflect two aspects of the credit market. First, creditors, especially finance houses, are now lending over longer periods with the result that smaller proportions are repaid each year. Secondly, default related to economic recession has increased (Parker, 1986; and see Chapter 14).

This increase in the amount of credit extended has been paralleled by an increase in the numbers of people who use credit to finance their buying. Almost 80 per cent of the adult population have used consumer credit of some sort and, at any one time, at least 50 per cent are using credit to finance consumer purchasing (Office of Fair Trading [OFT]/NOP, 1979; National Consumer Council [NCC], 1980). In addition, there is now more frequent use of more than one credit agreement at a time (OFT/NOP, 1979) reflecting not only opportunity but also a change in attitudes towards consumer credit.

In sum, more people are now using credit more often, and over longer periods, than ever before. Despite this, access to credit is not evenly spread and, moreover, the price which is paid for the use of credit facilities varies widely between different social groups. These inequalities will now be examined.

Using Credit

The range and forms of credit that are available to a would-be borrower are determined by three distinct, but inter-related, sets of variables: the policies and practices of credit granters; the reasons why credit is sought; and the social and cultural milieu in which the individual consumer makes choices about credit use. These will now be considered in turn.

The Policies and Practices of Credit Granters

There are substantial differences in the cost of different forms of credit. These differences reflect, on the one hand, the degree of security which the borrower is able to offer the lender in the way of property or goods and, on the other hand, the 'security' which he is able to offer in terms of his ability to repay. This first relationship is quite straightforward: a mortgage taken out on a house is secure as long as the loan is not greater than the value of the house and house values do not fall. Even if the buyer stopped making repayments soon after taking out a mortgage it is likely that the lender would be able to recoup all or most of the money loaned. Thus the annual percentage rate of charge (APR) on loans secured against property, land or goods tends to be low (around 12.5 per cent for a first mortgage, and 18 per cent for a second mortgage at the time of writing, January 1987).

In contrast, interest rates on unsecured lending are around 22 per cent APR for bank personal loans, without tax relief, and between 24 per cent and 32 per cent APR for loans from finance companies. Hire-purchase agreements cost between 22 per cent and 45 per cent APR while the interest on shopping checks and vouchers[1] can range up to 97 per cent APR. Using a credit card can cost the consumer up to 27 per cent APR but may, of course, cost nothing if the account is cleared each month (all APRs taken from *Which?*, May 1986).

Thus, when security is not available to, or not sought by, the lender the average APR rises, being determined by the lender's assessment of the borrower's ability to pay.

All credit granters operate some form of vetting of their potential borrowers, although this can vary from a careful, personal appraisal of the individual's financial circumstances, through the application of computer credit-scoring programs, to a cursory 'weighing-up' of risks carried out on the doorstep. The rigour of this assessment usually closely parallels the cost of the credit being offered: the lower the rate of interest, and therefore the profit margin, the more confident the lender needs to be of the likelihood of repayment.

Whatever the rigour of the assessment for credit-worthiness, most creditors use the same indicators of the borrower's likely ability to repay. Most important among these indicators are income and socio-economic status. As a consequence, both the extent of credit use and the type of credit used vary significantly with these two characteristics.

Those consumers who make the most use of any credit are those whose jobs give them a high socio-economic status (OFT/NOP, 1979; NCC, 1980). Moreover, people in managerial or professional occupations are more likely than others to be using three or more different types of credit at a time (NCC, 1980).

Socio-economic group also influences the type of credit individuals use. Bank loans, bank credit cards and budget accounts in stores are particularly associated with professional and managerial groups (Ison, 1979; OFT/NOP, 1979; NCC, 1980). Skilled manual workers seem particularly likely to have used finance company loans at some time although professional and managerial workers also make use of them. Hire-purchase use is more likely among non-professional, non-manual workers while professional and managerial workers seem to be more likely than others to use credit sale as a means of purchasing goods (Ison, 1979; OFT/NOP, 1979; NCC, 1980). The use of shopping or trading checks is restricted almost exclusively to people in manual jobs, especially when semi-skilled (Ison, 1979; NCC, 1980). Finally, while manual workers are the major users of mail-order credit it is also used a good deal by those in professional and managerial occupations (Ison, 1979; OFT/NOP, 1979; NCC, 1980).

Although socio-economic class and income are obviously related, differences in credit use between groups of people at different income levels can be more marked than those between people in different socio-economic groups. Household income is closely linked to whether or not credit has ever been used, those with the lowest incomes being the least likely ever to have done so (OFT/NOP, 1979; NCC, 1980). Further, those with low incomes are less likely to have made recent credit purchases (NCC, 1980).

The types of credit used by households also vary with income. Those with higher incomes are most likely to have bank personal loans and overdrafts, credit cards, credit or budget accounts at stores, and second mortgages for home improvements. In the middle-income bracket there is more use of hire-purchase, mail-order buying, loans from finance companies and credit sale. The lowest income groups rely on check and voucher trading and the tallyman[2] (OFT/NOP, 1979; NCC, 1980).

It can be seen then that to *describe* the profile of credit use among different socio-economic groups and at different income levels also serves to *explain* it. The relationship between income or socio-economic status and the type and cost of credit used is determined largely by the credit granter's assessment of the borrower's ability to repay.[3] By this process the paradoxical situation arises whereby those consumers least able to afford it pay the most for credit.

This process also interacts with other personal characteristics of the borrower which, per se, do not affect his or her ability to repay. For example, credit-scoring may rely on factors such as employment type and history, tenure, length of time in current place of residence, marital status, possession of a bank account and age. These indicators may seem sensible but will inevitably discriminate against women and young people and may also discriminate against certain ethnic groups. This discrimination is not, usually, overt but arises from the position which women, young people and blacks hold in the economic pecking order.

The Reasons for Using Credit

There is a variety of ways in which credit can be used in household finances. The Crowther Committee (Cmnd. 4596, 1971) drew a distinction between credit for improvement (i.e. for the acquisition of consumer goods and services that would not otherwise have been obtained) and credit for adversity (i.e. when used to tide a household or individual over a financial crisis). It may be more accurate, however, to see the use of credit as on a continuum with 'improvement' and 'adversity' at the extremes.

First, credit may be used to safeguard savings. Many consumers prefer to keep their savings intact, against some future need, and borrow money for large purchases (Katona, 1964; NCC, 1980).

Secondly, when ready cash is not to hand credit can be used to take advantage of some special circumstances — for example, a bargain in the sales, the purchase of a yearly season ticket for a commuter — which will save more money than the subsequent credit will cost. This method of credit card use, in particular, is one which figures prominently in advertisements. Additionally, a credit card may purchase an item in one month although money to pay for it will not be available until the next. In such a situation the credit is effectively interest free and, in both instances, its use can be regarded as a reasonable way of extending control over financial resources.

Thirdly, it is possible to use credit to even out demands on income or to bring them into synchrony. Thus, the cost of new winter coats and shoes for children can be spread over several months with weekly repayments to a mail-order catalogue or clothing club. Similarly, a bank budget account may be used to spread the burden of rates, car tax and insurance, fuel bills and other household expenses. A single monthly amount paid into a special account allows money to be drawn upon when necessary, up to an agreed maximum, regardless of whether or not sufficient funds are available at that time. This costs the user interest and service charges on the 'overdrawn' account but for those who are unable to save regular amounts to cover future commitments it provides a way of meeting large household expenses without juggling payments. The danger of this third group of strategies is the possibility of an unexpected fall in income which leaves the householder committed to weekly or monthly payments which can no longer be sustained.

The fourth way in which credit may be used most closely matches the 'credit for adversity' identified by the Crowther Committee. Some households find that their income is inadequate to sustain their needs and commitments. Consequently, money is borrowed either formally or informally, to meet these needs. For example, a household may buy items on credit and find that the repayments, plus housing and food costs, leave them nothing with which to pay the fuel bills. Instead of finding some way to reduce other outgoings until the fuel bills are paid, a short-term cash loan is taken out. Immediate relief from a pressing problem is certainly obtained, but it is at the expense of increased future commitments. Thereby a particularly vicious circle is created.

There is some empirical evidence to suggest, as might be expected, that the ways in which credit is used vary with socio-economic status. First, the attitudes of different groups to the advantages of using credit vary. Better-educated people and those in non-manual occupations are most likely to see credit as a way of protecting capital or of countering the effects of inflation (in 1979) than other consumers (NCC, 1980). By contrast, those in unskilled manual jobs are most likely to see one of the advantages of using credit as the ability to purchase goods when insufficient cash is available. It is interesting to note that the consumers most likely to mention the advantage of being able to buy goods immediately rather than having to wait are those in the professional/managerial group (NCC, 1980). These attitudes are largely reflected in actual purchasing behaviour.

Among consumers who have money problems (clients of a money advice centre) credit use very often falls into the third and fourth categories outlined above (Parker, 1985). Although these consumers use credit to buy household durable goods in much the same way as others do, they also use credit very often for buying clothes and shoes, especially for children. Further, there is a very heavy reliance on small cash loans to clear other debts or to finance everyday living expenses. It is interesting that it is not low income per se which determines the use of cash loans and credit for shoes and clothing in this group. Rather the presence, and number, of dependent children in the household is far more important. Even at a relatively high income level, children in the household make it more likely that there will be commitments of this type.

Social and Cultural Influences on Credit Use

It was suggested in the introduction to this chapter that the increase in the use of credit reflects not only its increased availability but also changed attitudes towards its use. Few people now consider that there is anything intrinsically 'wrong' with credit, unless they hold religious or moral objections to usury.

A recent survey of consumer credit use showed that only a minority of people (around three in ten) now feel that the use of credit is 'never a good thing'. Indeed, a quarter of respondents felt that credit was a convenient (20 per cent) or a sensible (6 per cent) way of buying, and the largest proportion (43 per cent) felt that it was 'occasionally necessary' when ready cash was not available

(NCC, 1980: 165). Evidence for a change in attitude towards credit is provided by the age-related pattern of credit use; people of retirement age are least likely ever to have used credit and are the least likely to be current users (NCC, 1980).

Although there has been a fundamental change in attitudes towards, and the use of, credit there are still differences in the types of credit which people use which are not explained solely by economic factors or by their ability to repay. The National Consumer Council showed in its 1979 survey that 'very few people buying on credit had considered any type of credit other than the one they had actually used' (NCC, 1980: 56). The conclusion drawn was that, while consumers do not feel that they are 'pushed' into using any particular type of credit, 'three powerful forces — habit, convenience and ignorance or diffidence about alternatives — propel most people into the decision, rather than any conscious evaluation of what is best for them' (NCC, 1980: 57).

These 'powerful forces' are very evident in the lives of those who have money problems (Parker, 1985). For some in this group, and indeed for low-income consumers who do *not* get into difficulties, credit use is an accepted and inevitable part of their way of life. This is especially so when a form of credit which is repaid weekly is used. When women carry all the responsibility for household budgeting and when they are tied, either by their own or their partner's income, to a weekly payment pattern the range of credit options open to them is limited (see Parker, 1987). Thus, 'mail order, check traders and other weekly callers such as tallymen are woven closely into the fabric of daily (or rather weekly) life as to be more than just a possible buying choice' (NCC, 1980: 58). Despite being made over seventy years ago, Maud Pember Reeves's observation about the attractions of weekly arrangements still holds for many when 51 per cent of manual workers are paid weekly in cash (CSO, 1986) and when 5 million others are reliant on weekly supplementary benefit payments (Financial Statistics, 1986).

> They like to buy the same things week after week, because they can calculate to a nicety how the money will last . . . So much a week regularly paid has a great attraction for them. If the club will, in addition to small regular payments, send someone to call for the amount, the transaction leaves nothing to be desired. (Pember Reeves, 1979: 63)

Payments to callers are thus a part of the weekly budget in much the same way as are rent and food.

It is difficult for some consumers to break out of this pattern, even when they do have sufficient resources to do so. Customers often build up a very personal relationship with their weekly callers which they may be reluctant to break. These callers usually come from well-established 'family' firms and women may do business with the same company that their mothers or grandmothers used. The reluctance to break with these forms of credit is further reinforced by their usefulness as a form of insurance against hard times. Women may keep a small, regular credit arrangement with such firms just so that, if needed, they can ask the caller for more substantial help. When the customer is already in regular contact with the creditor and is known as a good payer there is likely to be very little delay in obtaining credit in an emergency.

It is also difficult for those on weekly incomes to break away from weekly credit arrangements, which are inevitably the most expensive, to those which are monthly, and less expensive, without the benefit of a bank account.

Credit and Equity

Differences in patterns of credit use and the type of credit used would be of little consequence if the effect produced was *only* that some sorts of people used one form of credit and others used another. In fact these differential patterns have two major consequences.

First, as has already been shown, some people pay more for their credit than do others. Seminal work by David Caplovitz in the USA (Caplovitz, 1967), followed by that of UK researchers and commentators (NOP, 1971; Piachaud, 1974; Baldwin, 1975; NCC, 1975; Aird, 1977; Masey, 1977; NCC, 1980), has shown conclusively that the credit available to poorer or lower social class consumers is more expensive than that available to the more prosperous. Moreover, the goods available with the type of credit which poorer consumers use are often of poorer quality and value than those available to other credit users (Crowther Committee, 1971; Williams, 1977). Thus, poorer consumers pay more for credit, with which they often obtain poorer quality goods, than do their more prosperous counterparts.

Secondly, much of the credit which poorer consumers use is, in practice, unregulated by the Consumer Credit Act 1974 and thereby consumers are denied its protection.

Until the passing of the Consumer Credit Act, check trading was totally unregulated, existing in a 'legal limbo' (Crowther Committee, 1971) between hire-purchase and money-lending. Even with the implementation of the Act, however, much check trading and small-scale money-lending remains unregulated where the face value of the check sold or the money lent is less than £30. The Act defines such agreements as 'small' (Consumer Credit Act 1974, Section 17) and thereby exempt from Part V of the Act which regulates entry into credit agreements, the form and content of those agreements, signing, documentation, cancellation, 'cooling-off' and so on.[4]

Further, there is evidence that some lenders 'double-up' agreements, lending large amounts in multiples of less than £30 so that each agreement is exempt from the Act. This practice is illegal but goes on none the less (Borrie and Diamond, 1981).

Money-lending has always been difficult to regulate even given a legislative framework. Money-lenders in working-class areas in the nineteenth century were often women who lent on a small scale, using a nest-egg or a pension as the base on which to start their 'business'. Many 'drifted into lending on an informal basis at the behest of friends and neighbours [and] . . . were largely ignorant of the law' (Tebbut, 1983: 53). The rates charged by these, largely informal, lenders varied but were undoubtedly high, especially for loans of a few shillings on which a penny in the shilling was the usual charge.

The Moneylenders' Act of 1900 and the subsequent amending act of 1927 provided a framework which required lenders to be registered, and later licensed, and gave the courts power to reopen agreements which charged 'excessive' interest. The figure of 48 per cent was established in 1927 as *prima facie* excessive.

Despite this legislation, evidence suggests that there were as many, if not more, unofficial lenders as official ones in the years after 1900. These informal lenders were protected by the silence of a community which depended on their existence because 'while intimidation undoubtedly played its part in preventing [borrowers] giving the game away to the authorities, many were very grateful for the financial lifeline the lender extended' (Tebbut, 1983: 54). As Tebbut suggests, the position of the street money-lender had much in common with the back-street abortionist:

> Both originated in the desperation of the working class woman and aroused the ire of the philanthropist but the uncertain gratitude of their own community. The dependency of the relationship was such as to produce a frequent ambivalence which in the moneylender's case depended on the customer's relief at obtaining a loan and the likely recurrence of the same need in the future. The customer's very poverty meant that she had to keep on the right side of the lender. (Tebbut, 1983: 54)

Although the need for back-street abortionists has, by and large, disappeared with legislative change the same cannot be said of the money-lender. Concern about abuse has risen from time to time in public consciousness but the trade has continued more or less unchanged. Baldwin (1975) has documented the high interest rates and frankly dubious collection practices of money-lenders operating in Glasgow in 1973 and there have been occasional scandals about benefit books being used as security against 'back-street' loan sharks (Crossley, 1984).

The Moneylenders' Act was replaced by the Consumer Credit Act 1974 but it is probably as difficult now as it was at the turn of the century, and for the same reasons, to police money-lending practices. Although the Consumer Credit Act provides a more sophisticated licensing system than did the Moneylenders' Act, and makes substantial provision for the reopening of extortionate credit agreements, the *opportunity* to challenge money-lenders' practices is severely limited. Extortionate credit bargains can be reopened only when court proceedings are taken. As Cranston has pointed out:

> Almost invariably this means that [the provision in the Act] will be used as a shield when consumers are sued and not as a sword to challenge a wide range of interest rates, for consumers who enter extortionate credit agreements are those least likely to invoke the provisions of private law. (Cranston, 1978: 201)

Recourse to a money-lender is often a gesture of last resort; it is not surprising that people desperate for money would be reluctant to cut themselves off from their last source of credit by challenging the agreements in court.

Conclusions

This chapter has shown how important a part credit can play in household finances, yet not all households enjoy equal access to it. Income level, employment status, marital status, tenure and, by implication, gender and race can all influence the availability of credit. Further, the type of credit to which the most disadvantaged consumers have access disadvantages them further by costing more and buying less (in terms of the quality and price of goods). In addition, these consumers are afforded less protection through consumer credit legislation. When so much consumer buying depends on the use of credit, and when so much credit is extended to so many people, it can be argued that credit has become a resource in its own right. If credit *is* a resource then it follows that similar arguments as those put forward for the equitable distribution of income, educational opportunities, health care or housing could be expounded in favour of the equitable distribution of credit. Further, if credit is accepted as a social good in this way then a role in the credit market for the state or its agents becomes arguable.

The proposed Social Fund[5] is, of course, a form of social lending. Because of its cash-limited budget and the inevitable administrative complexities which will accompany it, it is unlikely to make much impact on the household finances of social security claimants. However, the Social Fund proposals do constitute an important breach in British governments' previous resistance to providing 'social' forms of credit.[6] If interest-free loans are to be available to benefit claimants, even if they do not want to use them, there seems to be no logical argument against providing cheap credit for other low-income groups as well.

The real need for low-income consumers is, of course, for an income which allows them to meet the normal contingencies of life, but the likelihood of substantially improved benefit levels or levels of pay at the lower end of the labour market seems remote.

The need for some form of social lending will become more acute as the division between those who hold capital resources (see Chapter 10) against which they can borrow cheaply and those who do not increases, compounding the disadvantage which the latter already experience.

Notes

1. Shopping (trading) checks are documents giving credit up to a fixed total (often £30) at certain shops; each purchase is deducted from the check, leaving a smaller credit balance; fixed instalments, including interest set at the start on the full value of the check, are usually collected weekly (often for twenty-one or -two weeks). Vouchers are similar to trading checks, but are usually for more expensive specific purchases from specific shops; fixed payments, including interest fixed at the start, may be collected weekly over one to three years (NCC, 1980: 21–2).

2. The tallyman is an itinerant credit trader, credit draper or clothing club offering doorstep credit for clothes or textiles costing up to about £30. Fixed instalments are collected weekly, often for twenty weeks, with interest fixed at the start (NCC, 1980: 21–2).

3. While the Crowther Committee accepted that 'down-market' lending carried a greater risk of default which led to higher rates of interest, it was not entirely convinced: '. . . we suspect that the considerable differences in interest charges which we have observed are more than can be reasonably justified by differences in the risk to which the lenders are exposed' (Cmnd. 4596, 1971).

4. Despite being 'exempt', in the terms of the Consumer Credit Act 1974, such agreements are liable to be reopened in the case of extortionate interest rates being charged and are still subject to the control of the Act regarding, for example, canvassing and the seeking of business.

5. The Social Fund will replace single payments with loans to claimants, repayable by automatic deductions from their benefits. These loans will be interest-free and restricted to amounts in excess of £30.

6. Apart from a brief flirtation with the idea of a '*mont de piété*', or municipal pawnbroker, the British state, unlike some other European states, has never entered the market to provide social lending facilities.

194   *Gillian Parker*

References

Aird, A. (1977) 'Goods and services', in F. Williams (ed.), *Why the Poor Pay More*. London: Macmillan/National Consumer Council.

Annual Abstract of Statistics (1966) No. 103. London: CSO.

Annual Abstract of Statistics (1976) No. 113. London: CSO.

Annual Abstract of Statistics (1985) No. 121. London: CSO.

Annual Abstract of Statistics (1987) No. 123. London: CSO.

Baldwin, S. (1975) 'Credit and Class Distinction', in K. Jones (ed.), *The Yearbook of Social Policy 1974*. London: Routledge and Kegan Paul.

Borrie, G. and A.L. Diamond (1981) *The Consumer, Society and the Law*. Harmondsworth: Penguin Books.

Caplovitz, D. (1967) *The Poor Pay More*. New York: Free Press.

Central Statistical Office (CSO) (1986) *Social Trends 16*. London: HMSO.

Cmnd. 4596 (1971) *Report of the Committee on Consumer Credit* (Crowther Committee). London: HMSO.

Cranston, R. (1978) *Consumers and the Law*. London: Weidenfeld and Nicolson.

Crossley, M. (1984) 'Tackling the Scandal of Illegal Money Lenders', *Municipal Review*, 647: 56.

Financial Statistics (1986) No. 295. London: Central Statistical Office.

Ison, T. (1979) *Credit Marketing and Consumer Protection*. London: Croom Helm.

Katona, G. (1964) *The Mass Consumption Society*. New York: McGraw Hill.

Masey, A. (1977) 'Savings, Insurance and Credit', in F. Williams (ed.), *Why the Poor Pay More*. London: Macmillan/National Consumer Council.

National Consumer Council (NCC) (1975) *For Richer, For Poorer: Some Problems of Low Income Consumers*. London: HMSO/National Consumer Council.

National Consumer Council (NCC) (1980) *Consumers and Credit*. London: National Consumer Council.

NOP Market Research Ltd (1971) *Surveys Carried out for the Committee on Consumer Credit, Department of Trade and Industry*. London: HMSO.

Office of Fair Trading/NOP Surveys Ltd (1979) *Consumer Credit Survey 1977*. London: Office of Fair Trading.

Parker, G. (1985) 'Patterns and Causes of Indebtedness: a Study of Clients of the Birmingham Money Advice Centre'. PhD thesis. Birmingham: University of Birmingham.

Parker, G. (1986) *Consumers in Debt*. Background paper for the National Consumer Council conference, 14 January 1986. London: National Consumer Council.

Parker, G. (1987) 'Making Ends Meet', in C. Glendinning and J. Millar (eds), *Women and Poverty*. Brighton: Wheatsheaf Books.

Pember-Reeves, M. (1979) *Round About a Pound a Week*. London: Virago (first published 1913).

Piachaud, D. (1974) *Do the Poor Pay More?* London: Child Poverty Action Group.

Tebbut, M. (1983) *Making Ends Meet: Pawnbroking and Working Class Credit*. Leicester: Leicester University Press, and New York: St Martin's Press.

Which? (1986) May. London: Consumers' Association.

Williams, F. (ed.) (1977) *Why the Poor Pay More*. London: Macmillan/National Consumer Council.

13

Earning, Sharing, Spending: Married Couples and Their Money

Jan Pahl

This chapter focuses on the complicated issue of money transfers within households, that is to say, on what happens to money between the point at which it is earned and that at which it is spent. For single people, earning and living on their own, this issue is not usually problematic: income is translated fairly directly into consumption and the main issue is whether it is spent sooner or later. In larger households, however, patterns of earning are not necessarily reflected in patterns of consumption.

In households with several members it is important to make a distinction between earning, controlling, managing and consuming, a distinction which is quite meaningless in the case of the single-person household where all these activities are carried out by the same individual. So, for example, an earning husband may keep overall control of household finances, handing over some of his income to his wife, who then has to manage the spending, taking into account the needs of different consumers within the household.

There is also an important but rather ill-defined distinction to be made between *household* and *individual* consumption. Clearly there are some items, such as housing, fuel and basic food stuffs, which most households consume collectively, and in respect of which there can be little or no variation between the standards of living of different members of the household. At the other extreme there are items which are typically consumed on an individual basis, such as cigarettes, clothes and entertainment. Here there can be consider-able variations in the standards of living of different people within the same household. These variations may, of course, reflect individual tastes, but they can also reflect access to income, whether earned or shared within the household. As we shall see, households differ between those within which the standards of living of all members are very similar and those within which large numbers of items are consumed on an individual basis and where, consequently, there may be considerable inequalities.

In conceptualising flows of money within the household, it is useful to see variables such as age, sex, marital status and kinship as *filter points* which control an individual's access to household income; these variables also affect the extent to which any one individual plays a role as a controller, a manager or a consumer of household resources. A child, for example, may have no control over the family finances, may manage only her or his own pocket money, yet may be a privileged consumer. A non-earning wife who receives a housekeeping allowance from her husband may have little control over household income, while playing a major role as a manager; her husband's role as an earner and controller of income enables him to hand over the work of spending to someone who will protect his interests as a consumer. The filtering effects of age, sex, marital status and kinship may be seen more clearly in a cross-cultural context. In our society marriage typically marks the point at which a woman takes on responsibility for managing collective expenditure on behalf of a household, in contrast to many Muslim societies in which married people may remain in their parents' households and men are the main spenders (Cain, 1987). In many parts of Africa a wife is likely to prefer separate control of income, partly so that her husband cannot use her wages to fulfil his responsibilities to his own elderly parents (Fapohunda, 1987; Munachonga, 1987; Oppong, 1981).

This chapter presents some of the evidence on patterns of allocation of money within households in Britain, drawing on a fast-growing body of research on this topic. The topic raises many questions. To what extent are individual earnings seen as earmarked for household as opposed to individual expenditure? How do different households allocate the money that earners contribute? Which members of the household are likely to be responsible for spending on which particular items? How significant are the variations in standards of living between individuals within households? Answers to these questions are central to building up a better understanding of the economic aspects of family life.

My own empirical study of the control and allocation of money within families was carried out in 1982–4. The study involved interviewing 102 married couples, all with at least one child under sixteen. The couples were selected at random from age-sex registers held by three health centres in Kent. Husband and wife were interviewed together as a couple, and then separately but simultaneously in different rooms. The interviews covered patterns of income and expenditure, transfers of money between the spouses, standards of living, debts and savings, and decision-making within the household. All the tables in this chapter, except those attributed to other sources, are taken from this study. The full results of the research will be published as a book (Pahl, forthcoming).

Her Money, His Money, Our Money

Conflicting ideologies surround earned money. On the one hand, there is the individualistic approach represented by the statement 'It's my money: I can do what I like with it', while, on the other hand, there is the assumption that the couple can be regarded as an economic unit. Being a breadwinner is often regarded as a burden, but it can also be a source of pride and power. Income contributed by wives keeps thousands of British families out of poverty, but wives' earnings are often still regarded as 'pin money' for 'extras'. Exploring the meanings attached to money once it enters particular households can help to elucidate these apparent contradictions.

Table 13.1 shows the answers which husband and wife, being interviewed simultaneously but in different rooms, gave to the question, 'How do you feel about what you earn: do you feel it is your income or do you regard it as your husband/wife's as well?' Many respondents amended the question, explaining that they saw their income as belonging to 'the family', rather than to themselves as a couple. There were substantial differences between husbands and wives on this issue, and also between answers relating to the income of the respondent and the income of the other partner. Men's income was more likely to be seen as pertaining to the family than was women's income. However, both men and women were more likely to see their partner's income as belonging to the individual, while they preferred to see their own income as belonging to the family as a whole. A very similar pattern was found in Australia by Edwards (1981a and b).

TABLE 13.1 *'How do you feel about what you earn: do you feel it is your income or do you regard it as your husband/wife's as well?'*

	Husband's income		Wife's income	
Income belongs to	Husband's answer (%)	Wife's answer (%)	Wife's answer (%)	Husband's answer (%)
The earner	7	24	35	52
The couple/family	93	76	65	48
Total per cent	100	100	100	100
Total number	99	100	52	56

The evidence presented in Table 13.1 is very relevant to the debate about the extent to which members of families see themselves as individuals or as part of a collectivity within which money is shared. First, both partners in general appear to operate a collective rather than an individualistic model of the family and to see sharing of income as the norm. Secondly, both tend to see the husband as the main earner, the breadwinner whose income should be devoted to the needs of the family, in contrast to the wife whose earnings are seen as more marginal. Thirdly, there is the minority of earners who see their income as their own, a minority which would probably have been larger had the interviews not been specifically focused on the issue of money management. Finally, it is interesting to see that both partners assume a higher degree of collectivity, in the form of income sharing, for themselves than for their spouse; this suggests that earners welcome the role of breadwinner and the self-esteem it entails. The more frequent attribution of the breadwinner role to men reflects partly the desirability of this role and partly the larger wages men are typically able to command and the freedom from responsibility for child-care which facilitates continuity of employment. In 1984 the average gross earnings of full-time female employees was 65 per cent of the average earnings of male employees (Central Statistical Office, 1986). Being a breadwinner can bring privileges: the wife of an accountant, who had herself been an accounts clerk before having children, said:

> His income is his. I respect him as the worker. It's our money, but if he was really against something I would go along with him — it's him that has to go to work to earn it.

In several interviews it appeared that the husband was trying to convince his wife that his income was really hers as well, but the sharing ideology being promoted by husbands tended to be received with some scepticism by wives. Thus, two other women said:

> He would like me to regard it as ours but I feel it is his.

> Now I regard it as mine as well, but I think it has taken a long time to feel like that — and him as well.

The difficulty which some women experience in regarding their husband's income as their own, even when encouraged to do so, has also been noted by Cragg and Dawson (1984). Perhaps some wives were reluctant to see their husband's incomes as shared because the husband's sharing of money was seen as a reward for the wife's domestic work, while her earnings were seen as outside the system. A milkman, whose wife worked part time as a nursing auxiliary said:

Her earnings are hers. A woman cooks, cleans, dusts — she ought to be
able to get a bit of pin money after looking after us ungrateful lot!

Similarly, a warehouseman, whose wife did a paid job washing
up, said:

Hers. What she does with her money is up to her. The work she does in
the home is enough — I keep the roof over our heads. It's up to her if
she works or not.

A nurse, who kept her earnings separate from those of her factory
worker husband, said of her husband:

He likes to think he is still running the house and is the breadwinner and
my job is just an extra thing that I do because I want to.

Yet this couple had already agreed, in the joint interview, that
her earnings were used to pay the bills for the telephone, the
purchase and running costs of the car, hire-purchase commitments,
and clothes for the wife, the husband and their three children.

What, in practice, did wives do with the money they earned? At
the time of the interviews half of the women in the sample were
earning and a few others had recently been in employment, so
information about what wives did with their earnings was collected
from fifty-three couples. The great majority of women made their
wages available for household consumption. Of the fifty-three,
twenty-one placed their earnings in a joint account or in a common
pool, another thirteen added their wages to the housekeeping
money and four used their earnings for specific bills, such as those
for fuel, milk or television. Ten other women described their
earnings as being for 'extras' or 'luxuries', mentioning holidays,
clothes, consumer goods or improvements to the house as the sorts
of items on which their money was spent. Only five wives kept their
money separate from the rest of the household income and only one
of these saw her earnings as her personal spending money. These
results are very similar to those of other research. For example, a
recent review of the links between household finance management
and labour market behaviour concluded:

Two general patterns are apparent in the data on married women's
financial attitudes and the use of the woman's wage. One is a marked
desire for independence . . . the other is the overwhelming tendency for
women to use their wage to augment housekeeping. (Morris and Ruane,
1986: 84)

Husbands had very different attitudes to their own earnings as
opposed to those of their wives. As Table 13.1 showed, 93 per cent
of men saw their own earnings as belonging to the family, while only
48 per cent defined their wives' earnings in this way. There was also

a contrast between how husbands and wives saw the wife's earnings: while 48 per cent of husbands said that the wife's earnings belonged to the family, 65 per cent of wives saw their earnings in this way. A salesman, whose wife worked as a fruit packer on a casual basis, described a common situation when he said:

> I like to regard her income as hers but it usually winds up going on the family.

A miner who gave his wife a weekly housekeeping allowance, and spent much of the remainder of his earnings on alcohol and fruit machines, said:

> I feel I'm delegated by the family to earn money. Her job is looking after the house and family, but she feels she has to get out of the house because of boredom. We always discuss what we've got to buy and who's going to pay for it. But her money is hers.

His wife, who said she used her earnings as a school cleaner for 'extras for the family' and most recently for new windows for the house, saw her income as belonging to them both, adding:

> If he needs a new bit for the car, I'll hand the money over.

Earning was important to wives, both because their families needed the money and because of the independence and self-esteem it brought them. Two-thirds of all the women said that it was important for them to 'have some money you know is your own'. When asked, 'If your husband's income were to be increased by the same amount as you now earn, would you want to go on doing paid work?', 84 per cent of earning wives said 'yes'. Thus a nurse said of her income:

> It gives you a feeling of independence — a feeling you're not absolutely reliant on your husband. You feel you're somebody — more confident.

A sales assistant in Marks and Spencers, who saw her income as her own, still commented:

> It's mine, but I'm happy to contribute to the household expenses. I like saying 'I paid for that' sometimes.

These comments suggest that being a breadwinner can be a source of great satisfaction, an idea supported by Table 13.1 in which both husbands and wives tended to see their own income as being for the family, their partner's income as for the individual earner. The association between contributing money to the household and having power in household decision-making is well known (McDonald, 1980; Safilios Rothschild, 1976; Scanzoni, 1979). This study also showed that wives who saw their earnings as being for 'the family' had more power when the couple were making decisions than did wives who saw their earnings as being for themselves as individuals (Pahl, forthcoming).

The Allocation of the Husband's Income

There are wide variations in the proportion of their earnings which husbands contribute to collective expenditure, in the extent to which wives have access to their partners' earnings, and in the degree to which husbands retain control over spending decisions. Table 13.2 presents a four-part typology of allocative systems and makes comparisons between this and other studies. The typology is, of course, a simplification of the complexities of reality, but has proved sufficiently useful to have been adopted by a number of other researchers (Pahl, 1984).

The four allocative systems are:

The whole wage system. One partner, usually the wife, is responsible for managing all the financial affairs of the household. The husband hands over his pay packet, keeping back only a small amount of personal spending money. This system is typical of poorer households.

The allowance system. The husband gives his wife a set amount each week or month out of which she has to purchase specific items such as food, clothes and so on. The rest of the money is retained by the household and used to pay for goods for which he is responsible. This system is most often found in households where the husband is the sole earner.

The pooling system. Both partners contribute earnings to a

TABLE 13.2 *Frequency of different types of allocative system*

	Pahl 1982–3 (%)	Family Finances Group 1983 (%)	Birds Eye 1983 (%)	Graham 1985 (%)	Homer et al. 1985 (%)
Whole wage: wife	14	18	14	17	21
Whole wage: husband	—	—	5	8	22
Allowance system	22	24	26	41	49
Pooling system	56	54	51	31	5
Independent management	9	4	—	3	4
Other/don't know	—	—	5	—	—
Total per cent	100	100	100	100	100
Total number	102	250	711	64	78

common pool, to which both have access. Both can spend the money in the pool, though they may have individual expenditure responsibilities.

The independent management system. Each partner keeps his or her income separate and each is responsible for paying for specific items needed by the household.

Table 13.2 shows that in general there has been considerable agreement about the prevalence of different ways of organising money in Britain in the 1980s. About half of all households use the pooling system, about a quarter the allowance system, about a sixth the whole wage system and about a twelfth the independent management system (Family Finances Group, 1983; Birds Eye, 1983). However, we have to remember that in the first three columns of Table 13.2, the results came from couples who knew they were taking part in a study of financial matters and who chose to discuss this very sensitive aspect of marriage with an interviewer. It is likely that these samples were biased towards couples who were reasonably happily married and for whom money was not particularly problematic. The fourth column gives data from families with pre-school-age children, who were being interviewed about the organisation of health care, and as such may have included fewer earning wives and more couples for whom money was a problem area (Graham, 1985).

A very different situation was described by the abused women interviewed at the Cleveland refuge by Homer et al. (1985). For many of these women physical violence was associated with a high degree of financial control on the part of husbands. In 22 per cent of cases the husband kept control of all the money coming into the household and many women were effectively left without any money at all. This was categorised as the 'whole-wage-husband' system and its effects, in leaving non-earning wives with no money at all, have been documented in other studies of battered women (Binney et al., 1981; Pahl, 1980; Evason, 1982). Even when money was transferred to the wife for housekeeping expenses, many violent husbands expected to get cash back for their own personal use, for example for drinking and gambling. The financial problems associated with these marriages were reflected in considerable material deprivation among the wives and in the fact that 55 per cent reported that they felt 'better off' living on supplementary benefit after the marriage ended (Homer et al., 1985). It seems likely that financial arrangements change in marriages which are near breaking point and that earners become less willing to share with non-earners. The result is that women who are contemplating divorce may have severe financial problems. This is likely to exacerbate the difficulties they face after the marriage ends (see Chapter 7).

What is the relationship between patterns of allocation of money within the household and patterns of spending? Does the allocative system itself function as a filter which makes it more likely that one partner or the other will be responsible for spending on particular items? To some extent this is bound to be the case, since allocative systems are in part defined by the pattern of expenditure responsibilities. In the space available here it is impossible to discuss spending patterns in detail. However, expenditure does appear to be influenced both by the organisation of finances within the household and by gender differentiation. In an important unpublished study, carried out in the late 1960s, McLeod demonstrated a link between the control of finances and the amount identified as the housekeeping allowance. He showed that as the husband's net income increased the proportion of the income paid to the wife as an allowance for household spending decreased. Where couples managed the finances jointly a higher proportion of total income was devoted to collective expenditure than was the case when the husband retained control and gave his wife an allowance (McLeod, 1977).

In the study reported here patterns of spending were sex-linked, with food, cleaning materials, things for the children and presents typically being the responsibility of wives, while housing and telephone bills, the car and spending related to alcohol tended to be the responsibility of husbands. This pattern is rather different from that identified by Gray, who found rent, rates and fuel to be female responsibilities in Edinburgh in the late 1960s. This difference probably reflects different patterns of control and allocation of money within the household. In the Edinburgh study 54 per cent of households used the whole wage system (Gray, 1979). Table 13.3 illustrates this point, taking spending on fuel as an example. It shows that in 41 per cent of households husbands were responsible for fuel bills compared with 30 per cent of households where wives paid for gas, coal and electricity: thus, though in general husbands were more likely than wives to be responsible for fuel bills, the difference was not great. There were striking differences however, between allowance system couples, where 68 per cent of fuel bills were paid by husbands, and whole wage system couples where 86 per cent of fuel bills were paid by wives. This last finding has important implications for all who are concerned about fuel poverty. Since households with whole wage systems are among the poorest households, wives are likely to be the ones who struggle to pay fuel bills out of inadequate incomes (Bradshaw and Harris, 1983; Parker, 1987).

TABLE 13.3   *Responsibility for expenditure on fuel by allocative system*

Fuel paid for by	Whole wage system (%)	Allowance system (%)	Pooling system (%)	Independent management (%)	Total sample (%)
Wife	86	9	28	11	30
Husband	0	68	39	56	41
Either or both	14	23	30	33	27
Other answers	0	0	2	0	2
Total per cent	100	100	100	100	100
Total number	14	22	57	9	102

It is impossible to know whether seeing himself as responsible for fuel underlies a husband's choice of the allowance system or whether the choice of allocative system precedes the division of expenditure responsibilities. In pooling households fuel tended to be paid out of a joint account or a common kitty, and this was reflected in the fact that it was equally likely to be paid by wife or husband or by them jointly.

Spending on food was the responsibility of wives in 74 per cent of households, of husbands in 9 per cent of households and of both partners in 18 per cent of households. However, spenders do not necessarily control how much money they have to spend, so a series of questions investigated this issue, exploring spending on food under the broader heading of 'housekeeping money'.

Who Decides How Much to Spend on Housekeeping?

The term 'housekeeping money' is itself ambiguous. For some couples the 'housekeeping money' means the allowance which the husband gives his wife, out of which she is expected to buy a specific range of goods for the household. This range of goods usually includes food and cleaning materials, but may also cover such items as clothes, transport costs for the wife and the children, pocket money and so on. In this chapter the term 'allowance' is used to describe this category of money.

The other meaning of the term 'housekeeping money', and the one which is being used in this section, is both narrower and looser. Here it signifies the sum of money which a couple, explicitly or implicitly, earmark for day-to-day living expenses, and especially for food and cleaning materials. Half the couples who took part in the study said they had a specific sum which they spent in this way, an amount which varied from £20 to £85 per week. Most of the rest of the couples could name an approximate amount, often commenting that it might vary from week to week; fifteen husbands did not know how much was spent on day-to-day housekeeping. The average amount spent, according to wives' estimates, was £42.

It was often difficult to be precise about how the amount spent on housekeeping was determined. Indeed, in many households it was not determined at all, the word 'housekeeping' was rarely used and it appeared, if at all, as a retrospective concept describing the money which had been spent on food. As one husband said, when asked how they decided how much to spend on housekeeping, 'The girl at the checkout tells you what it comes to.' At the other extreme about a quarter of households kept careful accounts and had a clear notion of how much should be spent each week or month on particular items.

TABLE 13.4   *Decision on amount of housekeeping money by allocative system*

	Whole wage system (%)	Allowance system (%)	Pooling system (%)	Independent management (%)	Total sample (%)
Wife decides	64	18	54	67	49
Husband decides	—	68	19	22	27
Joint decision	—	9	25	11	17
Poverty controls the decision	36	5	2	—	7
Total per cent	100	100	100	100	100
Total number	14	22	57	9	102

Table 13.4 shows four different ways in which couples made the decision about how much to spend. The most common method was for the wife to decide what was appropriate, or to buy what she considered necessary: nearly half the couples fell into this category. By definition, wives in whole wage households were responsible for deciding how much of the income should go on housekeeping, but this system was also common among pooling couples. Here wives simply took a given sum of money from the pool every week, raising it to keep in line with wage and price increases, or in response to particular needs, without consulting their husbands. As a lorry driver commented, 'Why should a husband decide what a wife has for housekeeping when she knows the prices?'

For at least seven of the couples the amount spent as housekeeping was severely limited by their poverty. Unlike those affluent households who simply bought what they wanted and called the money they had spent 'housekeeping', these poverty-stricken couples usually budgeted carefully, paying their bills for rent and fuel first and using what was left as economically as possible. One wife, unemployed herself and with an unemployed husband, in response to the question, 'How do you decide how much to spend on housekeeping?', said:

> It's what's left after paying the bills really! We pay out for the bills and then the rest is housekeeping. Our meals are getting smaller all the time and we eat differently from how we did a few years ago. More sausages and mince dishes, though I do insist on a Sunday roast every week, otherwise it doesn't seem like Sunday.

This remark is also a reminder of the symbolic significance of particular types of meat and of the ways in which hierarchies in meat can provide markers of inequality both within and between families (Kerr and Charles, 1986).

In other households the amount spent on housekeeping was decided by the husband, or was negotiated between husband and wife. Some husbands controlled the money tightly, which could force their wives into adopting a variety of strategies when it became impossible to feed the family on the money provided. A quarter of the couples in the study fell into this category. One wife with three teenage children and an unemployed husband answered the question, 'How do you decide how much to spend on housekeeping?', by saying:

> It used to be £10 till a year ago. Then my daughters got on to my husband. We kept rowing, we have more rows over money than anything else. Eventually he gave in. I'd asked him before but he'd taken no notice. He raised it another £10 so now I get £20.

This money, together with £16 contributed by the eldest daughter and £5.85 child benefit, had to cover food, pocket money, presents, dog food, gas bills, cleaning materials and clothing for a household of five people. When asked what she did if the money ran out she said:

> It always runs out. I've found I've got to be very, very careful what I buy. I make a shopping list and buy just those things but it still mounts up. I ask my husband for more but he often says no. If I don't get any more I go without myself. I live from hand to mouth.

The secrecy which surrounds marital finances served to maintain great inequalities between couples. Many wives who had to cajole or beg to get an increase in the housekeeping money were unaware that other wives were not forced into these sorts of strategies. These wide variations were revealed in answers to the question 'How do you go about getting an increase in the housekeeping?' One wife replied, 'I just have to ask, like most women. He'll cough up in the end.' The wife of a technical services manager said she got a rise, 'by rowing':

> The present amount was decided eight months ago. My husband did the shopping for one month and decided the amount. There should be government legislation about how much housekeeping should be.

Her husband's answer was rather different. He said housekeeping money was decided:

> By mutual agreement, with an eye to what we can afford. She would like more and I would like her to have less because we just don't have it. I know it's not enough.

One wife, in a couple who saw their money as pooled, explained how she negotiated an increase in the sum set aside for food:

> I ask, there's no problem, but I don't like actually asking. I do choose my moment and work my way round to it. He is normally OK but he might want to complain for an hour and a half or so, but he lets me have it if I say I really need it.

All these answers are very different from those of the genuinely pooling wife who said simply, 'I just go and cash more from the bank.'

Conclusions on Consumption

There has been considerable debate about the extent to which standards of living vary within households and in particular about whether married women have lower standards of living than married men. Since women's wages are on average two-thirds of men's wages, and about two-fifths of married women are not in paid employment at any one time, achieving a similar standard of living for both partners in a marriage depends on married men sharing at least part of their incomes.

Traditionally, economists and policy-makers have made the assumption that the household can be treated as a unit within which individuals have the same standard of living: 'The analysis of consumption patterns and their relationship to income are necessarily based on households since many essential items are consumed jointly by all or several members of a household' (Nicholson, 1979: 61; quoted in Land, 1983).

Empirical support for this stance was produced by a re-analysis of the Breadline Britain Survey by Taylor-Gooby (1985). This analysis suggested that there was considerable homogeneity between the living standards of married men and married women. In addition, while married men were rather better off than single men, married women appeared to be much better off than single women.

Yet there is a considerable body of evidence to suggest that at least some married women are worse off than the men with whom they live. Thus, for example, the lower meat consumption of women and children has been documented by Kerr and Charles (1986), while the structural basis for the assumption that women need less food, and less nutritious food than men has been examined by Delphy (1984). Married women's lack of access to private transport, relative to married men, is well established (Dale, 1986). Further, women were found to be more generally deprived than men, and housewives more deprived than other adults, in Townsend's study of poverty (Townsend, 1979). Summarising the available evidence on this topic Land concluded: 'The available evidence, then, shows that resources are distributed and consumed unequally within the family, and that, in particular, the mother's needs are accorded less importance than the needs of other members of the family' (Land, 1983: 63).

This issue is particularly relevant to debates about tax and social security policy. For tax and benefit purposes the legally married couple, together with their dependent children, are treated as a single unit. Money income is assumed to flow between the different members of the family so that each gets an equal, or at least equitable, share of the household income. This assumption lies behind the proposal to introduce transferable tax allowances, for example. In this tax system both husband and wife would have their own tax allowances, and if either did not earn, her or his allowance could be transferred to the other partner. The system can, however, create considerable problems for wives who do not earn. A wife who wishes to take up paid employment faces a choice between leaving her allowance with her husband and paying tax on all of her earnings, or taking her allowance back so that her husband has to pay more tax on his earnings (Morris and Ruane, 1986; Pahl, 1986). Debates about allowances for dependent children raise similar issues. Some commentators suggest that support can be given through male wage packets or through social security payments to the 'head' of household, while others argue that child support should go to the person responsible for day-to-day care of the child (Franey, 1986; Henwood and Wicks, 1986; Pahl, 1985). All these debates imply fundamental differences of opinion about whether household income is shared equally between husband and wife.

Is it possible to reconcile the disagreement between those who

hold that married partners ha
who suggest that some marri⟨
husbands? I would put forwar

First, the data suggest that
members share a common stan
stantial minority of households
small proportion of their incom
the consumption pattern of the h
his wife. This 'concealed poverty
income level, but is particularl⟨
especially where there are young
their mother to earn. Thus the Br
'in low income households it is tl   a
greater extent than their husbands   ⟨y, 1985: 281; see
also McKee and Bell, 1985). Extreme examples of the 'concealed
poverty of dependence' are revealed in studies of wife abuse,
marital breakdown and divorce; unfortunately it is just these
households which tend to refuse to take part in surveys of family
finances.

Secondly, it is important to take account of the ideologies which
surround earning and spending. In contemporary Britain, earning
carries more status than financial dependence, and it is expected
that dependents will show a certain deference towards those who
support them. A number of researchers have shown that, in
general, husbands expect to have their own personal spending
money in a way that wives often do not (Edwards, 1981a; Gray,
1979; Hunt, 1978; McLeod, 1977). The consequence is that when
non-earning wives need something for themselves they have to buy
it with money which they see as earmarked for household
expenditure and they often feel guilty as a result. Thus, one reason
why some wives are less well off in terms of consumption is that they
do not feel they have the right to spend on themselves. As many of
the quotations in this chapter imply, financial dependence often
seems to be associated with a deference which can have the effect of
increasing inequalities between earners and spenders.

The data presented in this chapter suggest a discrepancy between
theory and practice in the attitudes of husband and wife to earning
and spending. As has been shown, both partners were likely to
define the husband's income as earmarked for collective expenditure; yet in practice many husbands did not make all their income
available to the family, especially in households with allowance or
independent management systems. By comparison, wives' incomes
tended to be seen, especially by husbands, as earmarked for
individual expenditure; yet in practice most wives added their

ping or used it to buy things for the family.
ween earning, spending and consuming have
complex, being structured both by patterns of
cial management and by ideologies about gender
arriage.

The research on which this chapter is based was funded by the Economic and Social Research Council and the Joseph Rowntree Memorial Trust.

References

Binney, V., G. Harkell and J. Nixon (1981) *Leaving Violent Men: A Study of Refuges and Housing for Battered Women*. London: Women's Aid Federation (England).

Birds Eye (1983) *Housekeeping Monitor 1983*. Walton on Thames: Public Relations Department, Birds Eye Walls Ltd.

Bradshaw, J. and T. Harris (1983) *Energy and Social Policy*. London: Routledge and Kegan Paul.

Cain, M. (1987) 'The Consequences of Reproductive Failure: Dependence, Mobility and Mortality among the Elderly in Rural South Asia', in D. Hilse Dwyer and J. Bruce (eds), *A Home Divided: Women and Income in the Third World*. New York: Population Council.

Central Statistical Office (1986) *Social Trends 16*. London: HMSO.

Cragg, A. and T. Dawson (1984) *Unemployed Women: A Study of Attitudes and Experiences*. London: Department of Employment Research Paper, No. 47.

Dale, A. (1986) 'Differences in Car Usage for Married Men and Married Women: A Further Note in Response to Taylor-Gooby', *Sociology*, 20(1): 91.

Delphy, C. (1984) *Close to Home*. London: Hutchinson.

Edwards, M. (1981a) *Financial Arrangements within Families*. Canberra: National Women's Advisory Council.

Edwards, M. (1981b) 'Financial Arrangements within Families', *Social Security Journal*, December: 1–16.

Evason, E. (1982) *Hidden Violence*. Belfast: Farset Press.

Family Finances Group (1983) *Marriages and Money: Forms of Financial Arrangement within the Family*, mimeo, University of Surrey: Department of Sociology.

Fapohunda, E. (1987) 'The Non-pooling Household: A Challenge to Theory', in D. Hilse Dwyer and J. Bruce (eds), *A Home Divided: Women and Income in the Third World*. New York: Population Council.

Franey, R. (1986) *Past Caring: the Government's Plans for Pensions and Social Security*. London: Child Poverty Action Group.

Graham, H. (1985) *Caring for the Family*. The Report on a Study of the Organisation of Health Resources and Responsibilities in 102 Families with Pre-school Children. Milton Keynes: Open University.

Gray, A (1979) 'The Working Class Family as an Economic Unit', in C. Harris (ed.), *The Sociology of the Family*, University of Keele Sociological Review Monograph. Keele: University of Keele.

Henwood, A. and M. Wicks (1986) *Benefit or Burden: The Objectives and Impact of Child Support*. London: Family Policy Studies Centre.

Homer, M., A. Leonard and P. Taylor (1985) 'The Burden of Dependency', in N. Johnson (ed.), *Marital Violence*. London: Routledge and Kegan Paul.

Hunt, P. (1978) 'Cash Transactions and Household Tasks', *Sociological Review*, 26(3): 555–71.

Kerr, M. and N. Charles (1986) 'Servers and Providers: The Distribution of Food Within the Family', *Sociological Review*, 31(1): 115–57.

Land, H. (1983) 'Poverty and Gender: the Distribution of Resources within the Family', in M. Brown (ed.), *The Structure of Disadvantage*. London: Heinemann.

McDonald, G.W. (1980) 'Family Power: The Assessment of a Decade of Theory and Research: 1970–1979', *Journal of Marriage and the Family*, November: 841–54.

McKee, L. and C. Bell (1985) 'Marital and Family Relations in Times of Male Unemployment' in B. Roberts, R. Finnegan and D. Gallie (eds), *New Approaches to Economic Life*. Manchester: Manchester University Press.

McLeod, K.D. (1977) *The Family Economy and the Standard of Living*. End of Grant Report. York: Joseph Rowntree Memorial Trust.

Morris, L. and S. Ruane (1986) *Household Finance Management and Labour Market Behaviour*. Durham: Work and Employment Research Unit, University of Durham.

Munachonga, M.L. (1987) 'Income Allocation and Marriage Options in Urban Zambia: Wives Versus Extended Kin', in D. Hilse Dwyer and J. Bruce (eds), *A Home Divided: Women and Income in the Third World*. New York: Population Council.

Nicholson, J.L. (1979) 'The Assessment of Poverty and the Information We Need', in *The Definition and Measurement of Poverty*. London: DHSS.

Oppong, C. (1981) *Middle Class African Marriage*. London: George Allen and Unwin.

Pahl, J. (1980) 'Patterns of Money Management within Marriage', *Journal of Social Policy*, 9(3): 313–35.

Pahl, J. (1984) 'The Allocation of Money within the Household', in M. Freeman (ed.), *The State, the Law and the Family*. London: Tavistock.

Pahl, J. (1985) 'Who Benefits from Child Benefit?', *New Society*, 25 April: 117–19.

Pahl, J. (1986) 'Personal Taxation, Social Security and Financial Arrangements within Marriage', *Journal of Law and Society*, 13(2): 241–50.

Pahl, J. (forthcoming) *Money and Marriage*. London: Macmillan.

Parker, G. (1987) 'Making Ends Meet: Women, Credit and Debt', in C. Glendinning and J. Millar (eds), *Women and Poverty*. Brighton: Wheatsheaf Books.

Safilios Rothschild, C. (1976) 'A Macro- and Micro-examination of Family Power and Love', *Journal of Marriage and the Family*, 37 (May): 355–62.

Scanzoni, J. (1979) 'Social Processes and Power in Families', in W. Burr, R. Hill, I. Nye and I. Reiss (eds), *Theories about the Family*. New York: Free Press.

Taylor-Gooby, P. (1985) 'Personal Consumption and Gender', *Sociology*, 19(2): 273–84.

Townsend, P. (1979) *Poverty in the United Kingdom*. Harmondsworth: Penguin Books.

14
Indebtedness

Gillian Parker

Indebtedness could be said to be at the heart of the matter of this book because it results from a mismatch between resources and needs which may or may not be mediated by budgeting behaviour, access to capital resources and the perquisities of employment. Yet despite its continual and continuing association with various personal misfortunes, consumer debt has attracted little research attention until relatively recently. Thus, while debt was described in association with unemployment (Clark, 1978), low pay (Knight and Nixon, 1975) and lone parenthood (Marsden, 1973), there was little attempt to examine it in its own right. For a variety of reasons this position has changed and concern about personal indebtedness has grown.

The first of the three main reasons for this change is the growth of the incidence of debt. Since the early 1950s a collective emphasis on the 'consumer society' has led to increasing consumer aspirations. These aspirations, together with the expectation of continuing improvements in living standards and with changes in the credit market, have led to massive increases in both the number of people using credit and the amount of credit being taken on by individuals (see Chapter 12). Consumers are now more highly 'geared' in relation to credit commitments — that is, a higher proportion of their income goes towards servicing credit commitments — than in the past (Leigh-Pemberton, 1986). Even if no other change had taken place, this higher level of gearing would have created a greater incidence of default; coupled with increased unemployment, it has led to considerable increases, not only in consumer credit default but also in rent, fuel and mortgage arrears.

Secondly, the location of certain services in the public rather than the private or commercial domain has brought some forms of debt to public attention for the first time. For example:

> Before the introduction of gas and electricity supplies a household's ability to keep warm and well-lit was entirely a matter of finding sufficient money from their budget to pay for wood, coal, lamp-oil and candles. If the money could not be found it was of concern only to that

household and, possibly, charity but certainly not the state. Even after the introduction of domestic gas and electricity supplies difficulties in paying for them remained 'hidden' for as long as pre-payment meters were used. It is only with the demise of alternative heat and light sources and the replacement of slot meters with credit meters that fuel debt has become an issue of public concern. (Parker, 1983: 58)

Similarly, the fact that so much rented accommodation is now owned by local authorities 'ensures that statistics [about arrears] are available, and it stimulates interest in the size, nature and handling of the arrears problem' (Ashley, 1983: 126).

Thus, both fuel and housing default have become public issues by virtue of the transfer of responsibility from private enterprise to the state. This transfer has made the problem of debt more obvious, alerting the interest of those concerned with social welfare. However, it has also had the effect of changing default in these areas from an issue of commercial concern to one of public accounting.[1]

Thirdly, the increased incidence of indebtedness has aroused interest because of the strain it puts on the machinery of the state. The number of cases dealt with by the county courts of England and Wales increases every year; there were over two million plaints in 1985. The Scottish civil judicial system is similarly hard-pressed; indeed, the largest research study of debt proceedings to date was carried out as part of a review of Scottish legal processes (Adler and Wozniak, 1983; Gregory and Monk, 1983). More recently, the Lord Chancellor's Department has examined the whole process of debt enforcement in England and Wales as part of its wider ranging Civil Justice Review (Lord Chancellor's Department, 1987a).

Because of this recent emergence of debt as a problem in its own right, statistical evidence about its extent usually stretches back only a short distance. In addition the statistics are fragmented, relating only to the particular type of debt with which the collecting body is concerned. Similarly, studies of the causes of debt have often been confined to specific types of debt and have ranged from the frankly anecdotal, through properly controlled interview studies, to econometric analyses of area variations in debt. The purpose of this chapter is to bring together information from these various sources in an attempt, first, to quantify the true extent of consumer debt and, secondly, to pinpoint the causes of debt.

The Extent of Indebtedness

Increases in the level of indebtedness are evident across the whole range of personal goods and services. It is not just that more people are buying more by 'going into debt' (as shown in Chapter 12) but rather that more people are failing to make payments for these items when due. This section of the chapter is thus about the extent of these 'bad debts'.

Housing

Local authority. Since local government reorganisation in 1974, local authority rent arrears in England and Wales have risen from less than 2 per cent of rents collectable to 4.4 per cent in 1981–2 to 4.9 per cent in 1983 (Audit Commission, 1984). The most recent available figures suggest that the proportion is now some 5.6 per cent (Chartered Institute of Public Finance and Accountancy [CIPFA], 1986).

Some of these arrears, approximately 45 per cent, are 'technical' — caused by administrative and accounting practices, arrears owed by public bodies and individuals other than current council tenants, and arrears of rates included in rent arrears figures. Even when this is taken into account the amount of money outstanding has risen from 55 million in 1981–2 to 108 million in 1984 to £110 million in 1985. This increase is all the more striking given the introduction of housing benefit which, other things being equal, was expected to reduce the absolute level of arrears by about a third (Audit Commission, 1984, para. 25).

It is estimated that over a million local authority tenants (about one in four) have arrears although the proportion varies from area to area. In London, for example, around four in nine tenants have arrears (Audit Commission, 1984).

Mortgaged housing. In 1979, when the Building Societies Association (BSA) started to collect statistics on a national basis, properties taken into possession represented 0.048 per cent of all loans (2,530). In 1986 this proportion had risen to 0.296 per cent (20,550). Over the same period, loans six to twelve months in arrears have risen from 0.16 per cent (8,420) to 0.64 per cent of all loans (44,600) (BSA, 1987). In addition, at June 1985 loans which were between three and six months in arrears represented 1.63 per cent of all loans. In total, arrears of three months or more represented 2.44 per cent of all building society loans in June 1985 (BSA, 1985). The numbers of loans which are three months or more in arrears could, then, be as high as 169,300 (around 2.44 per cent of the number of loans at the end of 1986).

While building societies provide the vast majority of mortgages in the UK they are not the only institutions involved in this market. In

1985 building societies advanced £26,223 million, banks £6,157 million, insurance companies and pension funds £564 million and local authorities £267 million in mortgages (Department of the Environment [DoE], 1986).

In 1983, around 2.5 to 3 per cent of local authority mortgage loans to private individuals in England and 0.75 to 1 per cent of loans specifically for the purchase of council houses were at least six months in arrears (BSA, 1985). More recently the level of local authority mortgage arrears, in metropolitan areas only, has been estimated at one per cent of the total loan debt outstanding (Culley and Downey, 1986). The figures for the proportion of loans in arrears are more substantial: 3.28 per cent are three to six months in arrears; 2.5 per cent six to twelve months in arrears; and 1.4 per cent over twelve months in arrears.

Fuel
Despite concern about the increased level of fuel debt in recent years its scale is not large relative to the number of consumers. The majority of fuel bills are paid before final notices are issued and disconnection takes place in only a tiny proportion of domestic consumer households (Berthoud, 1981). However, although the *proportion* of consumers affected by disconnection is small the *numbers* are not. Further, the rate of disconnection is not the only indicator of fuel debt. The numbers of consumers who arrange repayment plans or elect to have pre-payment meters also indicate some level of difficulty in meeting fuel bills.

Electricity. Concern about the level of electricity disconnections led, in 1980, to a revision of the voluntary Code of Practice entered into by fuel boards. This revision contributed to a fall in the number of disconnections from a peak of 123,000 in 1980. Recent evidence suggests that the decline from this peak has now levelled out and that the number of disconnections is beginning to rise again. In the twelve months to September 1986, 101,379 households in England and Wales had their supply disconnected — some 0.56 per cent of the total number of domestic credit consumers (Electricity Consumers' Council [ECC], 1986). In the previous year 98,361 households had been disconnected; thus the 1986 figure represents an increase of 3.1 per cent. The number of consumers who remain disconnected is also rising. At 30 September 1985, 23,512 consumers were still without supply (having been disconnected at some time during the previous twelve months); a year later this figure had risen by 5.7 per cent to 24,855.

The Code of Practice, referred to above, encourages fuel boards to offer to consumers who are having difficulty meeting their bills the opportunity to enter into repayment plans or to have pre-payment meters installed. It would be expected then that some potential disconnections would be 'translated' into the increased use of repayment arrangements or the installation of more pre-payment (coin) meters.

The Electricity Consumers' Council has calculated that about 3 per cent of consumers each quarter are offered repayment plans when they have failed to pay their bill but only around a third of these consumers actually take up the offer. The remainder make sufficient payment to avoid disconnection although there is no indication of the proportion of these consumers who borrow money from other sources to avoid the repayment plan and/or disconnection (see also Berthoud, 1981).

Repayment plans often fail: the proportion of all disconnections which result from the breakdown of such a plan rose steadily from 22 per cent (of all disconnections) in 1981 to around 40 per cent in 1984 (ECC, 1985). An increase was to be expected, in that a greater proportion of consumers with payment difficulties were being offered plans to avoid disconnection, but without systematic research it is difficult to be categorical about the real causes of these failures. However, it has been suggested that the Boards may be 'requiring terms that are too strict or that the Boards are allowing debts to mount up too much before suggesting a payment plan' (ECC, 1985: para. 4.4).

The number of pre-payment meters for electricity supply installed each quarter has more than doubled (to around 49,000 a quarter) since 1980; moreover, since the beginning of 1982 these installations have exceeded the number of cash meters being removed (ECC, 1985: para. 5.1). This trend indicates a clear reversal in previous electricity board policy which reflects the changes in the Code of Practice. Many pre-payment meter installations are now directly related to the threat of disconnection. The ECC reports that 45 per cent of pre-payment meters installed in 1984 were put in after the Boards had made repayment plan offers to consumers who had not paid their accounts. A further index of consumers' difficulties in paying for fuel is the use of 'fuel direct' payments through Supplementary Benefit. At the end of 1984 there were approximately 140,000 fuel direct cases, an increase of around 90,000 since 1980. The ECC believes that this increase reflects rising unemployment but also the fact that Boards have stopped applying arbitrary ceilings on the debts for which they will accept fuel direct arrangements (ECC, 1985) thus enabling more claimants to make use of these arrangements. It is difficult, even given the figures produced by the ECC in its latest report, to judge what is the true extent of repayment difficulties experienced by electricity consumers. However an 'educated guess' would put the figure at one and a half million or 7.5 per cent of all domestic electricity consumers.[2] Even if all those consumers who pay their bill after an offer of a repayment plan were excluded, the number experiencing difficulty would still be around one million or 5.5 per cent of all domestic consumers.

Gas. Figures for gas disconnection show the same pattern for those of electricity; a fall from a peak in 1980 but rising again since mid-1982. In the twelve months to March 1986, 36,948 domestic gas consumers were disconnected for non-payment of their accounts. This represented around 0.23 per cent of all domestic consumers (National Gas Consumers' Council [NGCC], 1986).

The use of 'alternatives' to disconnection has also increased. The number of payment arrangements entered into to avoid disconnection in the year ending September 1983 was 528,490 (NGCC, 1985). This represented around 3.84 per cent of all domestic credit consumers; a similar proportion at March 1986 would account for around 566,630 consumers.

The number of pre-payment meters installed for gas supply has increased fourfold since a low point in 1980, although this increase now appears to be levelling off. Around 64,000 cash meters were installed in the twelve months to March 1984 compared with around 57,000 in the twelve months to March 1985 and 51,500 to March 1986. The NGCC report (1985) implies that *all* cash meter installations represent cases of hardship so this policy is clearly making a considerable impact on the number of disconnections that would otherwise have taken place.

Recent figures about the use of fuel direct arrangements for paying gas are unavailable. Extrapolation from 1983 data, when 2.75 per cent of all credit consumers had made such arrangements, suggests that almost 406,000 consumers would have been on 'fuel direct' in March 1986.

Taking all these estimates together it seems likely that around a million gas consumers experienced some difficulty in paying for their gas supply in the twelve months to March 1986. This represents around 6.3 per cent of all domestic credit and pre-payment consumers.[3]

Consumer credit
Evidence from the late 1970s and early 1980s suggests that between 5 and 10 per cent of all consumer credit extended creates some

'difficulties' in regard to repayment and that around one per cent will eventually become irrecoverable (National Consumer Council [NCC], 1980; Ison, 1979; Office of Fair Trading [OFT]/NOP, 1979). Even if these proportions have not increased in the interim it can be estimated that between £1,300 million and £2,600 million of the credit extended in 1985 will cause repayment difficulties and that £260 million will never be recovered. Given that at least half of the adult population is borrowing or buying on credit at any one time (NCC, 1980) between 0.9 million and 2.05 million people will experience payment difficulties on average credit commitments of between £1,300 and £1,450. Of these a quarter of a million might eventually fail altogether to repay credit commitments of around £1,000 each.

These figures can give no more than a broad indication of the incidence of consumer credit default. For example, some individuals will have multiple consumer credit debts thus increasing their average indebtedness but reducing the total number of individuals in default. Despite these reservations the data seem to indicate a substantial problem. Another partial indicator of the extent of default is the number of proceedings started in the county courts for hire-purchase debts, outstanding loans, the recovery of goods sold, and similar. The use of judicial statistics is not without problems, as the number of plaints issued is not necessarily related to the amount of credit advanced in any particular year. For example, it could be that creditors now pursue their claims through the courts more often than in past years. Moreover, a large part of the work done within the county courts relates to debts to the state — local authorities, fuel authorities — rather than to consumer credit granters (Goode et al., 1984). Thus, while the number of plaints issued has quadrupled over the past thirty years, it is difficult to judge whether this is merely a function of the increased use of consumer credit, whether it reflects some change in creditors' policies, or whether it indicates a real increase in the incidence of default. Because of the intermittent raising of the maximum amount which may be pursued through the county courts, the judicial statistics do not allow any accurate analysis of increases or decreases in default over long periods. For example, the number of proceedings started dropped steadily between 1974 and 1979, when the maximum amount pursuable was £2,000. When the maximum was increased to £5,000 in 1980 the number of proceedings started to rise again: from 1.5 million in 1978 to 2.2 million in 1986 (Lord Chancellor's Department, 1987b). However, even with this intermittent reduction in the number of plaints, clearly the work of the county courts in the pursuit of debt has increased substantially in the past twenty-five years.

Within this increase of total proceedings started there are considerable differences between different types of plaint. Plaints for the repayment of bank and finance house loans have more than trebled since 1980. By contrast, the number of plaints for hire-purchase and the recovery of goods has dropped. This 'excess' of plaints entered for bank and finance house loans adds further weight to the argument in Chapter 12 that increased levels of finance-house lending might account for the recent, accelerated growth in amounts of retail credit outstanding at the end of each year.

The number of petitions in bankruptcy issued has also started to rise again in recent years following a drop as a result of administrative changes in 1976. The number of petitions of 1984 was the highest it had been for at least twenty-five years (7,253) although this dropped somewhat in 1985 to 6,493 (Judicial Statistics, 1986).

Finally, while the number of warrants of execution against goods has remained more or less steady the number of sales eventually made has increased since 1978 although, again, the actual numbers are small.

Despite the reservations expressed about their use, the judicial statistics do seem to point to a general increase in default, with default on some types of consumer transaction increasing more rapidly than on others.

The Causes of Indebtedness

The 'cause' of personal indebtedness is, of course, not having enough money to meet all one's commitments but the ways in which such a mismatch can arise are various. As other chapters in the book show, the extent to which individuals and households can manipulate resources to meet needs is not determined solely by the income that they can command in the labour market. Home ownership, participation in occupational pension schemes, other forms of occupational welfare and work-related perks can, in addition to enhancing financial and quasi-financial resources, increase the control which individuals have over those resources. Further, certain circumstances mediate the *demands* which are made on resources. For example, the impact of unemployment is not felt so keenly by those who have savings or investment incomes, good occupational pension schemes buffer the loss of income on retirement, home owners can borrow against the equity in their property to even out demands across the life cycle, and so on. Consequently, predicting whether any individual or household will experience difficulty meeting the demands made on their financial resources should not depend simply on a Micawberish comparison of income and expenditure.

Unfortunately, the opportunity to carry out such a wider-ranging investigation of the phenomenon of indebtedness has not yet arisen. Relatively little is known about the way in which 'middle-class' and higher socio-economic groups order their household finances or the extent to which they become indebted because research attention has focused on those who have low incomes and those who become the clients of advice and social welfare agencies. Inevitably, the rest of this chapter relies heavily on this type of research.

Employment and Income

The relationships between unemployment and indebtedness and between low income and indebtedness have been demonstrated in many studies. Studies of unemployment (Daniel, 1974; Clark, 1978; Smith, 1980) have shown that households with unemployed heads experience a wide range of money difficulties and debts (see also Chapter 6). Households with rent arrears are more likely to have an unemployed breadwinner than households without (NCC, 1976a; Ungerson and Baldock, 1978; Duncan and Kirby, 1983) and households experiencing difficulties paying for fuel, or which are disconnected from their supply, are likely to have experienced disruptions to income through unemployment or ill-health of the household head (Hesketh, 1975; NCC, 1976b; Berthoud, 1981; Parker, 1983).

As might be expected, many of these studies have also demonstrated a connection between low income, particularly low per capita income, and debt. However, when most households containing an unemployed head are in receipt of low incomes (see Chapter 6) it is not entirely clear whether it is loss of paid employment, or the resulting low income, or both which 'cause' indebtedness. When asked about the cause of their money problems, people who are already in debt are likely to mention reduced or lost income due to unemployment, sickness, bereavement or divorce (Caplovitz, 1974; Adler and Wozniak, 1981; Gregory and Monk, 1981; Parker, 1985). While this might indicate that a reduction in income, rather than low income per se, is responsible for money problems, such an interpretation is not unequivocal (Ashley, 1983). There is evidence, for example, that debts 'cluster' in a different way and are of a different type depending on whether income has been low for a long time or has fallen recently. 'Primary' debt for housing or fuel is thus more a feature of long-term low income whereas 'secondary' debt, for less essential items, is more likely to occur among recently unemployed people who have previously enjoyed relatively adequate incomes (Parker, 1985).

Some indication of the relative contributions of low income and reduced income to indebtedness is available from analysis of the Family Finances Survey (Parker, 1986). This showed that among households with similar incomes unemployment increased the likelihood of householders experiencing difficulty paying for fuel and housing. *Recent* unemployment was strongly associated with difficulties paying for housing and a high level of recent credit commitments. Long-term unemployment was associated with money borrowing and housing arrears. In sum, the analysis suggested that: 'differences between the employed and the unemployed, and between the short-term and long-term unemployed [were] substantial enough to warrant the conclusion that unemployment, of itself, causes debt in households which already have low resources' (Parker, 1986: 44).

Household Composition and Size
The composition and size of the households in which indebted people live also appear to be implicated in the causation of debt. For example, there are more likely to be dependent children in households with rent arrears, with fuel debts, and with consumer credit debt than in households without these problems (Duncan and Kirby, 1983; Berthoud, 1981; Adler and Wozniak, 1981; Gregory and Monk, 1981).

The presence of young children may be important in causing debt in at least two ways. Young children both increase demand on resources — they require extra heat, food and clothing that their parents might otherwise be prepared to do without (see Chapter 3) — and reduce per capita income.

Households headed by single parents are also more susceptible to housing and fuel debt than other households (Duncan and Kirby, 1983; Berthoud, 1981; Parker, 1985). As lone-parent households are smaller than other households containing dependent children (see Chapter 7) it seems that the very low incomes which these households have are more important in predisposing them towards debt than is family size.

By contrast, single parents are no more likely to appear in the courts with consumer credit debt than other householders but this probably reflects their lack of access to such credit as much as any other causative factor (Gregory and Monk, 1981).

Budgeting and Financial Decision-making
While structural elements such as low income and disruptions to

income through unemployment play very important roles in the causation of indebtedness, not all people who are in debt have low incomes. Conversely, not all who have low incomes get into debt (though a substantial proportion do). It is obvious, then, that there must be an elective element in the process which leads some people into debt. As was pointed out earlier, most of the research which has attempted to examine budgeting and other forms of financial decision-making has concentrated on the behaviour of people with low incomes. The few indicators to budgeting in high income households that are available come from studies of the impact of unemployment on more affluent workers (Berthoud, 1979). Such studies underline the importance of savings and income from sources other than paid employment in cushioning the effects of unemployment (see Chapter 6).

By contrast, low-income households rarely have such buffers to prevent them becoming indebted. For example, tenants with housing arrears have been found to plan their expenditure as often as do other tenants. However, they find it difficult to keep to such plans when unexpected, or unexpectedly large, demands crop up because their low income makes it unlikely that they would have savings (Duncan and Kirby, 1983).

It is very easy to identify 'poor budgeting' among low-income households because it is only in such households that the consequences of this behaviour become evident. No one cares if the well-paid worker is profligate as long as his or her bills are eventually met.

The Experience of Indebtedness

Presenting statistics about the extent of debt and describing the empirically determined relationships between certain variables and indebtedness give insight into the 'what' and 'why' of this phenomenon. However, they can give little flavour of how it feels to be in debt. While the *experience* of disadvantage is not the focus of this book it is worth presenting the details of some composite examples here in order to convey something of the desperateness of debtors' lives.

Those with 'primary' debts, as described above, are usually in households which are heavily dependent upon state benefits and have often been so for some time. For example, Mrs A was a lone parent with two children of school age, dependent on supplementary benefit after her husband had left her. Mrs A's rent was paid directly to the local authority but she was paying £1 per week extra to repay arrears incurred after her husband had left and before her benefit position had been established. Clothes and household goods were bought using mail-order catalogues and shopping checks. Mrs

A managed to keep up payments on these and put away small amounts towards other commitments such as fuel bills. An unexpectedly large electricity bill, however, caused her to miss several weeks' payments on her catalogues and shopping checks. The caller who normally collected these repayments suggested that Mrs A should have a cash loan to enable her to catch up and to put some money towards the gas bill which had just arrived. Mrs A borrowed £50 and paid off her arrears and the gas bill. She then started to pay back the cash loan at £5 a week over thirteen weeks, in addition to the payments she had already been making before taking out the loan. Six weeks later another electricity bill arrived.

It takes little imagination to predict the outcome of this sort of situation; cases such as this provide citizens' advice bureaux and money advice services with their most frustrating work because there is so little scope for improvement. It is extremely difficult to restore the balance between income and outgoings once it is lost because there are usually no extras in the budget which can be cut until the financial crisis has passed.

Those with 'secondary' debts often find that their problems start with a reduction in previously adequate, or more than adequate, income because of illness or job loss. For example, Mr B was a semi-skilled manual worker with two children at junior school. His wife had a part-time clerical job and, on the strength of both their incomes, they had chosen to buy the local authority house in which they lived. The family enjoyed a good standard of living but most of their income was committed to the mortgage, home improvement loan and hire-purchase agreements for furniture and carpets. The money saved for fuel bills and for car tax and insurance left little spare after food and clothing had been bought.

Mr B was then made redundant and for a while the family managed to juggle the repayments, cut back on food and family outings and, eventually, sold the car. As time passed it became more difficult to maintain all the payments and Mr and Mrs B stopped paying the hire-purchase and home improvement loan. The furniture was repossessed after a county court action and the finance company who had given the home improvement loan (which was secured on the house) started to threaten legal action which could result in the Bs' having to sell their house.

Even if Mr B found another job immediately it would take several years to clear the legacy of debt. If unemployment persisted the family could well find themselves homeless. Many local authorities consider repossession of a home because of mortgage arrears to demonstrate 'intentional' homelessness and refuse to rehouse the families so displaced.

These two 'types' of debt are not mutually exclusive, of course; prolonged income reduction among 'secondary' debtors will eventually bring with it 'primary' debt.

Conclusions

With a million local authority tenants in arrears, one and a half million electricity consumers and a million gas consumers experiencing difficulty paying their fuel bills, between a million and two million people having problems meeting their credit commitments, 169,300 building society mortgage loans in arrears, and 20,550 properties repossessed by building societies, it is clear that personal debt is substantial. Even if there were considerable overlap between the different categories of debt it is unlikely that the total population experiencing these difficulties in England and Wales alone could be much under two million. Neither is it likely that the numbers will decrease substantially in the near future; indeed, the continued growth of the consumer credit market and of long-term unemployment are likely, in their different ways, to trigger further increases.

Even given the growth of credit use among affluent consumers, those most likely to be in debt are individuals and households who are *not* affluent. Debt is largely a function of unemployment and of low per capita income. It is related to the expenses of child-rearing and to the poverty suffered by many lone parents after divorce and separation. The welfare and advice agencies who help debtors, and the county courts who eventually have to deal with them, are thus unlikely to see any reduction in their workload without substantial improvements in the conditions of the most impoverished consumers.

Notes

1. It remains to be seen whether this change will be reversed by the recent return of gas supplies to the private sector.

2. Calculated thus:

Disconnections: 12 months to 31.9.85	101,379
Payment plans agreed (1984)	721,296
25% of those paying after offer of payment plan (1984)	385,340
50% of pre-payment meter installations (1984) say,	98,000
All 'fuel direct' cases (1984)	140,000
	1,437,492
Total domestic electricity consumers 1984–5 (ECC, personal communication)	19,212,000

3. Calculated thus:

Disconnections: 12 months to March 1986	36,948
Payment plans, minus disconnections, 12 months to March 1986, say	529,682
All meter installations, 12 months to March 1986	51,541
All 'fuel direct', 12 months to March 1986, say	405,784
	1,023,955

Total domestic gas consumers, March 1986 (12 months average)   16,129,000

References

Adler, M. and E. Wozniak (1981) 'The Origins and Consequences of Default: an Examination of the Impact of Diligence'. Edinburgh: Department of Social Administration, University of Edinburgh.

Ashley, P. (1983) *The Money Problems of the Poor: a Literature Review*. London: Heinemann Educational Books.

Audit Commission (1984) *Bringing Council Tenants Arrears Under Control*. London: HMSO.

Berthoud, R. (1979) *Unemployed Professionals and Executives*. London: Policy Studies Institute.

Berthoud, R. (1981) *Fuel Debts and Hardship*. London: Policy Studies Institute.

Building Societies Association (BSA) (1985) *Mortgage Repayment Difficulties: Report of a Working Group*. London: BSA.

Building Societies Association (BSA) (1987) *BSA News* 7(2): 3.

Caplovitz, D. (1974) *Consumers in Trouble: a Study of Debtors in Default*. New York: Free Press.

Chartered Institute of Public Finance and Accountancy (CIPFA) (1986) *Housing Revenue Accounts Statistics 1984–5 Actuals*. London: CIPFA Statistical Information Service.

Clark, M. (1978) 'The Unemployed on Supplementary Benefit: Living Standards and Making Ends Meet on a Low Income', *Journal of Social Policy*, 7(4): 385–410.

Culley, L. and P. Downey (1986) *Mortgage Arrears: Owner Occupiers at Risk*. London: Association of Metropolitan Authorities.

Daniel, W.W. (1974) *A National Survey of the Unemployed*. London: Political and Economic Planning.

Department of the Environment (DoE) (1986) *Housing and Construction Statistics June Quarter 1986 Part 1*. London: HMSO.

Duncan, S. and K. Kirby (1983) *Preventing Rent Arrears*. London: HMSO.

Electricity Consumers' Council (ECC) (1985) *Debt Collection, Disconnections and Electricity Consumers: Report of the Operation of the Code of Practice*. London: ECC.

Electricity Consumers' Council (ECC) (1986) *Statistics on the Disconnection of Domestic Consumers for Non-Payment*. London: ECC.

Goode, R., R. Cotterell, H. Gravelle, B. Davies, J. Phipps and T. Davis (1984) 'The Recovery of Judgement Debts in the County Court: Some Preliminary Results.' London: Faculty of Law, Queen Mary College, University of London.

Gregory, J. and J. Monk (1981) *Survey of Defenders in Debt Actions in Scotland*, Research Report for the Scottish Law Commission No. 6. London: HMSO/OPCS Social Survey Division.

Hesketh, J.L. (975) *Fuel Debts: Social Problems in Centrally Heated Council Housing*. Manchester: Family Welfare Association.

Ison, T. (1979) *Credit Marketing and Consumer Protection*. London: Croom Helm.

Knight, I.B. and J.M. Nixon (1975) *Two-parent Families in Receipt of Family Income Supplement, 1972*. London: HMSO.

Leigh-Pemberton, R. (1986) 'Structural Change in Housing Finance'. Speech to the 17th World Congress of the International Union of Building Societies and Savings Associations, Vienna, September 1986.

Lord Chancellor's Department (1987a) *Civil Justice Review Consultation Paper No. 4: Enforcement of Debt*. London: Lord Chancellor's Department.

Lord Chancellor's Department (1987b) *Judicial Statistics 1986*. London: HMSO.

Marsden, D. (1973) *Mothers Alone: Poverty and the Fatherless Family*. Harmondsworth: Penguin Books.

National Consumer Council (NCC) (1976a) *Behind with the Rent — a Study of Council Tenants in Arrears*. London: NCC.

National Consumer Council (NCC) (1976b) *Paying For Fuel*. London: HMSO.

National Consumer Council (NCC) (1980) *Consumers and Credit*. London: NCC.

National Gas Consumers' Council (NGCC) (1985) *Fuel Debts and Hardship: the Working of the Revised Code of Practice*. London: NGCC.

National Gas Consumers' Council (NGCC) (1986) *Gas Disconnection Figures*. London: NGCC.

Office of Fair Trading (OFT)/NOP Surveys Ltd (1979) *Consumer Credit Survey 1977*. London: OFT.

Parker, G. (1983) 'Debt', pp. 56–68 in J. Bradshaw and T. Harris (eds), *Energy and Social Policy*. London: Routledge and Kegan Paul.

Parker, G. (1985) 'Patterns and Causes of Indebtedness: a Study of Clients of the Birmingham Money Advice Centre'. PhD thesis. Birmingham: University of Birmingham.

Parker, G. (1986) 'Unemployment, Low Income and Debt' in I. Ramsay (ed.), *Debtors and Creditors: Socio-legal Perspectives*. Abingdon: Professional Books.

Smith, D.J. (1980) 'How Unemployment Makes the Poor Poorer', *Policy Studies*, 1(1): 20–6.

Ungerson, C. and J. Baldock (1978) 'Rent Arrears in Ashford'. Canterbury: Department of Social Policy and Administration, University of Kent.

THE DISTRIBUTION OF FINANCIAL WELFARE

15
Income Distribution over the Life Cycle

Michael O'Higgins, Jonathan Bradshaw
and Robert Walker

Unlike many other books about the distribution of income and wealth, this volume attempts, through its structure and content, to focus attention explicitly on the relationship between families' needs and resources. In this, it is much influenced by the pioneering work of Seebohm Rowntree in York at the turn of the century. Rowntree (1901) identified five stages in the life of a labourer, 'five alternating periods of want and comparative plenty': childhood, early working adulthood, having children, working life after children grow up and old age. Four of these five stages are reflected in chapters included in the first part of the book.

While grounded in detailed research and observation, Rowntree's five stages are perhaps best viewed as an idealised model of the life cycle, or as an 'ideal type' (Weber, 1946). Although based on the experience of a labourer, the model, with its emphasis on periods of *comparative* want and plenty over an individual's lifetime, is equally applicable to persons in other social classes. However, not all individuals will necessarily pass through every stage, nor will each person's life path follow precisely the same sequence. Moreover, the model, though it finds echoes in, for example, the four stages (āśramas) of Hindu life (Sen, 1961), is nevertheless culturally and temporally specific. Divorce and separation, certainly on a large scale, are recent phenomena which post-date Rowntree's inquiries by six decades. Divorce and remarriage (or the possibility of new, more or less, permanent unions outside marriage) mean that increasing numbers of individuals are repeating certain of Rowntree's life-cycle stages. Moreover, both separation and divorce add a new 'stage' of relative want which fits uneasily into Rowntree's model (see Chapter 7).

Likewise, the periods of want associated with unemployment and disability do not fit neatly into the Rowntree model. This does not mean that either phenomenon had escaped Rowntree's attention; rather, in 1901 the finding which most impressed Rowntree's contemporaries was the extent of poverty found among the gainfully employed (Harris, 1977: 54). Less than one in twenty of families in 'primary poverty' were poor because of irregularity of work or unemployment, whereas a half were in regular work. By the 1930s the situation had changed, as indeed had theories about the nature of unemployment and the potential role of government (e.g. Keynes, 1936). In Rowntree's study in 1935 (in which he employed a different measure of poverty), a third of recorded poverty was the result of inadequate pay and over a quarter was caused by unemployment (Rowntree, 1941; Veit Wilson, 1984).

Rowntree did not distinguish disability from illness in either his 1901 or 1941 study. In the former, illness itself was coupled with old age and it was concluded that about 5 per cent of 'primary poverty' was due to the incapacity of the chief wage earner through 'accident, illness or old age'. In both studies Rowntree was more interested to determine the impact of poverty on health rather than in estimating the importance of ill-health as a cause of poverty. In 1941 he considered old age and illness separately as causes of poverty and concluded that, in quantitative terms, old age was more than three times more important than illness.

A further weakness with Rowntree's formulation, as Jane Millar explains in Chapter 7, is that it assumes that the family is a 'self-contained unit within which all family members share in the same fortunes and misfortunes'. That this is not always the case will be plain from reading Chapter 13. There are important distinctions to be made between earning, controlling, managing and consuming within families. There is also evidence that in a substantial minority of households 'men contribute a relatively small proportion of their income to collective expenditure, so that the consumption pattern of the husband is more affluent than that of his wife' (p. 209 above). Unfortunately, neither the methodology nor the data are yet available to explore intra-familial inequality adequately on a national scale (though, see Taylor-Gooby, 1985).

It is nevertheless appropriate, despite criticisms of Rowntree's model, to conclude this volume with an analysis of the distribution of income and expenditure over the life cycle. It brings together much of the material discussed in the sections devoted to 'costs' and 'resources' and facilitates consideration of the extent to which the allocation of resources equates with the distribution of financial needs. But, more than this, it enables a simulation of the pattern of inequality based on income flows and changing needs across peoples' lives which results in a different, and arguably, more meaningful picture of financial welfare than is possible from traditional cross-sectional studies. For example, take two men with the same income: their circumstances would be treated as identical under the more usual cross-sectional analysis. In reality, however, one individual may have worked for fifteen years and be almost at the peak of his earning capacity. He may then be made redundant at fifty and, after retirement, have only a relatively small occupational pension with which to supplement his pension. By contrast, the other may, after five years of work, have just established himself successfully on a career ladder, so that with salary increments and promotions a consistently-rising real income is assured; he may have marketable skills, and may retire with a handsome capital sum and an occupational pension relative to which his state pension is merely a minor supplement. These sketches or typologies are not simply extreme examples of an occasional occurrence: they represent patterns of life chances common in different groups in society. Consequently, the lifetime inequalities which are concealed by a snapshot of annual equality are predictable and account needs to be taken of them in analyses of the distribution of income.

Simple cross-sectional analysis may also operate to conceal *equalities*, that is, to portray as inequalities income differences which if measured over a lifetime might amount to nothing. Thus, the fact that one person's annual income is twice as large as another's may simply indicate that the first is nearing the peak of his career while the second, with precisely the same career, may still be on the early rungs of the ladder.

The foregoing discussion suggests two focuses for analysis which occupy a central place in this chapter: first, a consideration of the degree of inequality which exists *between* life-cycle groups and, secondly, an examination of the inequalities *within* life-cycle groups and which, therefore, cannot be attributed to life-cycle effects. Later, the chapter returns to three major themes which have emerged elsewhere in the book. The first addresses the impact of recent economic, social and demographic developments on the pattern of inequality. The second concerns the way in which some people are able to manage the different financial needs which they experience at various stages in their lives by, for example, saving or by investing in owner occupation. Finally attention shifts to the response of the state to the vertical and horizontal inequalities existing in British society. But, first, some discussion is warranted of the life-cycle groups used in the analysis.

Defining the Life Cycle

Although the analysis of life-cycle inequalities presented in this chapter was conceived independently of the book, the life-cycle groups employed closely mirror the distinctions drawn in earlier chapters. Table 15.1 lists ten life-cycle categories defined in terms of a number of characteristics: age of adults, marital status, age of the youngest and/or oldest child, number of children, number of adults and economic status (specifically, whether retired or not). Within a general aim of including as large as possible a proportion of the overall sample, and constrained by the vagaries of the Family Expenditure Survey (FES) data (see, for example, Hakim, 1982; Bulmer, 1986), the intention was to confine membership of each category to households which are among themselves highly comparable and which represent clear phases or stages of life. Furthermore, though the categories are discrete, the life-cycle groups represent a progression of stages through which a household might pass; in that sense, the categories represent sets of adjacent points on a continuous variable. As with Rowntree's original formulation, however, this is not to deny the importance or legitimacy of other patterns of progress through life, or to suggest that movement from one group to the next is part of some inevitable, ordered sequence.

The first two groups, younger adults and couples without children, belong to the first of Rowntree's two periods of comparative plenty in adulthood prior to having children. Comparatively

TABLE 15.1   *Life-cycle groups in 1982*

Life-cycle group[1]	Percentages
1 Young single (one adult aged under 35)	3.2
2 Young married (married couple, female under 35)	5.3
3 Family formation (married couple, children all under 5)	7.2
4 Middle childrearing (married couple, at least one under 5 rest aged 5–15)	5.7
5 Complete family (married couple, children all aged 5–15)	12.9
6 Early dispersal (married couple, one child 5–15, one or more 16+)	4.7
7 Two generations (married couple, no children under 16, at least one 16–24)	6.7
8 Empty nest (married couple, male 45–65)	9.8
9 Early retirement (married couple, both pensioners)	8.4
10 Old and single (one adult, pensioner)	13.2
11 Lone parent (lone parents with children under 16)	3.2
Unclassified	19.8

[1] Total number of households = 7,428.

few people fall into these two categories, 8.5 per cent in 1982, reflecting the relative brevity of this period of affluence.

Three stages in childrearing are recognised — an entirely pre-school stage (family formation), a mixed pre-school and compulsory school stage (middle childrearing) and an entirely compulsory school stage (complete family). The rationale for these distinctions are evident from reading Chapter 3. Most important are the opportunity costs imposed on families by pre-school-age children which mean that only 26 per cent of mothers are gainfully employed (compared with 64 per cent with older children), and the increased consumption of older children (General Household Survey [GHS], 1986). Almost 26 per cent of the sample fall in these three stages which together typically account for a substantial proportion of an adult's pre-retirement years.

The stages of 'early dispersal' and 'two generations' are conceptually straightforward. The first, as defined, consists of couples with children both of compulsory school age and also aged over sixteen; it is the period when children start being old enough to take a job, to go to college or leave home, and are thus beginning to be less dependent on their parents. The 'two generation' stage comprises couples who only have children aged between sixteen and twenty-four living at home; the children are all old enough to take jobs or to enter further education and training and are becoming independent of their parents. Unfortunately, data limitations prevent fully comparable definitions being used for the years prior to 1982 (see Table 15.6 below).

The 'empty nest' stage forms the core of Rowntree's second period of comparative plenty, since it consists of couples without children where the husband is in middle age but not yet retired. This is the third largest group, with around one-tenth of sample households.

The final two groups are pensioner households, although not all of the individuals are necessarily fully retired from the labour market. Together they account for more than one-fifth of households with twice as many elderly single adult households as elderly couples. As would be expected from the discussion in Chapter 4, women comprise the majority of the second group and for some of them this stage may be one of the longest that they experience.

One-fifth of the sample does not fit into the classification and includes such household types as lone-parent families, multi-adult, non-nuclear family households, and middle-aged unmarried adults. As Chapters 2 and 7 show, lone-parent families are a growing group that is important to policy, not least because typically they have relatively few resources in relation to their needs. Nevertheless, in

1982 they still formed only 3.2 per cent of households in the FES sample although, of course, a much higher proportion of children are likely to spend some time in a lone-parent family. Moreover, lone-parent families are difficult to place in the life cycle because they do not form a homogeneous group; they range from the young unmarried mother, through the separated and divorced to the middle-aged widow (see also Chapter 2, Figure 2.1). For this reason they are treated as a separate group in the discussion which follows.

Patterns of Inequality

Following Rowntree, the contention is that a part of the inequality evident in the distribution of income is associated with life-cycle factors. It is explicable, therefore, though not necessarily justifiable, in terms of the changes in the nature of a household which may be expected to take place over time and which, in the British context, are often associated with changes in family needs and resources. This component of inequality is considered first before examining the evidence of inequality which cannot be attributed to life-cycle effects.

Life-cycle Inequalities: Income and Expenditure
Table 15.2 presents the average income and expenditure for each of the life-cycle groups (income is defined net of direct taxes and national insurance contributions). No account is taken of differences in household composition. On this basis income is greatest

TABLE 15.2   *Net household income and expenditure by life-cycle groups, 1982*

Life-cycle group	Net income (£ p.w.)	Expenditure (£ p.w.)	Expenditure relative to net income (%)
Young single	95	92	96
Young married	189	156	83
Family formation	151	140	93
Middle childrearing	158	148	94
Complete family	178	167	94
Early dispersal	221	209	95
Two generations	234	228	97
Empty nest	149	134	90
Early retirement	93	90	98
Old and single	54	54	99
Lone parent	86	86	100

among young couples before children arrive, and among families containing children over sixteen; many wives in the latter group will have returned to work and the older children may themselves be contributing to total family income. Income is lowest among both the young and old who are living alone.

The comparison of income with expenditure in Table 15.2 is also of interest. Due to the way in which income and expenditure are measured in the Family Expenditure Survey the difference between them cannot be interpreted as a direct measure of savings (FES, 1986). However, the relative difference between the various life-cycle groups, when interpreted as an indication of their relative savings potential, probably reasonably reflects the true situation. On this basis it would appear that young married couples have the greatest potential and may be saving about a fifth of their income. They may be deliberately setting aside resources in the expectation of starting a family or buying a home of their own. Alternatively they may be saving simply because their outgoings happen to fall short of their income. Likewise, couples at the 'empty nest' stage of the life cycle seem to be saving hard, presumably in preparation for retirement.

Considering, next, Rowntree's periods of relative 'want', child-rearing and old age, two different patterns are evident. The estimates of income and expenditure for households of pensionable age are virtually identical, suggesting that little income is left over for saving. Indeed, some pensioners will be running down their savings while others will be living off the interest (see Chapter 4 and below). Families with younger children, on the other hand, do appear on average to be setting modest sums aside. One may speculate that this reflects the 'responsibility' inherent in the parental role with a need to plan for unexpected contingencies. Alternatively, and perhaps in addition, it could be that they are saving for those future expenses which can be predicted well in advance, for example, the costs of older children and, thinking further ahead, of retirement and old age.

Life-cycle Inequalities: Financial Welfare
The central theme of this volume is that the living standards available to households may be as much affected by their different sizes and composition as by their varying incomes. Consequently, in Table 15.3 net income and expenditure are adjusted for household size to yield approximate measures of financial welfare (see Appendix, p. 250). Figure 15.1 illustrates the effect of this transformation by plotting adjusted and unadjusted net income for each life-cycle group.

TABLE 15.3   *Net equivalent household income and expenditure for life-cycle groups, 1982*

Life-cycle group	Equivalent net income (£ p.w.)	Equivalent net expenditure (£ p.w.)	Rank order of affluence[1]
Young single	156	150	2
Young married	189	156	1
Family formation	112	104	5
Middle childrearing	88	82	10
Complete family	103	96	6
Early dispersal	94	89	7/8
Two generations	123	121	4
Empty nest	149	134	3
Early retirement	93	90	8/7
Old and single	89	88	9
Lone parent	69	69	11

[1] First number is rank on equivalent income, the second on equivalent expenditure.

Rowntree's predicted pattern of periods of relative want and plenty is clearly evident in Table 15.3. Periods of want coincide with childrearing and old age, and periods of relative plenty with early adulthood before the arrival of children and with the years that follow their departure. The effect of the transformation to equivalent income and expenditure (see Chapter 1), as Figure 15.1 shows, is to highlight the relative deprivation of families with children. No family type with children aged under sixteen has a standard of living more than two-thirds that of a young married couple. But, underlining what is said in Chapter 7, lone parents are by far and away the least affluent group with an average living standard little more than three-quarters of that of single pensioners. Single pensioners and families in the middle stage of childrearing suffer similar degrees of deprivation. However, the level of expenditure, or consumption, of these families is noticeably lower than for pensioners since, as was noted above, they may be managing to set small sums aside, presumably to meet future expenditures.

To recap, the model of alternating phases of relative want and prosperity which Rowntree identified as coinciding with clear stages in the life cycle would appear to be as appropriate in 1982 as it was in 1899. The impact of children on living standards is profound. Moreover, the substance of this conclusion is little affected by the choice of equivalences as the Appendix to this chapter indicates. As

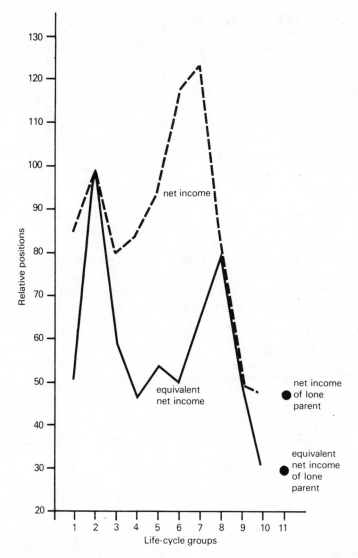

FIGURE 15.1 *Patterns of well-being of life-cycle groups comparing equivalent net income with net income*

See Table 15.1 for a description of each numbered group.

Cooke writes in Chapter 4: 'Children bring a mixture of pleasure and pain to parents, but they also invariably represent an economic cost.'

Inequalities within Life-cycle Groups

The discussion so far has assumed a fair degree of homogeneity of circumstances within the life-cycle groups and statistical tests in fact confirm that the differences between life-cycle groups are greater than the differences within them. However, as Table 15.4 shows, the variation in living standards *within* each life-cycle group is nevertheless considerable. In each life-cycle group some households have sufficient incomes to place them in the top quintile of living standards, while others are found in the lowest quintile.

Some of the reasons underlying these inequalities have been highlighted in earlier chapters, especially Chapters 8 to 11. Moreover, there is a very extensive literature which discusses the nature and causes of income inequalities and within which many nuances of interpretation and fundamental differences of opinion exist (see Atkinson, 1983). Suffice it to say that a family's position in relation to the labour market proves to be a critical determinant of their financial welfare and that this is in turn determined by a wide range of structural and individual influences (some of which may themselves be related to life-cycle factors). Additional considerations such as the ownership and transfer of physical assets and wealth (see Chapter 10) and the redistributive role of the state are also important (see below and, for example, Nolan, 1986; O'Higgins, 1985; Le Grand, 1986).

Some indication of the importance of class and employment on

TABLE 15.4   *The distribution of equivalent income within life-cycle groups, 1982*

Life-cycle group	Quintiles of equivalent net income[1]				
	Bottom (%)	2nd (%)	3rd (%)	4th (%)	Top (%)
Young single	14	8	14	20	44
Young married	3	2	5	21	70
Family formation	16	15	27	25	18
Middle childrearing	31	21	27	15	6
Complete family	23	19	25	21	13
Early dispersal	26	23	25	19	7
Two generations	6	12	26	36	21
Empty nest	8	11	16	26	39
Early retirement	28	32	20	12	9
Old and single	22	41	19	11	7
Lone parents	65	19	8	5	3

[1] The figures represent the percentage of households in a particular life-cycle group who are in each quintile, i.e., except where there are discrepancies due to rounding, they sum across the rows to 100 per cent in each life-cycle group.

household resources is given in Table 15.5. Occupational class is often treated as a surrogate for the impact of structural and economic factors on a person's life chances. Table 15.5 shows that *within* each life-cycle group up to a quarter of the variation in net income can be attributed to differences in occupation. As might be expected, occupational differences have the least marked impact on income in the early stages of life before the careers of young professionals and managers have taken off. They are also less important when older children are contributing substantially to families' incomes.

TABLE 15.5   *Factors affecting the distribution of equivalent income within life-cycle groups, 1982*

| Life-cycle group | Percentage of variation within life-cycle group due to occupation of head of household[1] | Percentage of households with | | Income of households with no worker as a % of income where someone is in work[2] |
		no earner	more than one earner	
Young single	6	20	—	39
Young married	15	3	88	47
Family formation	24	5	31	50
Middle childrearing	22	8	30	57
Complete family	16	5	67	53
Early dispersal	11	2	83	51
Two generations	16	1	88	62
Empty nest	21	16	47	55
Early retirement	N/A	86	3	68
Old and single	N/A	94	—	78
Lone parents	19	52	4	72

[1] Occupation (excluding those retired, unoccupied or members of HM forces) categorised into professional and managerial, clerical, skilled manual and other manual.
[2] Equivalent net income.

The impact of employment, and the lack of it, is also evident from Table 15.5. The reasons why households might lack somebody in employment vary by life-cycle group. Most pensioners have retired — indeed, for many the state pension is conditional on retirement — while child-care responsibilities keep many single parents out of employment. Unemployment is more of a factor among the young (20 per cent were not employed though some of these will have been students) and among many couples in the 'empty nest' phase of life, although sickness and disability is also important at this age. The net incomes of households with nobody in employment are usually little more than half those of corresponding households where somebody is working. The discrepancy in incomes is greatest among single young people and, more generally, where there are younger children in the household. The latter phenomenon probably reflects the less generous rates paid for younger children under most social security schemes. Even for couples over retirement age, many of whom stand to lose part of their pension if they work, having a job appears to boost average net incomes by 28 per cent, other things being equal.

The presence of two or more earners can add considerably to the financial welfare of a family. Walker, for example, demonstrates in Chapter 2 that a second income is a virtual prerequisite for a couple to purchase a house of their own, and this largely explains the high incomes of young married couples recorded in Tables 15.3 and 15.4. The presence or absence of a second earner helps account for the widely different levels of financial welfare found *within* each stage of childrearing (see Tables 15.4 and 15.5). For example, 43 per cent of families in the 'family formation stage' have equivalent incomes in the top two quintiles. Of these families, 46 per cent have two earners compared with just 6 per cent of those with equivalent incomes in the lowest quintile. Moreover, variations in the propensity for both parents to work — reflecting, for example, the constraints imposed by pre-school-age children — also explain some of the differences in financial welfare which exist *between* the childrearing stages in the life cycle. Finally, in similar vein, the relative prosperity of 'early dispersal' and of 'two generation' families is often due to the earnings of wives and particularly of older children, although whether the additional income generated by children is pooled to the equal benefit of all members of these households is doubtful (see Chapter 2; Cusack and Roll, 1985).

Whatever the other factors which impinge on individuals' life chances it is clear that life-cycle factors are very important. Seventy per cent of young childless couples have equivalent incomes in the top quintile while about 60 per cent of pensioner households have incomes in the lowest quintile. Lone-parent families, in particular, are concentrated in the lowest quintile while the position of other families, though more variable, tends towards the lower half of the equivalent income distribution.

Recent Changes

Earlier chapters have drawn attention to the rapid pace of economic and social change evident in Britain during the 1970s and 1980s. The growth of unemployment (see Chapter 6) is perhaps the most obvious development, but there have been other economic changes, including the marked shift in employment away from manufacturing towards the service sector and, with it, an increase in employment opportunities for women, albeit often in low-paid, part-time jobs (see Chapter 8). Council house sales, and to a lesser extent privatisation, have broadened the base of the ownership of wealth (Chapter 10). There has been a substantial increase in non-cash transactions including, for example, non-monetary payments from employment (see Chapter 9) and the growth of credit sales (see Chapter 12); these have rapidly expanded the opportunities for some groups to adjust their income flows better to match current and future demands.

Turning to social changes, people are marrying and having fewer children later, while their offspring are leaving home earlier — often to set up on their own (see Chapter 2). Separation and divorce and the number of lone-parent households have all increased (see Chapters 2 and 7), while, within marriages, it seems likely that conjugal roles are shifting, albeit slowly, partly in response to the new economic and social opportunities open to women (see Chapter 13).

These social and economic changes are likely to have an impact on different types of households in a variety of ways, some of which have been considered in earlier chapters. Table 15.6 attempts to summarise their impact on living standards, as evidenced in the Family Expenditure Survey. The analysis is unavoidably partial. Some changes — for instance, in non-money incomes — may not be picked up at all. Others will take a long time to work through the system: the growth in owner occupation, for example, entails short-term costs and longer-term gains for different life-cycle groups. Additionally, the cross-sectional nature of the data is somewhat problematic. The life-cycle groups do not comprise the same people eleven years later although they are drawn from the same population cohort. More importantly, it cannot be assumed that differences over the eleven years reflect the outcome of processes operating during the intervening years; they may simply reflect generational differences that in turn result from processes existent prior to 1971.

Despite these very real limitations, a perusal of Tables 15.4 and 15.6 together proves to be rewarding. First, comparison of the relative values of equivalent net income between the two years reveals that the living standards of families with children have fallen both in relation to the index household (young married couples) and in relation to pensioners and young single people. However, there

TABLE 15.6 *The change in the distribution of equivalent income, 1971–82*[1]

| Life-cycle group | Quintiles of equivalent net income 1971[2] | | | | | Relative value of equivalent net income[3] | |
	Bottom (%)	2nd (%)	3rd (%)	4th (%)	Top (%)	1971 (%)	1982 (%)
Young single	3	8	17	26	46	84	84
Young married	2	3	7	21	67	100	100
Family formation	10	20	33	25	12	61	59
Middle childrearing	33	30	21	11	6	48	46
Complete family	17	23	28	21	12	58	54
Early dispersal[4]	22	32	28	13	5	50	49
Two generations[4]	7	17	34	22	18	66	60
Empty nest	6	12	14	29	39	86	79
Early retirement	45	27	15	8	6	45	49
Old and single	43	30	11	9	7	48	47

[1] See also Table 15.4.

[2] The figures represent the percentage of households in a particular life-cycle group who are in each quintile, i.e., except where there are discrepancies due to rounding, they sum across the rows to 100 per cent in each life-cycle group.

[3] Average equivalent income for each life-cycle group expressed as a percentage of the average equivalent income for young married couples (the index group).

[4] Older children aged 16 and 17; compare Table 15.1.

are important differences between the experiences of families at different stages of childrearing, which are partly explicable in terms of changing demographic factors and the selective impact of unemployment. Take, for example, younger families with children. These groups experienced quite substantial falls in income (relative to childless couples) between 1971 and 1982. For complete families this fall was translated directly into a 4 per cent fall in living standards relative to couples. However, in the case of families in the middle of childrearing, the impact of an even larger fall in income was lessened by a compensating fall in household size reflecting the lower birthrates in the 1970s. In fact, Table 15.6 suggests that changes in this group led to the living standards of families with above average incomes being squeezed while the relative position of those with below average earnings advanced somewhat.

In marked contrast to families in the middle of childrearing, the 1970s witnessed an increase in inequality among newly formed families. The proportion with equivalent incomes falling in the bottom decile increased from 10 to 16 per cent between 1971 and 1982 while the proportion with incomes in the top decile rose from

12 to 18 per cent. The mechanisms by which this change was brought about are unclear. The simple explanation of increased opportunities for female employment for some groups generating more two-earner families, juxtaposed with higher levels of unemployment for others, does not seem in accord with the facts; the transformation had already happened by 1976 before the main rise in unemployment occurred.

Marked changes also occurred in the financial circumstances of families with older children. Unfortunately, a direct comparison between 1971 and 1982 is only possible for 'early dispersal' and 'two generation' families with older children aged sixteen or seventeen. Early dispersal families, defined in this way, experienced the largest relative fall in living standards of any family type (six percentage points), while 'two generation' families experienced the smallest fall of any family with children (one percentage point). In 1971 both family types were relatively common, reflecting the baby boom of the late 1950s. By 1982 the numbers had dropped by over 50 per cent, partly because the effects of the baby boom had passed and partly because of youngsters leaving home earlier (the number of young single-person households in the sample increased by 246 per cent between 1971 and 1982). Moreover, the families were, on average, smaller in 1982 than in 1971. Reflecting this fact, and perhaps also the higher levels of unemployment among teenagers, average net income, unadjusted for household size, fell in relation to the incomes of childless married couples, by between 16 per cent (early dispersal stage) and 24 per cent (two generation stage). For families in the early dispersal phase this substantial relative fall in resources was almost entirely offset by changes in the size and composition of families within the group. To a lesser extent this was also true of two generation families but the proportion of them that were very affluent (top quintile) fell by half, probably due to the collapse of employment opportunities for young people.

Two final observations are appropriate, one concerning the impact of unemployment, the other relating to the economic welfare of the elderly. First, some of the financial consequences of higher levels of unemployment among the young and among older workers (see Chapter 7) can be deduced from Table 15.6. In the eleven years to 1982 the chances of a single person falling in the bottom quintile of the equivalent income distribution more than quadrupled. Likewise, the edge was taken off the spell of affluence prior to retirement.

Secondly, Table 15.6 highlights the improvement that has taken place in the financial welfare of retired households. In 1971, almost half of the households in each of the two retired life-cycle groups were in the bottom quintile of the equivalent income distribution, and more than a quarter of each were in the second quintile. By 1982, the proportion of each in the bottom quintile had been almost halved to around a quarter. While some of this shift is reflected in the second quintile, which in 1982 contained almost a third of retired couples and two-fifths of retired single adults, much of it goes higher up the distribution: the proportion of retired couples in the top three equivalent quintiles increased from 29 per cent in 1971 to 41 per cent in 1982; the corresponding figures for retired single adults are 27 per cent and 36 per cent. These changes are substantial and not fully explained simply by the replacement of retired persons in the lower quintiles by the new poor created by unemployment (see Chapter 4). In part they reflect the increased numbers of pensioners retiring with better occupational pensions. The net effect is that inequality among pensioners is increasing: those without resources other than the basic state pension remain as poor as ever, but newer cohorts contain greater numbers of more affluent pensioners (see Chapter 4). However, despite these changes, it remains true that retirement is a period of relative want as severe as any experienced in other life-cycle stages (single parents excluded).

Managing Resources over the Life Cycle

It is arguable that the periods of relative want and plenty which are experienced over the life cycle would be even more extreme were it not for the fact that they are, in broad terms, predictable. In practice individuals, either through personal saving or by collective action through state or private agencies, attempt to even out flows in their lifetime incomes. As a consequence one might expect the principal sources of income to change over the life cycle; Table 15.7 illustrates that this is the case.

The structures which facilitate life-cycle management of resources are most developed with respect to retirement. For those reaching retirement age in Britain exclusion from the labour market is almost unavoidable (see Chapter 4) but, because this eventuality is known well in advance, it is easy to plan for. Table 15.7 shows that, on average, about 8 per cent of the income of retired households comes from investments and, in the case of couples, another 16 per cent from private and occupational pensions. Both these sources of income reflect savings in earlier life, although not all saving is voluntary: contributions to occupational pension schemes are often compulsory and reflect a social, rather than a personal response to the inevitability of retirement. Some 60 per cent of the average pensioners' income takes the form of a national insurance pension

TABLE 15.7 *Sources of income for all life-cycle groups, 1982*

	Young single (%)	Young married (%)	Family formation (%)	Middle child-rearing (%)	Complete family (%)	Early dispersal (%)	Two genera-tions (%)	Empty nest (%)	Early retire-ment (%)	Old and single (%)	Lone parent (%)
Earnings/self-employment	73	93	84	78	83	84	86	72	4	2	26
Investment	2	1	1	1	1	2	2	5	8	8	1
Occupational pensions/ annuities	0	0	0	0	0	0	2	6	16	11	1
NI pensions	0	0	0	0	0	0	1	2	63	62	3
Unemployment benefit	2	1	3	0	1	1	2	2	0	0	0
Health-related benefits	0	1	0	2	1	3	3	8	2	1	1
Child benefit	0	0	5	9	6	5	1	0	0	0	14
Means-tested benefits	11	2	6	7	5	3	2	4	5	12	43
Other state benefits	0	0	0	0	0	0	0	0	0	1	0
Other income	12	2	1	2	1	2	1	0	0	0	11
Total[1]	100	100	100	100	100	100	100	100	100	100	100

[1] Gross Income: some columns do not add to 100 because of rounding.

which is the state's principal response to the social inevitability of retirement (see Chapter 2).

Social responses to two other life-cycle contingencies are also evident from Table 15.7. One is childrearing and the payment of child benefit to families with children. The second is the increasing prevalence of sickness and disability which accompanies later working life and is reflected in social security payments to the pre-retirement households.

Earlier (Table 15.2) evidence was presented suggesting savings to meet these contingencies, especially prior to having children (although in the middle childrearing years as well) and in the years just before retirement. Individual saving, however, is obviously conditional upon having sufficient resources to set money aside as well as having the inclination and reason to do so. This is illustrated by Table 15.8 which considers those life-cycle groups for which expenditure recorded in the Family Expenditure Survey is substantially less than their disposable income; that is, those groups which on average appear most likely to be saving. The higher a household's income in relation to its needs, the larger the weekly amount which would appear to be 'saved'. It is also evident that higher social classes tend to 'save' more than lower social classes

TABLE 15.8 *Weekly income less expenditure according to equivalent net income and social grade (£ per week)*

Life-cycle group	Quintiles of equivalent net income				
	Bottom (£ p.w.)	2nd (£ p.w.)	3rd (£ p.w.)	4th (£ p.w.)	Top (£ p.w.)
Young married	−35	—	−9	10	46
Family formation	−15	−1	8	5	57
Middle childrearing	−12	3	12	14	138
Complete family	−13	−5	6	19	75
Empty nest	−14	−7	−1	12	35

	Social grade[1]			
	AB (£ p.w.)	C1 (£ p.w.)	C2 (£ p.w.)	DE (£ p.w.)
Young married	59	18	26	1
Family formation	26	7	8	−6
Middle childrearing	23	−18	11	−2
Complete family	33	5	3	−5
Empty nest	20	8	−5	−2

[1] Social grade roughly translates as: AB — higher-paid professionals, managers and administrative staff; C1 — lower-paid administrative and clerical staff; C2 — skilled manual; DE — other manual. The smallest number in any cell (middle childrearing C1 families) is 40.

(noting, though, that manual workers in class C2 average higher net — but not net equivalent — incomes than do non-manual workers assigned to class C1).

The failure, or inability, to save, is likely to have serious financial repercussions later in life. It is impossible directly to confirm this using the Family Expenditure Survey since one cannot know what the financial circumstances of those now in their twenties will be when they retire. Likewise, it is difficult to estimate the income flows generated by investing in owner occupation (see Chapter 10). However, Table 15.9 shows that the financial circumstances of pensioners belonging to social groups that are currently most likely to be saving are much more secure than those of other pensioners. The investment income of retired AB couples is virtually four times that of any other group and sixteen times that of DE households. Indeed, over half of the gross income of retired AB couples (itself much above the average income for all types of households) is derived from savings and deferred income, that is from investments, occupational pensions and annuities, compared with less than a third of the income of C1 and C2 pensioners and only a tenth of the income of DE pensioners.

TABLE 15.9   *The investment and pension income of retired couples, 1982*

| Source of income | Social grade of household head | | | |
	AB	C1	C2	DE
Investments				
Amount (£)	48	13	8	3
% of gross income	20	11	8	4
Occupational pensions and activities				
Amount (£)	70	21	20	5
% of gross income	36	18	21	7
Total gross income (£)	205	113	97	72
Total net income (£)	169	105	92	69

The labour market, fiscal regime and opportunities for saving have, of course, changed radically since many current pensioners were at work and were preparing financially for retirement. Recent changes are likely to have an impact on future generations. For example, unemployment has differentially affected older workers in the 'empty nest' stage of the life cycle and, linked to this, increasing numbers are effectively retiring prematurely on health grounds (see, also, Bosanquet, 1987). These groups will therefore enter old age without benefiting from Rowntree's second period of prosperity and having missed out on this opportunity to set money aside for retirement. The result may be that the traditional pattern in retirement of the risk of poverty increasing with age may be substantially modified by the arrival of a cohort of younger but less financially secure pensioners. At the same time, the maturing of SERPS (the State Earnings Related Pension Scheme) and the spread of occupational pension schemes will improve the position of other groups of pensioners, thus adding to the inequality among pensioners.

Similarly, the very high level of unemployment among young single people is likely to deny them rapid access to owner occupation on marriage. This is likely not only to increase current expenditure on housing, and therefore to inhibit saving, but also to mean that owner occupation is achieved later in life when the front loading of mortgage interest payments is likely to coincide with periods traditionally associated with high levels of saving.

Developments of this kind may have profound effects on individuals' attempts to manage their lifetime resources and to necessitate substantial changes to be made to the tax and social security systems and require new responses from savings institutions.

The Role of Government

Table 15.7 illustrated the varying contribution which the state makes, through the social security system, to the financial well-being of families at different stages in the life cycle. First come family benefits for children and parents, then sickness and disability benefits followed by retirement pensions in early old age. Pensions are then often supplemented by means-tested benefits in the later years when assets fall and occupational pensions are eroded by inflation or cease with the husband's death. Within this sequence the state responds to less predictable contingencies such as marital breakdown, widowhood and, of course, unemployment.

The state also responds to life cycle needs with provisions in kind through, for example, the education, health and domiciliary services. Moreover, similar concerns are evident in the tax system: direct taxes ostensibly seek to tax people according to their ability to pay; indirect taxes sometimes attempt to avoid having an impact on particular groups (for example, the VAT exemption on childrens' clothing).

By raising and spending money in this way the government effects a transfer of resources between families at different stages in the life cycle, and hence with different needs (horizontal redistribution), and between families with different resources in the same stage of life (vertical redistribution). It also makes provision for the compulsory transfer of resources from one stage in a person's life to another. However, governments' actions are seldom informed directly (or even indirectly) by analyses of individual needs and requirements such as those presented in this volume. In practice, the outcomes of government activity are frequently mutually confounding, often because separate policies have been evolved on the basis of narrow objectives and because the actual effects of these policies have been ignored (Sandford et al., 1980; Walker, 1982; Atkinson et al., 1986).

It cannot be assumed that individual behaviour is not in turn affected by government policies (Ross et al., 1985; Burtless and Haveman, 1985). For example, it is possible, if unlikely, that people save less for retirement because they know that they will receive a state pension and can supplement this by claiming some form of means-tested assistance (Munnell, 1987). Moreover, Rowntree noted as long ago as 1936 how employers were reacting to government provisions on pensions: the 'tendency for employers to dismiss old workers more readily than they would have done had there been no scheme of state pensions [as in 1899]' (Rowntree, 1941, p. 114).

Several studies have discussed in detail the distributional consequences of public expenditure and fiscal policies and have also rightly underlined the technical difficulties of providing an accurate picture (Central Statistical Office [CSO], 1985; Le Grand, 1982, 1986; Smeeding, 1984; O'Higgins, 1980). However, none has adopted a life-cycle perspective (though see Layard, 1974; Hedström and Ringen, 1985; Nicholson, 1981; Rottman et al., 1982; and, also, Jenkins, 1986). One simple, albeit partial, description of this process of state transfers is provided by comparing the social security benefits received by a family and the amount paid in direct taxation. Clearly, this index excludes the impact of benefits in kind and the effect of the indirect tax system although, for 1982, it reflects most government subsidies to owner occupation (though not those going to local authority housing). Its value lies less in describing the transfers achieved than in giving a glimpse of the state's perception of relative needs.

Figure 15.2 plots the value of benefits minus taxes for each life-cycle group according to the level of the household's equivalent 'original' income, that is their income prior to receipt of benefits and before the levying of taxes after accounting for differences in household needs. It shows that for most life-cycle groups the break between receiving a net gain and making a net loss through the tax-benefit system occurs between the second and third quintiles of

original income, although the average benefit received by households in the second quintile is generally very small. The exception is
pensioners who continue to receive a net gain up to the fourth
quintile of net income reflecting the fact that the state pension is not
means-tested.

The treatment of households in the bottom quintile of original

	Quintiles of equivalent original income				
Life-cycle group	Bottom (£ p.w.)	2nd (£ p.w.)	3rd (£ p.w.)	4th (£ p.w.)	Top (£ p.w.)
Young single	+30	+1	−7	−19	−44
Young married	+51	[+9]	−2	−29	−64
Family formation	+64	+1	−16	−32	−62
Middle childrearing	+88	0	−25	−41	−105
Complete family	+80	+2	−23	−43	−97
Early dispersal	+90	+10	−36	−66	−121
Two generations	+72	+30	−21	−58	−102
Empty nest	+57	+34	−11	−28	−64
Early retirement	+60	+49	+30	+18	−22
Old and single	+42	+31	+22	+9	−13
Lone parent	+63	+26	−10	−23	[−46]

FIGURE 15.2 *Net benefit/tax gain, 1982 (£ per week)*

Bracketed numbers are based on 10 families or less.

income varies considerably between life-cycle groups (the average weekly original income in this quintile — that is, income before state intervention — is equivalent to £5 for a married couple). Families, particularly those with older children, receive substantially larger sums than do pensioners and other groups without children. However, if the income from the state is converted to take account of household needs a very different pattern emerges (not shown in Figure 15.2): pensioner couples receive 52 per cent more, and single young people 25 per cent more, than a 'complete' family or one in the middle stages of childrearing. Families with younger children also appear to receive substantially more than families with older ones. Single pensioners receive 39 per cent more than single young people.

Turning to families with higher incomes who experience a net loss of income, similarly inequitable patterns are evident. Families in the fourth and top quintile of the original income distribution pay markedly larger sums in tax and national insurance than do families at other stages in the life cycle. The reason is that at these levels of income child benefit payments are swamped by the effect of the tax system which is largely insensitive to variations in households' needs as opposed to differences in gross income. For example, the needs of single people and complete families are very different: the equivalence scale used in this chapter implies that to be placed in the top quintile of equivalent net income a complete family would require a net income (i.e. not equivalenced) of £420 per week and a single person only £182. Yet, the average tax rate (net of benefits) for a complete family and a single person in the top quintile of equivalent net income is virtually identical (namely, 23 and 24 per cent respectively).

Before leaving the subject of the state's role in supporting financial welfare, it is important to reiterate how limited the preceding analysis has been. A much more sophisticated analysis taking account of service provision, indirect taxation and the impact of policies on individual behaviour is required before firm conclusions can be drawn. Nevertheless, an a priori case has been made that the state's activity is rather less in tune with variations in life-cycle factors than it might be.

Conclusions

This chapter has argued the importance of the life-cycle perspective in income distribution analysis and has defined and described a set of life-cycle groups which account for more than 80 per cent of households in the 1982 Family Expenditure Survey.

The equivalent income analysis strikingly demonstrated the relatively low levels of financial welfare available to families with children. For the main life-cycle groups with children, these levels were little more than half those available to younger married couples; in some cases the relativities were less than half, leaving certain life-cycle groups with children with average standards of living marginally below those of retired households. During the 1970s, families with children first joined and then gradually over-took retired households as the group with the highest probability of occupying the bottom quintile of financial welfare. Correspondingly, the proportion of retired households likely to be at higher levels increased.

The chapter has not examined the arguments for particular differentials in economic welfare — a major theme in the first part of the book, nor have criteria been suggested whereby particular differences might be judged appropriate. Moreover, it has been possible only to begin to explore the detailed causes of the patterns and changes which are revealed. Regardless of detailed causation, however, two conclusions emerge clearly.

First, Rowntree's categorisation of periods of 'want' and 'plenty' remains valid: childrearing and old age are periods of (almost equal) relative want while adulthood before and after childrearing is a time of relative plenty. Second, it suggests that the horizontal redistri-butive mechanisms — those aimed at achieving equity between family types — are ineffective: they do not appear to redistribute an adequate quantity of resources. Policies which reduce the resources available to families with children in order to provide benefits to those without children would further exacerbate these inequities.

Appendix

In order to establish that the results were not simply a function of the equivalence scales used a 'sensitivity analysis' was conducted using two other equivalence scales and the results are compared for 1982 in Table 15.10. The equivalence scales used in the analysis above weight children rather higher than is common. This reflects a judgement based on the work of Muellbauer (1979), Piachaud (1979) and Godfrey and Baldwin (1983) on the relative living standards of families. The first alternative tried was to weight all children equally as 0.27 of an adult — the ratio used in the Royal Commission on the Distribution of Income (Cmnd. 7175, 1978). The effects of this was, as would be expected, to reduce the relative position of couples with pre-school children (group 3) and improve that of families with older children (groups 5 and 6). The second

TABLE 15.10 *Comparisons of results using different equivalence scales for children, 1982*

Quintile	Life-cycle groups[1]										
	1 (%)	2 (%)	3 (%)	4 (%)	5 (%)	6 (%)	7 (%)	8 (%)	9 (%)	10 (%)	11 (%)
1. Children 0–4 = 0.25; 5–11 = 0.35; 12–15 = 0.45[2]											
Top	44	70	18	6	13	7	21	39	9	7	3
4th	20	21	25	15	21	19	36	26	12	11	5
3rd	14	5	27	27	25	25	26	16	20	19	8
2nd	8	2	15	21	19	23	12	11	32	41	19
Bottom	14	3	16	31	23	26	6	8	28	22	65
2. All children = 0.27											
Top	42	67	15	6	18	9	20	37	9	7	5
4th	22	22	24	17	25	20	33	26	10	10	4
3rd	13	7	26	27	23	29	27	17	18	16	12
2nd	9	2	16	21	17	22	13	11	30	42	25
Bottom	15	3	19	30	17	20	6	9	33	25	54
3. Children 0–4 = 0.25; 5–11 = 0.30; 12–15 = 0.35											
Top	43	68	17	6	15	7	20	38	9	7	4
4th	22	21	23	17	23	20	34	26	11	10	5
3rd	13	6	27	27	24	28	27	16	19	17	10
2nd	8	1	15	21	18	22	13	12	30	42	24
Bottom	15	3	17	29	20	23	6	8	31	24	57

[1] Life-cycle groups:

1	Young single	7	Two generation
2	Young married	8	Empty nest
3	Family formation	9	Early retirement
4	Middle childrearing	10	Old and single
5	Complete family	11	Lone parent
6	Early dispersal		

[2] From Table 15.4.

alternative tried was to reduce the weights given to older children. The effect of this was, again as would be expected, to reduce the relative position of couples with older children (groups 5, 6 and 7). However, in both alternatives tried the changes were relatively small — shifting the proportions in each quintile only by, at most, a few percentage points and certainly not altering the overall picture obtained.

References

Atkinson, A.B. (1983) *The Economics of Inequality*. Oxford: Oxford University Press.

Atkinson, A.B., J. Hills and J. Le Grand (1986) *The Welfare State in Britain 1970–85: Extent and Effectiveness*. London: Welfare State Programme, Discussion Paper 9.

Bosanquet, N. (1987) *A Generation in Limbo*. London: Public Policy Centre.

Bulmer, M. (1986) 'Continuous Social Surveys', in M. Bulmer (ed.), *Social Science and Social Policy*. London: George Allen and Unwin.

Burtless, G. and R. Haveman (1985) *Taxes, Transfers, and Labor Supply: The Evolving views of US Economists*. Wisconsin: IRP Discussion Paper 778–85.

Central Statistical Office (CSO) (1985) 'The Effects of Taxes and Benefits on Household Income 1984', *Economic Trends*, 376 (December).

Cmnd. 7175 (1978) *Royal Commission on the Distribution of Income and Wealth. Report on Lower Incomes*. London: HMSO.

Cusack, S. and J. Roll (1985) *Families Rent Apart*. London: Child Poverty Action Group.

FES (1986) *Family Expenditure Survey 1985*. London: HMSO.

General Household Survey (GHS) (1986) *General Household Survey 1986*. London: HMSO.

Godfrey, C. and S. Baldwin (1983) *Economies of Scale in Large Low Income Families*. York: Social Policy Research Unit Working Paper.

Hakim, C. (1982) *Secondary Analysis in Social Research*. London: George Allen and Unwin.

Harris, J. (1977) *William Beveridge*. Oxford: Clarendon Press.

Hedström, P. and S. Ringen (1985) *Age and Income in Contemporary Society*. Luxembourg: Luxembourg Income Study, Working Paper 4.

Jenkins, S. (1986) *Distinguishing Horizontal Inequity from Reranking: A Partial Symmetry Approach with Empirical Illustrations*. Bath: Bath University, Papers in Political Economy, 86/02.

Keynes, J.M. (1936) *The General Theory of Employment*. London: Macmillan.

Layard, R. (1974) 'On Measuring the Redistribution of Lifetime Income', pp. 45–72. in M.S. Feldstein and R.P. Inman, *The Economics of Public Services*. London: Macmillan.

Le Grand, J. (1982) *The Strategy of Equality*. London: George Allen and Unwin.

Le Grand, J. (1986) *On Researching the Distributional Consequences of Public Policies*. London: Welfare State Programme, Discussion Paper 6.

Muellbauer, J. (1979) 'McClements on Equivalence Scales for Children', *Journal of Public Economics*, 12: 221–31.

Munnell, A.H. (1987) 'The Impact of Public and Private Pension Schemes on Saving and Capital Formation', in *Conjugating Public and Private*. Geneva: International Social Security Association, Studies and Research, 24: 219–36.

Nicholson, J.L. (1981) *Inequalities of Income over the Life Cycle*. Paper to the International Association for Research in Income and Wealth Policy Studies Institute (mimeo).

Nolan, B. (1986) 'The Distribution of Social Security Transfers in the UK', *Journal of Social Policy*, 15(2): 185–205.

O'Higgins, M. (1980) 'The Distribution Effects of Public Expenditure and Taxation: An Agnostic View of the CSO Analyses', pp. 28–46 in C. Sandford, C. Pond and R. Walker (eds), *Taxation and Social Policy*. London: Heinemann.

O'Higgins, M. (1985) 'Inequality, Redistribution and Recession: the British Experience 1976–82' *Journal of Social Policy*, 14(2): 279–307.

Piachaud, D. (1979) *The Cost of a Child*. London: Child Poverty Action Group.

Ross, C., S. Danziger and E. Smolensky (1985) *Social Security, Work and Poverty among Elderly Men 1939–79*. Wisconsin: IRP Discussion Paper 785–85.

Rottman, D.B., D. Hannan, N. Hardman, and M. Wiley (1982) *The Distribution of Income in the Republic of Ireland: A Study in Social Class and Family Cycle Inequalities*. Dublin: The Economic and Social Research Institute, Paper 109.

Rowntree, B.S. (1901) *Poverty: A Study of Town Life*. London: Macmillan.

Rowntree, B.S. (1941) *Poverty and Progress: a Second Social Survey of York*. London: Longman.

Sandford, C., C. Pond and R. Walker (eds) (1980) *Taxation and Social Policy*. London: Heinemann.

Sen, K. (1961) *Hinduism*. Harmondsworth: Penguin Books.

Smeeding, T. (1984) 'Approaches to Meaning and Valuing In-kind Subsidies and the Distribution of their Benefits', in M. Moon (ed.), *Economic Transfers in the United States*. Chicago: University of Chicago Press.

Taylor-Gooby, P. (1985) 'Personal Consumption and Gender', *Sociology*, 19(2): 273–84.

Veit Wilson, J. (1984) 'Seebohm Rowntree', in P. Barker (ed.), *Founders of the Welfare State*. London: Heinemann.

Walker, A. (1982) (ed.) *Public Expenditure and Social Policy*. London: Heinemann.

Weber, M. (1946) *From Max Weber, Essays in Sociology* (Trans. H. Gerth and C.W. Mills). New York: Oxford University Press.

Index

abatement (benefit), 67, 93
Adler, M., 213, 220, 221
adults (relative needs), 168–72
affluence, 3, 49
   see also plenty (relative)
age factor
   childrearing costs, 36–7, 38, 39–40
   temporal divisions (elderly), 55–7
ageing (costs), *see* elderly people
Aird, A., 190
allowance system, 201, 202, 204, 205,
   209
Alpren, L., 87
Altmann, R.M., 50
Annual Abstract of Statistics, 183
Anthony, S., 101
Ashley, P., 213, 220
assets, 91
   personal sector, 149, 150–54, 163
Atkinson, A.B., 82, 236, 247
attendance allowance, 64, 71, 179
Audit Commission, 214
Avery, L., 71

babies (costs), 30
Baldock, J., 220
Baldwin, S., 4, 32–3, 41, 67, 69, 71–3,
   89, 96, 173, 190, 192, 250
bank loans, 185, 186
Bank of England, 160
bankruptcies, 219
basket of goods (costs)
   childrearing, 4, 29–37
   housing expenditure, 9, 23–4
Beckman (of Shelter), 159
behavioural estimates (child costs), 29,
   37–40
Bell, C., 209
benefits
   national insurance, 67, 168–71, 175
   non-wage, *see* non-wage benefits
   -taxation model, 82, 106, 247–8
   unemployment, 84–5, 87–9, 92–4,
      168–9, 175, 176–7

benefits, *cont.*
   see also social security benefits;
      supplementary benefits; welfare
      benefits
Bennison, B., 18
Berthoud, R., 89, 90–91, 175, 215, 216,
   220, 221, 222
Beveridge, W., 67, 177, 180
Beveridge Report (1942), 27–8, 63,
   170–72, 173, 179
Binney, V., 202
Birds Eye, 202
black economy, 132, 134–5, 141–6
Board of Inland Revenue, 137, 145
Bonnerjea, L., 74, 75–6
Borrie, G., 191
borrowing (and credit), 90–91
Bosanquet, N., 245
Bradshaw, J., 33, 86, 91–3, 106, 112,
   170, 174, 175, 203
Breadline Britain, 126, 207, 209
British Gas, 152
Brown, J., 27, 67
Buckle, J., 70, 71
budget accounts, 185, 186, 187
budget standards, 29, 32–7, 43–4, 96
budgeting (and debt), 2, 5, 221–2
building societies, 150–51, 153–4, 224
Building Societies Association, 14–15,
   17, 87, 158, 214
Bulmer, M., 230
Burghes, L., 88, 93
Burtless, G., 247
Business Decisions Limited, 142

Cain, M., 196
capital accumulation, 158–60, 162
Caplovitz, D., 10, 220
carers/caring (costs), 62–4, 71–6, 77–8
Casserley, J., 67
Central Policy Review Staff, 51
Central Statistical Office, 6, 111, 115,
   128, 155, 168, 189, 198, 247
Chambers, A., 104

Charles, N., 206, 208
Charles, S., 2
check trading, 185, 186, 189, 190
child benefit, 107, 172, 178, 244
children
    disabled, 69–70, 72–3
    relative needs, 169, 172–4
childrearing, 3, 27–8
    direct costs, 4, 29–41, 43–4, 234–5
    income distribution, 234–5, 238–41
    indirect costs, 4–5, 29, 41–3, 231
Christopher, T., 145
Clark, B., 67
Clark, M., 86, 88, 90–91, 212, 220
clothing clubs, 187
community care, 63, 71–6, 77–8
company welfare, 132, 135–40
'complex' households, 10–11
consumer credit, *see* credit
Consumer Credit Act (1974), 190–91,
    192
consumer goods, 9, 182, 183, 188
consumption patterns, 195, 203,
    207–10, 228
contributory benefits, 177–8, 180
Conway, J., 19
Cooke, K., 32–3, 67, 89, 91, 93, 96, 173
cooling-off period (credit), 190
costs (financial), 2, 3–5
    ageing and retirement, 46–60
    childrearing, 27–44
    disability, 63–78
    household formation, 9–25
    marital breakdown, 99–112
    unemployment, 81–96
council housing, 13, 19, 158, 213, 214
    legislation, 14, 20, 54, 157, 163
Cragg, A., 198
Craig, C., 123
Cranston, R., 192
credit, 6, 90–91, 212, 217–19
    equity and, 190–92
    expansion, 182–4
    granters, 184–6
    as social good, 182, 192–3
    using, 184–90
    see also debt
credit cards, 183, 185, 186, 187
Crossley, M., 192
Crowther Committee, 186–7, 190

Culley, L., 87, 215
cultural influence (credit), 188–90
Cusack, S., 23, 238

Dale, A., 208
Daniel, W.W., 86, 88, 220
Darnborough, A., 65
Dawson, T., 198
Deacon, A., 106, 170
Deaton, A., 39
debt, 86–7
    causes, 212–13, 219–24
    credit default, 212, 217–19
    extent, 212, 213–19
'decency threshold', 121
Delphy, C., 208
Desai, M., 32
Dex, S., 66
DHSS, 46, 58, 82–3, 88, 90, 93–4, 106,
    108, 124, 125–6, 145
Diamond, A.L., 191
Dickinson, K., 111
differential costs (unemployment),
    87–9
Dilnot, A.W., 28, 83, 84, 85, 88, 145
disability (costs), 3, 63–4, 228
    benefits, 64, 67, 71, 74–5, 77, 175,
    177–9, 180, 244
    caring/carers, 62–4, 71–6, 77–8
    impact, 65–71, 76–8
Disability Alliance, 67, 71, 77
Disabled Persons (Employment) Act,
    65
disregards (earnings), 92–3, 178
divorce, *see* marital breakdown
Divorce Reform Act (1969), 100
Doling, J., 87
Downey, P., 87, 215
Duncan, S., 220, 221, 222
Dunnell, K., 12

earnings
    of carers, 72–5
    of disabled, 64, 65–6, 77
    household allocation, 196–204, 209
    importance of, 5, 115–17
    income distribution, 117–19
    inequalities, 121–6, 128–9
    part-time, 119, 120, 121, 122–3, 126
    pay structure, 119–21

earnings, *cont.*
  policy reforms, 128–30
  replacement ratios, 81–5
  single parents, 103, 105–6, 109, 112
  tax burden, 5, 115, 126–8
  of unemployed, 92–3
earnings-related supplements, 84, 87,
    89, 93, 177
  SERPS, 59, 66, 74, 146, 246
economic change, 238–9, 240–42
economies of scale, 20, 22–3, 32, 40–41,
    168–74
Edwards, M., 197, 209
Eekelaar, J., 101, 102, 103, 104, 113
elderly people, 4, 10–11, 163
  class divisions (welfare), 52–5
  disability in, 70–71, 75, 76
  gender divisions, 57–60
  income distribution, 237–8, 241–6
  pensions, *see* retirement pensions
  retirement costs, 46–52
  temporal divisions, 55–7
electricity bills, 215–17, 224
employment, 220–21
  of carers, 72–5
  of disabled, 64, 65–6, 77
  income distribution, 236–7, 239
  non-wage benefits, 6, 132–47
  policies, 125–6, 128–30
  in retirement, 50, 54–5
  see also earnings; part-time work;
      self-employment;
      unemployment
Employment, Department of, 50, 105,
    111, 119
Engel, E., 38
Environment, Department of the, 18,
    54, 215
equivalence scales, 2, 38–40, 171–3,
    180, 234–7, 239–40, 244, 249–51
Ermisch, J., 10, 11–12, 13, 19
Evason, E., 105, 202
executives, 89–91, 139, 185–6, 188
expenditure, 46–52, 110–11, 232–3, 234
  see also consumption patterns

Fair Wages Resolution, 125
family allowance, 27, 28, 173
Family Budget Inquiry, 170–71, 173

Family Expenditure Survey, 21, 84,
    109–10, 117
  childrearing costs, 33, 35–7, 39
  distribution of family welfare, 7,
      230, 232–3, 239, 244, 249
  retirement costs, 51–2, 55, 57, 59
Family Finances Group, 202
Family Finances Survey, 41, 86, 91,
    103, 104, 105–7, 108, 221
Family Income Supplement, 106, 169,
    172, 178
family life cycle, *see* life cycle
Family Policy Studies Centre, 112
family size, 38, 82, 88–9, 221
Fapohunda, E., 196
Fiegehen, G.C., 48, 51
Field, F., 94, 126, 173
financial decision-making, 2, 221–2
financial needs, *see* needs
financial resources, *see* resources
financial welfare, 1–3, 7
  changes, 238–42
  government role, 246–9
  inequality, 229, 232–8, 250–51
  life-cycle stages, 227–8, 230–32, 249
  resource management, 242–6
Finch, J., 72
Fogelman, K., 112
Forrest, R., 19
Franey, R., 67, 208
fringe benefits, 115, 132–4
  inequality, 138–40, 146
  taxation, 6, 130, 132, 134–8, 141–7
  value, 135–40
fuel bills, 21, 22, 203–4
  arrears, 87, 212–13, 215–17, 224
furniture and furnishings, 23–4

Garganas, N.C., 39
gas bills, 217, 224
gearing ratios, 159, 160–61
gender
  divisions of welfare, 57–60
  see also men; women
General Household Survey, 11–13, 17,
    19, 53, 83, 103, 105, 139, 231
Glendinning, C., 67
Godfrey, C., 250
government (welfare role), 229, 246–9
Graham, H., 75, 202

Gray, A., 203, 209
Green, F., 135, 138, 139
Gregory, J., 213, 220, 221
Groves, D., 56, 58, 60, 70, 72, 112
Grunfeld, N., 24

Hakim, C., 230
Hannah, L., 56
Harbury, D., 149
Harris, A.I., 66, 67–8
Harris, C.C., 11
Harris, J., 228
Harris, T., 203
Hartley, J.F., 89
Haskey, J., 101
Haveman, R., 247
Hedges, A., 18
Hedström, P., 247
Henwood, A., 208
Henwood, M., 76
Hesketh, J.L., 220
Hill, M., 86
Hill, P., 33
hire-purchase, 182, 183, 185, 186
Hirst, M., 66, 73
Hitchens, M.W.N., 149
Holmans, A., 12, 16, 18, 19
Home Equity Conversion, 163
Homer, M., 202
Homes, P., 18
horizontal inequality, 2, 6, 108, 229
horizontal redistribution, 166, 246–7,
    250
household formation
    expenditure costs, 2, 20–25
    family size, 38, 82, 88–9, 221
    housing, *see* housing
    patterns, 9–13
household income, 2, 7, 139–40
    consumption patterns, 195, 203,
        207–10, 228
    earnings (sharing), 197–201
    housekeeping, 196, 203, 204–7
    husband's (allocation), 201–4
housekeeping money, 196, 203, 204–7
housing
    access to, 13–20
    benefit, 18–20, 22–3, 35, 47, 49,
        168–9, 178, 214
    childrearing costs and, 33–5

housing, *cont.*
    debt, 212–13, 214–15, 224
    expenditure, 2, 20–25
    prices, 14–15, 158, 159–60
    see also council housing; mortgages;
        owner occupation; rented
        housing
Housing Acts, 157
Houthakker, H.S., 4, 39
Hughes, J., 92
Hunt, A., 51
Hunt, P., 209
Hutton, S., 57, 174
Hyman, M., 70, 72

income
    debt and, 220–21
    disabled, 64, 65–8
    distribution, 117–19
    forgone (by unemployed), 81–5
    household, *see* household income
    one-parent families, 102–12
income distribution (over life cycle)
    government role, 246–9
    inequality (patterns), 232–8
    life-cycle groups, 230–32, 249–50
    one-parent families, 7, 231–2, 234,
        235, 238
    recent changes, 238–42
    resource management, 242–6
indebtedness, *see* debt
independent management system, 201,
    202, 204, 205, 209
industrial injuries, 63, 178–9
Ineichen, B., 12
inequality
    benefits, 6, 176–80
    earnings, 121–6, 128–9
    household income, 5, 7, 196, 202,
        206–10
    life-cycle factors, 5, 229, 232–8
    non-wage benefits, 138–40
inflation, 56–7, 60, 150–52, 158, 159
Inland Revenue, 124, 137, 141, 143,
    145, 154
Institute of Fiscal Studies, 28, 145
interest rates, 151–2, 159–60, 185,
    191–2, 193
    mortgage, 17, 159–60, 184–5

invalid care allowance, 64, 74–5, 77, 177, 178
invalidity benefit, 67, 175, 178–9
investment income, 242, 243, 245
Ison, T., 185–6, 218

James, C., 53, 57
Jenkins, S., 247
Job-Start, 125
Job Release Scheme, 50
Job Training Scheme, 125
Jones, G., 12
Jordan, D., 65, 66, 77
Joshi, H., 41–2, 74, 102

Karn, V., 163
Katona, G., 187
Kemeny, J., 160
Kerr, M., 206, 208
Keynes, J.M., 228
Kilroy, B., 162
Kinrade, D., 65
Kirby, K., 220, 221, 222
Kleinman, M., 13, 19
Knapp, M., 2
Knight, I.B., 212

Labour, Ministry of, 170–71, 173
labour market, 125–6, 139, 140
    see also employment
Labour Research Department, 144
Land, H., 72, 99, 207, 208
Lansley, S., 113, 126
Lavers, G.R., 3
Lawther, G., 24
Layard, R., 66, 68, 83, 113, 247
Le Grand, J., 236, 247
leakage (of cash), 160–61, 163–4
Leete, R., 101
Leigh-Pemberton, R., 212
life assurance, 135, 136, 139, 152–3
life cycle, 7, 99–100
    income distribution, *see main entry*
    stages, 5, 227–8, 230–32, 249–50
Lister, R., 28, 93
Littlewood, J., 15, 17
living standards, 2, 5, 132, 212
    budget standards, 29, 32–7, 43–4, 96
    childrearing and, 29, 32–40, 43–4
    consumption and, 195–6, 207–9

living standards, *cont.*
    disabled, 63, 64, 76–7
    earnings and, 115, 128
    income distribution and, 232–41
    one-parent families, 104, 106, 109–11, 234
    in retirement, 51, 56
    in unemployment, 81, 85–7, 89–90, 96
    welfare benefits and, 166–8, 175, 179–80
loans, 185–6, 188, 190–93
    see also mortgages
local authority housing, *see* council housing
long-term benefits, 174–7, 180
long-term unemployment, 81, 84–5, 86, 90–91, 94, 221, 224
Lonsdale, S., 65, 66
Lord Chancellor's Department, 213, 218
Low Pay Unit, 119, 122, 124, 128–9, 140
Lynes, T., 30, 173

McClements, L.D., 4, 39
McDonald, G.W., 200
Mack, J., 113, 126
McKee, L., 209
McLanahan, S., 112
Maclean, M., 102, 103, 104, 113
McLeod, K.D., 203, 209
Madge, J., 12, 15, 16, 17, 19
mail-order, 186, 187, 189
maintenance payments, 102–5
Manpower Services Commission, 86, 91, 144
manual/non-manual work, 119–20, 185–6, 188
marital breakdown, 3, 12, 13, 99–101, 227
    financial impact, 102–7, 111–12, 202
    income inequality, 107–11, 112
marriage, 58
    breakdown, *see* marital breakdown
    income, *see* household income
Marsden, D., 212
Martin, J., 42, 59, 73, 105
Masey, A., 190
Mason, S., 15, 17

Matrimonial and Family Proceedings
    Act (1984), 103
Matthews, K., 145
means-tested benefits, 180
    for disabled, 67, 77, 177–8
    for one-parent families, 106, 107
    for unemployed, 82–3
Melville, J., 92
men, 73
    earnings, 119, 120, 197–204, 209
mental handicap, 70
middle class (debt), 220
Miles, I., 145
Millar, J., 107, 112
Mirror Group, 141
Mitchell, D.A., 33
mobility allowance, 64, 71, 179
money-lending, 190–92
Monk, J., 213, 220, 221
'moonlighting', 132, 134–5, 144–5
Morgan, J., 174
Morris, C.N., 83, 84, 85, 88, 145
Morris, L., 199, 208
mortgages, 20, 154, 186
    annuity schemes, 54, 159
    arrears, 86–7, 163, 212, 214–15, 224
    first-time buyers, 14–16, 17, 163
    interest rate, 17, 159–60, 184–5
    subsidies, 130, 136, 156–8, 159
Moylan, S., 83, 88, 90–91, 93
Muellbauer, J., 4, 39, 250
Munachonga, M.L., 196
Munnell, A.H., 247
Murie, A., 19
Murlis, H., 132
Murphy, M., 16

National Consumer Council, 87, 184,
    185–6, 187–90, 218, 220
National Freight Corporation, 152
National Health Service, 33, 118, 124,
    129, 146
national insurance
    benefits, 67, 168–71, 175
    contributions, 42, 51, 56, 127, 130
    pensions, 42, 46–50, 56, 58–9, 66,
    168–71
needs, 1–2, 171
    financial (and costs), 3–5
    relative, 168–74

needs, *cont.*
    resources and (mismatch), *see* debt
Neugarten, B.L., 50
New Earnings Survey, 76, 119, 120, 121
New Workers Scheme, 125
New York Community Council, 33–5,
    36–7
NFHA, 156
Nicholson, J.L., 207, 247
Nissel, M., 74, 75–6
Nixon, J.M., 212
Nolan, B., 236
non-contributory benefits, 177–8, 180
non-wage benefits, 132–4
    company welfare, 135–40
    tax evasion, 141–7
normative estimates (costs), 29–32, 43

Oakley, A., 42
occupational class, 236–7
occupational pensions, 46, 48–9, 242,
    245–6
    fringe benefit, 132–4, 136, 139, 146
    funds, 149, 152–3, 155, 163–4
    inequality, 52–3, 55–60, 66
OECD, 33
Office of Fair Trading, 184–6, 218
Office of Population Censuses and
    Surveys, 10–12, 50, 77, 82, 100,
    102, 111
O'Higgins, M., 143, 236, 247
one-parent families, 4, 221, 224
    benefit system, 178, 180
    financial costs, 9–13, 19
    income distribution, 7, 231–2, 234,
    235, 238
    income inequalities, 107–11, 112
    income sources, 102–7, 109, 111–12
    life-cycle stage, 99–100, 101–2
one-person households, 10–11, 18–19
Oppong, C., 196
opportunity costs, 5, 41–2, 43, 231
overdrafts, 186, 187
overtime, 120, 121, 122–3
Overton, E., 10, 11–12, 13, 19
Owen, S., 42
owner occupation, 13, 14–16, 246
    growth, 5–6, 149–52, 155–64
    in retirement, 51, 52, 54, 56
    see also wealth

Pahl, J., 99, 197, 200, 202, 208
Pahl, R.E., 6, 75, 144
Parker, G., 65, 87, 91, 184, 188, 189,
    203, 213, 220–21
Parker, H., 32–3, 106
Parker, S., 50, 51
Parker, S.R., 92
part-time work, 42, 59, 72–3, 74
    earnings, 119, 120, 121, 122–3, 126
    fringe benefits, 132, 139
    in unemployment, 92–3
Pember Reeves, M., 189
pensions, *see* invalidity benefits;
    retirement pensions; widows'
    pensions
perks, *see* fringe benefits
Perlman, R., 92
Phillips, H., 67
Phillipson, C., 50–51, 66
Piachaud, D., 30, 31–2, 38, 42, 44, 66,
    89, 174, 190, 250
Pile, Sir William, 145
plenty (relative), 3, 99, 227, 230–31,
    233–4, 245–6, 250
Policy Studies Institute, 87
Pond, C., 116
pooling system, 201–2, 204, 205
Popay, J., 103
population trends, 9–11
poverty, 3, 126, 130, 228
    childrearing and, 27, 28, 31
    disability and, 64, 67–8
    household income, 202–3, 205–6,
        209
    in retirement, 46–9, 51, 53, 57, 246
    see also want (relative)
Prais, S.J., 4, 39
pre-payment meters, 213, 215, 216
'primary' debt, 220, 222–3, 224
privatisation, 152, 164
process effects (pensioners), 56–7
productivity, 116, 121, 123, 124, 129
professionals, 89–91, 185–6, 188
profits, pay and, 123, 124
progressive taxation, 126–7, 129–30
public sector wages, 123–4

racial discrimination, 116, 123
Rahman, N., 124
Rathbone, E., 27

Reddin, M., 153
redundancy payments, 91–2
regional factors, 14–15, 120–21
rented housing, 16–19
    arrears, 86–7, 212, 213, 214, 224
    council, *see* council housing
repayment plans (fuel), 216, 217
replacement costs (childrearing), 41–2
replacement ratios, 81–5, 87–9, 94–5
resources (financial), 1–2, 5
    management, 6–7, 228, 229, 242–6
    needs and (mismatch), *see* debt
    see also credit; earnings; non-wage
        benefits; wealth (new patterns);
        welfare benefits
Retail Price Index, 20, 31, 33, 109, 121,
    150, 158, 183
retirement, *see* elderly people
retirement pensions
    occupational, *see main entry*
    SERPS, 59, 66, 74, 146, 246
    state, 42, 46–50, 56, 58–9, 66, 175
    women's, 42, 46–7, 56, 59–60, 112
Review Body of Top Salaries, 136
Right to Buy, 14, 20, 54, 157, 163
Rimmer, L., 72
Ringen, S., 247
Roberts, C., 42, 59, 73, 105
Robins, P., 111
Roll, J., 23, 30, 238
Ross, C., 247
Rottman, D.B., 247
Rowntree, B.S., 24, 170, 171, 173, 247
    plenty/want stages, 3, 99, 227–8,
        230–31, 233–4, 245, 250
Royal Commission on the Distribution
    of Income and Wealth, 53–4,
    116–17, 154–5, 250
Ruane, S., 199, 208

S-curve analysis, 35–6
Safilios Rothschild, C., 200
Sandford, C., 247
savings, 89, 90, 222, 229, 233, 242,
    244–5, 246
Scanzoni, J., 200
'secondary' debt, 220–21, 223–4
self-employment, 116, 132, 134–5, 141,
    142–4, 146
Sen, A., 32, 227

sensitivity analysis, 250–51
Severe Disablement Allowance, 177–9
Shelter, 157, 159
short-term benefits, 174–7, 180
short-term unemployment, 84–5, 91, 221
sickness benefit, 67, 175, 244
Simkins, J., 67
'simple' households, 10–11
Sinfield, A., 89, 92
Smail, R., 135
Smart, C., 112
Smee, C., 93
Smeeding, T., 247
Smith, D.J., 86, 87, 88, 220
Smith, S., 145
social change, 239
social class, 52–5, 190, 191, 244–5
Social Fund, 193
Social Security Act (1966), 176
Social Security Act (1986), 28
Social Security Advisory Committee, 92, 94, 180
social security benefits, 243–4, 246–9
    for disabled, 66–7, 244
    lone mothers, 106–7
    unemployed, 90, 93–4, 95–6
Social Security Pensions Act (1975), 53, 56, 153
Social Security Provision for Chronically Sick/Disabled People, 72
socio-cultural influences (credit), 188–90
socio-economic status (credit), 185–6, 188, 220
spillover costs, 4
State Earnings Related Pension Scheme (SERPS), 59, 66, 74, 146, 246
status, pay and, 115–17
Stern, J., 93
stocks and shares, 152
Sullivan, O., 16
superannuation, 133, 134, 136
supplementary benefits
    for children, 172–3, 174
    disabled, 67, 71
    lone mothers, 103–4, 105–7
    long/short-term, 169, 174–6

supplementary benefits, *cont.*
    non-contributory, 177, 178
    in retirement, 47–8, 49, 53, 57–8
    for unemployed, 93–5
Supplementary Benefits Commission, 94, 175
Survey of Personal Incomes, 143

tallymen, 186, 189
Tarpey, T., 112
taxation, 93, 130, 152, 162, 208
    avoidance, 6, 132, 134–5, 136–8, 146
    -benefit model, 82, 106, 247–8
    burden, 5, 115, 126–8
    evasion, 6, 132, 134–5, 141–7
    income distribution and, 5, 117–19, 246
    mortgage relief, 130, 136, 156–8, 159
    progressive, 126–7, 129–30
Taylor-Gooby, P., 207, 209, 228
Tebbut, M., 191
teenagers (cost), 38
Thatcher government, 125, 155
Thomas, A., 160
Thomas, A.D., 18
Thorns, D.C., 162
Thornton, C., 141
Tickner, V., 67
Titmuss, R., 46, 52
'total income support', 106
Townsend, P., 31, 32, 66, 68, 70, 77, 113, 140, 208
trade unions, 116, 123, 129
two-parent families, 4, 108–11

unemployment, 3, 50, 60, 66–7
    benefit, 84–5, 87–9, 92–4, 168–9, 175, 176–7
    debt and, 163, 212, 216, 219, 220–21, 222, 224
    differential costs, 87–9, 94–6
    income distribution, 7, 228, 237–8, 239, 241, 242
    income forgone, 81–5, 116
    living standards, 81, 85–7, 96
    long-term, 81, 84–5, 86, 90–91, 94, 221, 224
    short-term, 84–5, 91, 221
Unemployment Assistance Board, 173

Ungerson, C., 220

Van der Gaag, 39
Veit Wilson, J., 228
vertical inequality, 2, 6, 108, 229
vertical redistribution, 166, 247

wages, *see* earnings
Wages Act (1987), 140, 147
Wages Councils, 125
Walker, A., 49, 50, 51, 55, 57, 59, 65, 66, 67, 70, 72, 247
Walker R., 18, 50
want (relative), 3, 99, 227–8, 233–4, 250
war pensions, 63, 178
wealth (new patterns)
    distribution, 154–5
    inherited, 161–2
    owner occupation, 149–50, 151–2, 155–64
    personal assets, 144, 150–54, 163
Webb, A., 2
Weber, M., 227
Weitzman, L., 104
welfare benefits
    contributory/non-contributory, 177–8, 180
    disabled, *see* disability (costs)
    inequality, 6, 176–80
    living standards and, 166–8, 175, 179–80

welfare benefits, *cont.*
    means-tested, *see main entry*
    one-parent families, 178, 180
    short/long-term, 174–7, 180
    variation by size, 168–74, 179–80
Wheeler, R., 52, 54
Whiteford, P., 172
Whitehead, C., 13, 19
whole wage system, 201, 202, 203, 204–5
Wicks, M., 28, 71, 76, 208
widows' pensions, 56, 59, 60, 112, 175
Williams, F., 190
Winyard, S., 116
women
    care role, 63, 72–6
    earnings, 119, 120, 123
    earnings (allocation), 197–201, 209
    employment, 41–2, 105–6
    gender division of welfare, 57–60
    lone mothers, *see* one-parent families
    pension rights, 42, 46–7, 56, 59–60, 112
    widows' pensions, 56, 59, 60, 112, 175
Women and Employment Survey, 42, 73, 74, 105
Workmen's Compensation, 27
Wozniak, E., 213, 220, 221
Wynn, M., 173

DATE DUE